LIBRARIANS AS COMMUNITY PARTNERS

AN OUTREACH HANDBOOK

EDITED BY CAROL SMALLWOOD

AMERICAN LIBRARY ASSOCIATION
CHICAGO   2010

Carol Smallwood received her MLS degree from Western Michigan University and her MA in history from Eastern Michigan University. She is the author or editor of eighteen books, published by Scarecrow, McFarland, Libraries Unlimited, Pudding House, and others. Her magazine credits include *The Writer's Chronicle, Instructor, English Journal,* and *Michigan Feminist Studies.* She has worked in school, public, and special libraries as well as serving as a consultant.

The paper used in this publication meets the minimum requirements of American National Standard for Information Sciences—Permanence of Paper for Printed Library Materials, ANSI Z39.48-1992. ⊗

Library of Congress Cataloging-in-Publication Data
Librarians as community partners : an outreach handbook / edited by Carol Smallwood.
    p. cm.
  Includes bibliographical references and index.
  ISBN 978-0-8389-1006-1 (alk. paper)
  1. Library outreach programs—United States—Case studies. 2. Libraries and community—United States—Case studies. 3. Libraries—Public relations—United States—Case studies. I. Smallwood, Carol, 1939–
Z711.7.L52 2010
021.2'0973—dc22

2009020359

ISBN-13: 978-0-8389-1006-1

Printed in the United States of America
14 13 12 11 10   5 4 3 2 1

Mixed Sources
Product group from well-managed forests and other controlled sources
www.fsc.org Cert no. SW-COC-002283
© 1996 Forest Stewardship Council

CONTENTS

Foreword *by Kathy Barco* / **vii**

Preface / **ix**

PART I   A SAMPLER OF OUTREACH PROGRAMS

1   Bake a Book and They Will Come *by Iona R. Malanchuk* / **3**

2   Establishing a Library Docent Program *by Mary H. Nino* / **5**

3   Friends in Need: Involving Friends of the Library in
    Community Outreach Programs *by Vera Gubnitskaia* / **9**

4   Lifesaving Library Outreach *by Felicia A. Smith* / **11**

5   Planning a Library Anniversary Celebration *by Mary H. Nino* / **13**

6   Reading Matters in Mentor: Library Services at the Pools
    and Beaches on Ohio's North Coast *by Lynn Hawkins* / **15**

7   Small Grants Can Have Big Rewards *by Chelsea Dinsmore* / **17**

8   Using a Digitization Project to Produce a Book
    for Community Outreach *by John R. Burch Jr.* / **19**

9   Using Pilot Projects for Outreach *by Chelsea Dinsmore* / **21**

PART II   SENIOR OUTREACH IN PRACTICE

10   Beyond the Campus: Information Literacy Instruction
     for the Senior Community *by Susan M. Frey* / **27**

11   Memoir Writing for Older Adult Groups *by Mark Donnelly* / **29**

12   Outreach to the Senior Community:
     One Library's Activities *by Bob Blanchard* / **33**

13   Sí Se Puede! / Yes We Can! *by Meryle Leonard* / **35**

14   What Boomers Want: The Future of Outreach *by Ellen Mehling* / **37**

PART III   YOUTH OUTREACH IN PRACTICE

15   Better Than One: Collaborative Outreach for
     Homeschooled Teens *by Catherine Fraser Riehle* / **43**

16 Children's Initiative: Establishing a Successful Partnership
    with a Local Public School System *by Vera Gubnitskaia* / **45**

17 Hundreds of High School Students Study at the Library *by Tiffany Auxier* / **48**

18 Reaching Out to Create Outreach Programs
    among Teen Library Patrons *by Maryann Mori* / **51**

19 Reaching Out to Student Athletes, Two Students
    at a Time *by Maureen Brunsdale* / **53**

20 Teen Theater at the Public Library *by Licia Slimon* / **55**

21 Teens Will Respond *by Maryann Mori* / **57**

22 Upward Bound Outreach to Talented
    High School Students *by Jamie Seeholzer* / **59**

PART IV   CORRECTIONAL FACILITY OUTREACH

23 Freedom Readers in a Juvenile Correctional Facility *by Felicia A. Smith* / **65**

24 Has Your Public Librarian Been to Prison? Participation in
    Summer Reading Games *by Glennor Shirley* / **68**

25 Has Your Public Librarian Been to Prison? Participation in
    Shared Grant Projects *by Glennor Shirley* / **72**

PART V   SPECIAL COLLECTIONS

26 Breathing Life into the Circus Collection *by Maureen Brunsdale* / **75**

27 Bringing History to the People's Fingertips: University of Florida
    Digital Collections and Historical Florida Newspapers *by Melissa Shoop* / **77**

28 They Didn't Teach Me *This* in Library School:
    Managing a Library Art Gallery *by Karen Brodsky* / **79**

PART VI   USING LOCAL MEDIA TO REACH
OUT TO THE COMMUNITY

29 Lights, Camera, Libraries *by Nancy Kalikow Maxwell* / **85**

30 Partnering with a Local Newspaper to
    Digitize Historical Photographs *by John R. Burch Jr.* / **87**

PART VII   SUCCESS WITH BOOK FESTIVALS

31 Michigan Reads! Statewide Outreach Project *by Christine K. Heron* / **93**

32   Books That Shape Our Lives: A Community of Readers *by Jan Siebold* / **95**

33   Collaboration Creates a Successful Regional
     Low-Vision Fair *by Bob Blanchard* / **97**

34   One Community, One Story *by Florence M. Turcotte* / **99**

35   SOKY Book Fest *by Uma Doraiswamy* / **101**

36   University of Florida's George A. Smathers Libraries and
     the Common Reading Program *by Melissa Shoop* / **103**

PART VIII   CLASSROOM OUTREACH

37   Academic Connections: A College Librarian
     Reaches Out to a Middle School *by Margaret Keys* / **109**

38   Integrating Manuscripts into the Michigan Curriculum
     through Archival Outreach *by Marian Matyn* / **110**

39   Public School Teacher Workshops Conducted by the University of Alabama
     at Birmingham's Mervyn H. Sterne Library *by Delores Carlito* / **114**

40   Secondary Classroom Instruction in Birmingham *by Delores Carlito* / **116**

41   Teaching American History: Archivists Partnering with
     Public Schools *by Sharon Carlson* / **119**

42   A Different Kind of Science Project: A Partnership between
     a Community College Library and a High School Media Center
     by Nancy Kalikow Maxwell / **121**

PART IX   DIVERSITY OUTREACH

43   Día de los Niños / Día de los Libros *by Meryle Leonard* / **127**

44   Documenting the Experiences of African Americans, Native Americans,
     and Mexican Americans: Archivists Partnering with Oral Historians
     by Sharon Carlson / **129**

45   Ethiopia Reads *by Loriene Roy* / **132**

46   Homework Club for English Language Learners *by Licia Slimon* / **134**

47   If I Can Read, I Can Do Anything: A National Reading Club
     for Native Children *by Loriene Roy* / **137**

48   Laptop Literacy: Language and Computer Literacy Services to Refugees
     in Burlington, Vermont *by Barbara A. Shatara* / **139**

49   The Long Journey to Vermont: Immigration, Cultural Identity, and
     Book Discussions That Build Community *by Barbara A. Shatara* / **141**

50 Outreach to the Russian-Speaking Community in the
Arapahoe Library District *by Katya B. Dunatov* / **144**

51 Outreach to Newly Enrolled African American
College Students *by Jamie Seeholzer* / **146**

52 Serving Multicultural Patrons at the
Arapahoe Library District *by Katya B. Dunatov* / **148**

PART X COMMUNITY GROUP COLLABORATION AND OUTREACH

53 Community Groups Join Forces for Family Fun *by Tiffany Auxier* / **153**

54 Connecting with the Community: Partnering to Deliver a
Storytime Outreach *by Margaret Keys* / **155**

55 Creative Partnerships with Local Organizations *by Ellen Mehling* / **158**

56 Dinner with the Presidents: Teaming Up with the
Yours Truly Restaurant Chain *by Lynn Hawkins* / **161**

57 Faraway Places *by Uma Doraiswamy* / **163**

58 Fostering Community Engagement through a
Town and Gown Lecture Series *by Susan M. Frey* / **165**

59 A Friend in Need: Partnering with an
Employment Center *by Elaine Williams* / **167**

60 Guest Reader Storytime: Fenton Area Outreach Project
by Christine K. Heron / **170**

61 Local Artists-in-Residence at Your School Library *by Jan Siebold* / **172**

62 Partnering for Lifelong Learning: A Unique Collaboration
by Catherine Fraser Riehle / **174**

63 Partnering for Dollars: Using Grant Opportunities to Build Community
and Provide Programming *by Karen Brodsky* / **177**

64 Partnering with a Local Park or Historical Agency *by Florence M. Turcotte* / **179**

65 Partnering with Your Local Historical Society *by Elaine Williams* / **182**

66 A University Library Reaches Out to an
Entire Community *by Iona R. Malanchuk* / **185**

Afterword *by Edith Campbell* / **187**

List of Contributors / **189**

Index / **195**

FOREWORD

WHAT PART of a book does a reader look at first? If you're like me, you've already scanned the table of contents and the index. You might have read one or two articles whose titles were so irresistible that you had to turn right to them. Early on, you checked out the cover blurbs and the editor's biography. If you're one of the contributors, you no doubt looked yourself up in that list. And now you've come upon the foreword, which is supposed to be a short, introductory statement. I like to compare the foreword of a book to the appetizers section of a menu. Both should describe some tidbits to whet your appetite for what is to come: the main course. In this book, the main course is outreach.

Here are just a few of the entrées (or should I say entries?) you'll want to sample:

- unconventional outreach — partners such as juvenile correctional facilities, newspapers, local parks or historical agencies, and employment centers
- teen outreach — homeschooled teens, student athletes, teen thespians
- multicultural, senior, and baby boomer outreach
- and don't miss the articles on library anniversaries, beach outreach, a circus collection, and a library art gallery

When trying to come up with a synonym for outreach, you need look no further than the titles of the articles in this book. Connecting, delivering, partnering, collaborating, teaming up, joining forces, fostering engagement . . . these are a few of the words and phrases that describe the innovative, groundbreaking, and life-changing work being performed by today's librarians.

Kathy Barco
Children's Librarian, Albuquerque/Bernalillo County Public Library

PREFACE

THIS BOOK is a mosaic of sixty-six articles by thirty-four innovative librarians from across the United States who share their successful outreach activities with the reader. These unpublished articles (1,900–2,100 words each) by school, public, academic, and special librarians and LIS faculty convey the effectiveness of outreach and the dedication, inventiveness, and enthusiasm of librarians. This book was compiled for library and information studies students as well as professionals already in the field.

Librarians tend to share, and this bodes well for outreach—even in times of economic stress, the creativity of librarians opens fresh paths to reach patrons in their communities. There was so much variety that it was a challenge to group the articles into chapters.

It was difficult to select from so many librarians willing to share their experiences, and every effort was made to include variety. Contributors were encouraged to provide two examples of outreach and to follow Gustave Flaubert's advice to help busy readers: "Whenever you can shorten a sentence, do. And one always can. The best sentence? The shortest."

The outreach activities are grouped in the table of contents and are also indexed by subject and author.

It has been a pleasure working with these creative librarians who are willing to share their outreach experiences. Librarians are indeed dedicated professionals, and it has always been an honor to be counted among them.

PART I
A Sampler of Outreach Programs

1

BAKE A BOOK AND THEY WILL COME

Iona R. Malanchuk

WANT TO show just how sweet a good book can be? Try organizing an Edible Book Contest. A University of Florida library committee has been doing just that for the last six years with success. It is held in April in recognition of National Library Week, and there are only two rules of competition: each entry must be edible and must relate somehow to a book. Imagine colorful, detailed, and sometimes very large platters with an edible depiction of *War and Peace, Cinderella, Charlotte's Web, Treasure Island, Who Moved My Cheese?, The Grapes of Wrath, Memoirs of a Geisha, Eragon, Cloudy with a Chance of Meatballs, Beowulf,* and so on. Other equally fascinating and creative book-related entries have included an edible book truck, edible bookmarks, and others. Almost everyone stays until the very end to applaud the award winners and watch as each proud participant takes her cake back home to share with family or friends.

A DIVERSE GROUP OF PARTICIPANTS

Reading enthusiasts need time to design and create their colorful and delicious entries, so the detailed planning and advertising for this annual University of Florida Libraries competition begins in January, three months ahead of the April contest. This outreach effort to the entire community is promoted in a website that identifies dates, times, and procedures and includes an electronic submission/entry form. E-mails announcing and describing the contest are sent to various departments and groups both on and off campus. The University of Florida Libraries home page and local media outlets promote this fun event and encourage participation with regular announcements. Individual committee members start to make personal contact with other library staff throughout the Gainesville community, with individual teaching and research faculty, and with patrons and schools in the area. We continue to have the support of many undergraduate and graduate students who are novice pastry chefs-in-the-making, and we benefit from the creative participation of very capable high school students enrolled in a local Culinary Arts Institute. The event is held outdoors, and so we inevitably attract curious people who are just passing by and are drawn to the large crowd of eager participants and supporters. This competition is a friendly one that ends with some students coming forward to say they were amazed by the creativity shown and asking when and how they might submit entries for next year.

LOCATED JUST OUTSIDE THE MAIN LIBRARY'S FRONT DOOR

In order to accommodate easy viewing of the cakes as well as the lines of people who wish to vote for their favorites, it is appropriate to set up the viewing tables just

3

outside the main library on a covered walkway. If it rains, the display of edible books is brought to an inside lobby area. Colorful banners are hung in various strategic locations across the wide expanse of lawn so that there is no doubt of the sponsorship of our library system and the advertised connection to our observation of National Library Week. Edible entries arrive the morning of the contest between 8:30 a.m. and 10:30 a.m. Cake viewing begins when the tables are first set up by 10:00 a.m. and usually lasts for about an hour. All entries are brought to a location within the library where two committee members record each and every book title and author as well as the participant's name so that a brief, numbered information card sits in front of each entry during the viewing period. Judging and voting takes approximately forty-five minutes. The tabulation of votes is done by a separate, impartial group of volunteer library staff members. One year we relied on a group of six judges to select the award winners, but the next year we allowed voting by attendees.

ENTICE THEM TO COME AND CELEBRATE NATIONAL LIBRARY WEEK

Because this contest is only offered in April and in conjunction with a celebration of National Library Week, we seize the opportunity to connect with other libraries throughout our area. Although we make sure that all participants receive some recognition, five prizes are awarded to the best entries in each of the following categories: Most Creative, Least Edible, Best Overall Fiction, Best Overall Nonfiction, and Best Children's Book. Prizes are solicited by committee members during the preceding three-month planning period and come from popular local restaurants, bookstores, ice-cream parlors, and so on. Local businesses seize the opportunity to receive publicized recognition of their support for this library program via mention of their businesses on our website, banners, and in e-mails. The purpose of this joint venture by library staff, users, administrators, and other friends of libraries is to recognize and celebrate the necessary and valuable contributions that libraries make in their communities.

WE CONTINUE TO LEARN FROM EACH ANNUAL EDIBLE BOOK CONTEST

We continue to learn from our efforts and we revise our procedures as necessary. This past year we had double the number of cakes from the previous year, and we did not expect that many. Therefore, we needed to increase the number of people carrying the cakes from the holding area inside the library to the outside display tables. We needed additional display tables and taped-down table coverings that needed to be moved outside at the last minute.

Voting took longer and would have been easier if we had had the tabulators working in pairs. One person needs to unfold the ballot and read the award category and selected winner's name while the other person records the vote. It may be more efficient to have a vote collection box at the end of each table and a solid deadline for casting the ballot.

Other essentials would include possibly having your committee brainstorm other award categories that won't be confusing, such as Best Children's Book, Best Adult

Book, Most Creative, and possibly Least Appetizing. One year we had one cake that melted into a distorted, unappealing heap. Be sure to have enough trash bags to collect the leftover debris. All dishes need to have ownership identification and contact information on the bottom because some participants bring their entry and then leave for class or work or home. Each award presented should include recognition of the donating business. This basic courtesy may result in a repeat donation next year. Be prepared for complaining people demanding to know where exactly the contest was advertised because they "never heard about this" and "would have gladly entered the contest" if only they had known about it. This year we even publicized the event on Facebook and had a talented, artistic committee member design and touch up a chalk display on the sidewalk in front of the large and well-populated student union.

Something else that surprised us was the involvement of students from a local high school Culinary Arts program. Last year a number of these students entered an original cake in our competition, and they won the top prize in their category. This year the high school students were not able to compete, but the director of that program accepted our invitation to be one of our six judges, thereby continuing their support of our well-publicized contest. They have already indicated they will be back next year for our fourth annual Edible Book Contest, an event that many of our university people are looking forward to as well.

2
ESTABLISHING A LIBRARY DOCENT PROGRAM

Mary H. Nino

THE KING Library Docent program, established in 2003, is a very successful program where trained volunteer docents serve as tour guides and share the wonderful facility, resources, and art of the Dr. Martin Luther King, Jr. Library in San Jose, California, with the public. The King Library, which was named the 2004 Thomson Gale/Library Journal Library of the Year, is a unique partnership between San Jose State University and the city of San Jose. Opened in 2003, the 476,000-square-foot building serves as both the university library and the main branch of the San Jose Public Library system. It is comanaged and operated by these two institutions and has been popular beyond expectation from opening day.

WHY THE LIBRARY ESTABLISHED ITS DOCENT PROGRAM

Although there are several joint libraries in the county, a joint venture on this scale had never been attempted before. A visionary community member who anticipated the likelihood of many curious visitors approached the library dean and suggested establishing a docent program similar to museums. While the King Library is unique and larger than most, a docent program could be established on a smaller scale for any size library.

THE STEPS IN STARTING A DOCENT PROGRAM

Determine how the docent program can best help the library. It may be that the library is well established and does not often have requests for tours. Offering tours is a great marketing tool for both new and older buildings, however, and can rekindle interest in any long-established institution. Docents may be utilized in numerous other ways, too. Other possibilities include

- ambassadors or speakers at popular programs
- supporters at city council meetings
- assistants with school groups and visits
- outreach to senior or shut-in groups who can't visit the building

INITIAL PLANNING

Establish a docent team or planning committee. This group should include a staff member who enjoys working with volunteers and is good with details and follow-up. This individual provides continuity and should be familiar with library practices and policies. Involving an energetic library supporter from the community, who has the time and connections, is also strongly recommended. Additional staff members can offer ideas and staff buy-in. This is essential because personnel in smaller organizations may feel threatened that the docents are usurping staff duties.

DEVELOP A JOB DESCRIPTION AND TRAINING PROGRAM

Develop a well-written job description with clearly defined duties and expectations for the docents. Include both a monthly hourly commitment and a minimum number of months that each docent will commit to the program. Schedule training sessions and determine equipment needs. As much as possible, engage the most appropriate person to present each training session. Training should be comprehensive, with well-planned agendas and attractive, up-to-date materials. This type of intensive training can help position the program as prestigious and a notch above regular volunteer positions. Docents want to feel knowledgeable and well prepared when interacting with visitors and being asked questions. Topics to consider when developing training include the following:

1. History of the organization and building

2. Information about the library's parent organization—funding, lines of reporting, and so on

3. Library philosophy, mission, and services—could also provide updates on upcoming library bond measures

4. Library departments and staffing—function, training requirements, day-to-day responsibilities

5. Behind-the-scenes tour—library trainees are often fascinated by what goes on in nonpublic areas of the library. Provide an opportunity for them to observe the whole operation and feel like they have specialized information and expertise.

6. Art—does the library have any significant or unique art? Provide background information on any visiting exhibits or speakers.

7. Safety and facilities—in the event of a building or medical emergency, what is the plan? Where are the exits, phones, restrooms, fire alarms, and security personnel located? Are docents' emergency contact numbers readily available?

8. Technology—what kind of technology is available? Nuts-and-bolts questions such as "Is there Wi-Fi?" "How do I print?" or "How do I get on a computer?" may not be part of the tour, but familiarity with these services will make docents feel more prepared.

9. Communication skills—giving a good tour is an art. Docents should be coached in

    • how to show welcoming behaviors

    • how to keep a group together and engaged

    • how to keep stragglers from slowing down the process

    • how to avoid having the tour hijacked by a know-it-all or attention-seeking guest who wants to monopolize the group's attention

10. Housekeeping—is there a secure place for the docents' personal belongings? What is the process for calling in sick or getting parking validation if necessary?

11. Additional library services—what other areas could be promoted? Outreach to the disabled, literacy programs, special collections, classes, or innovative programming?

12. Practice tours—docents should be given the opportunity to do a training tour before working with a tour group.

RECRUITMENT

A well-connected and visible community member on the planning team can be a tremendous asset and can help determine the most effective places to advertise and to recruit for docent candidates. The library website is a great place to market the program and should include the job description, application form, and contact name and numbers. Local media outlets can also be utilized to spread the word. Retirement communities can be a good source of interested candidates. Descriptive brochures can be displayed prominently at library events.

STAFF SUPPORT AND SCHEDULING

Staff that help with training should make sure that the docents are introduced and feel welcomed. Docents who complete the training should receive identification badges and be treated with respect and appreciation for their willingness to share and promote the library. The staff member who serves as the primary liaison with the docents should handle tour requests and communicate with docents via e-mail. Available docents will volunteer for upcoming tours and the information is then entered into a Yahoo! Groups calendar (http://groups.yahoo.com), which is available for all docents to access. This staff member also handles record keeping and will compile an annual report on the program.

ADVERTISING

Initially, the King Library offered several tours each week. As the years passed, demand tapered off. We now offer prescheduled tours and one weekly tour. Tours are advertised on the library website, local newspaper, and through bookmarks that are available in the library, the convention center, and nearby hotels. In addition, the library utilizes a local organization's weekly upcoming events newsletter and the online services craigslist (www.craigslist.org) and Artsopolis (www.artsopolis.com) to promote the tours.

RETENTION

One way to further involve docents is to have the more seasoned members serve as mentors for new docent trainees. Not only is their knowledge recognized and valued, but they can also offer encouragement for new trainees, getting them up to speed more quickly. In addition, the docent team will hold quarterly meetings, often a potluck lunch, where docents can socialize, make suggestions or share stories, and receive any new training or information. Not only do the docents enjoy getting together, but these gatherings provide a great opportunity to acknowledge their contributions. Once a year, a holiday appreciation luncheon is held, with service pins being awarded for each year of service.

3

FRIENDS IN NEED

Involving Friends of the Library in Community Outreach Programs

Vera Gubnitskaia

STUDIES SHOW that adults who live below the poverty line often do not graduate from high school and many do not read well. Because the literacy level of children is closely linked to that of their parents, children from economically disadvantaged families often lack the necessary skills to enter kindergarten. The Head Start program was established in 1965 to address child development issues in low-income families. The program focuses on early literacy, kindergarten readiness, and parental involvement. Since its inception, the program has provided many educational benefits to families that live below the poverty line.

In Orange County, Florida, 10.5 percent of families with children under five years old live below the poverty line. It is clear that there is a need for the community to address issues arising from many children growing up in economically disadvantaged families. The Head Start program is one of the most important means of improving literacy and kindergarten-readiness level for children in a substantial portion of the Orange County population.

The Orange County Library System became involved with the Orange County Head Start program in the mid-1980s. The library staff worked with Head Start personnel and administrators to encourage bringing kids to the library and using it as one of Head Start's resources. Staff also began scheduling regular outreach programs at the Head Start centers. This marked the development of a long-term, mutually beneficial partnership.

After some time, the library felt that it would like to become more involved in promoting and developing family and early literacy. An idea was developed to supplement the practice of introducing children to books during story programs: give each child a book to take home, a book that had just been read to them. If children liked the program, they might ask their parents to read the book to them at home. This would allow us to achieve several goals: to develop children's interest in books and reading and to encourage families to read together. The money issue came up, of course, because there were over 1,500 children enrolled in the Head Start program. A donation or a grant was needed to make this idea come to life.

Enter the Friends of the Library. Organized in 1947, the Friends of the Orange County Library System (FOL) is a volunteer organization that supports our library system. Friends of the Library runs the library bookstore and the Gifts and Greeting gift shop. With funds raised from sales, FOL donates books to some of the library-sponsored community initiatives, such as the Head Start initiative.

For the past ten years, FOL has contributed $6,500 annually to the Head Start programs and the book giveaway program. Each year, library staff select a book title that the library will purchase with these funds. The requirements for title selections are as follows:

The title should be readily available for purchase in large quantities.

The title should be available in paperback. Hardcover books are more expensive, and we are not able to buy them in sufficient quantities. Board books are often abridged, and we prefer to have full-length stories. In addition, preschool children in Head Start programs view board books as "baby books" and are not as excited as when they get "big kid" books.

Maximum per-copy cost should not exceed $5.99 (with the library discount, it usually comes to just under $4.00, which makes it possible for us to order large quantities).

The title should be "presentable," that is, we should be able to use it in a story program for three- to five-year-olds. To achieve greater impact, we select books that we can act out, to make them more attractive to kids and encourage future family reading activities.

We give preference to titles that can also be found in a Spanish-language version. A total of 24.3 percent of the population in Orange County is Hispanic. When possible, we order one copy of the same title in Spanish for each Head Start's library.

We give special consideration to titles that are available in oversized format. Large books make stories more visual and are ideal for preschool story programs.

The rest of the process goes in the following manner:

1. The Youth Services staff select at least three titles to ensure that we have a backup in case our primary selection is not available in sufficient quantities.

2. Our Acquisitions Department works with vendors to check which title is available in 1,600 copies and ensure that the total cost is covered by the FOL funds.

3. The Youth Services manager submits an annual request to the Friends of the Library to include Head Start initiative funding in their budget. The budget is finalized at an FOL meeting, after which Youth Services and Acquisitions get a "go-ahead" to purchase materials.

4. After materials are purchased, delivered, and processed, library teen volunteers attach a special label to each book to acknowledge FOL as a donor.

After all materials are processed, the Youth Services staff contact each Head Start center and schedule the date for story programs and the book giveaway. At the same time, they verify the correct number of children at that center to ensure that every child receives their book during our visit. Staff prepare and conduct programs that include books, songs, stories, and games. Members of FOL along with a representative from Library Community Relations and the library director visit at least two programs to observe the programs' impact and participate in the book giveaway.

Head Start centers and the library enjoy several benefits from this partnership. The centers are able to introduce an additional free educational activity into their curriculum, ensure that each child receives a book recommended by a library expert, and enhance their curriculum. By promoting its services to over 1,500 kids, their families, and teachers each year, the library has an opportunity to increase the number of library card registrations, circulation numbers, door count, and program attendance. Last but not least is the positive impact of the initiative on the community that is achieved by increasing literacy levels and school readiness, developing lifelong reading and learning habits among low-income families, and raising children who are better prepared for success in the future.

4

LIFESAVING LIBRARY OUTREACH

Felicia A. Smith

THIS CHAPTER describes a successful marketing promotion on the first day of class designed to increase awareness of library services among students in a creative manner.

Before creating promotional items, I answered the five Ws: Who, What, When, Where, and Why. For this promotion, the Who was undergraduate students at the University of Notre Dame. When creating our marketing plan, I conducted a literature review to ascertain what challenges libraries are facing nationwide. This dealt with the Why. In 2005 OCLC produced *Perceptions of Libraries and Information Resources*, which is a survey of over 3,300 library users, including nearly 400 college students, to gain a better understanding of trends relating to the information consumer and to libraries.[1]

This left the two remaining Ws: the When and the Where. I decided to hand out my promotional materials on the first day of class, in front of DeBartolo Hall. As it is in real estate, "location, location, location" is everything in promotions. DeBartolo Hall contains two-thirds of the total campus classrooms, so I went to where the patrons were.

After writing the marketing plan and conducting the literature review, creating promotional items was quite simple and enjoyable. This particular promotion was made even easier due to budgetary constraints.

Step 1: Format and Content. I decided on a list of library services that could be read in less than one minute.

Step 2: Creative Presentation of Facts. I learned as a child that it is not what you say but rather how you say it. In marketing classes I learned that consumers will ask, "What's in it for me?" Consequently, I decided to use color fonts to add emphasis. In keeping with the different color theme, I added Life Saver candy rolls as a treat. Amazon.com had the best price online, so we ordered five hundred rolls of Life Savers for a total of $250.

Step 3: Quality Production. Production quality is vitally important to success. Therefore, I paid Kinko's $180 to print glossy postcards on sturdier paper stock.

Step 4: Manual Labor. I taped a Life Saver roll to each postcard using at least two layers of tape because I didn't want them falling off. I also wanted to increase the time it takes to remove the candy from the postcard, allowing more time to read the text.

Step 5: Distribution. I stood directly in the middle of the entrance of DeBartolo Hall with my cart about twenty-five minutes before the start of the first class. Fortunately, I had had the foresight to place postcards on the railing leading into the building, in case some people were walking farther away from me, or I had a long line. This actually ended up being extremely helpful, especially when I needed to open a new box of cards or when a crowd of students converged on me at once. All the postcards were gone in fifteen minutes! This was an effective promotion, even though it is a simple idea.

The students said they loved Life Savers and asked, "Why would the library do this?" I explained that we just wanted to make sure they knew that we are here to help. They were genuinely grateful, and this achieved our marketing goal to evoke positive responses to library communications. In conclusion, it is vital to

- get patrons' attention
- deliver a clear, concise message
- motivate students to absorb your message positively

It is essential to differentiate between promotions and marketing. Marketing requires an inordinate amount of analysis and planning. The following story is the best way to summarize the difference:

> If the circus is coming to town and you paint a sign stating "Circus Coming to the Fairground Saturday," that's advertising.
> If you put the sign on the back of an elephant walking through town, that's promotion.
> If the elephant walks through the mayor's garden, that's publicity.
> If the mayor laughs about it, that's public relations.
> If the residents go the circus, you show them the booths and answer questions, and they spend money at the circus, that's sales.
> And if you planned the whole thing, well now, that is Marketing! (source unknown)

NOTE

1. Cathy De Rosa, *Perceptions of Libraries and Information Resources: A Report to the OCLC Membership* (Dublin, OH: OCLC Online Computer Library Center, 2005).

5

PLANNING A LIBRARY ANNIVERSARY CELEBRATION

Mary H. Nino

THE DR. Martin Luther King, Jr. Library, which was named the 2004 Thomson Gale/Library Journal Library of the Year, is a unique partnership between San Jose State University and the city of San Jose. Located in downtown San Jose, California, and opened in 2003, the 476,000-square-foot building serves as both the university library and the main branch of the San Jose Public Library system. It is comanaged by these two institutions and has been popular beyond expectation from opening day. Initially, the joint library concept met with considerable resistance and protest, particularly from university faculty. After five years, even the most die-hard skeptics have come around, and the library has become a source of university and civic pride. It is often pointed to as a model for collaboration and has fostered a desire for more resource sharing. Given this history and despite the fact that the King Library was only five years old, personnel from both the university and the public library system agreed that an anniversary celebration would provide an ideal opportunity for reflection, promotion, and congratulations. The event required considerable planning, staff time, and coordination. Several factors contributed to the successful execution of our event.

The following suggestions will guide libraries considering a celebratory event in their own communities.

1. Establish a Planning Team. Ideally, the group should include people with varied roles and skills who can interact well and who have the power to move the process forward. We included outreach and programming librarians, our marketing expert, and even representatives from our parent institutions. We agreed to meet regularly and assigned responsibilities and deadlines.

2. Clarify Goals and Objectives. What does the team hope to accomplish? Is the event designed to promote library services and visibility? Will there be a theme? Will the focus be on speeches and recognition, or will there be activities that might be of interest to families with children? Our team agreed that we would kick off the anniversary with a one-day event complete with dignitaries, tours, music, and dance performances and follow it with a monthlong celebration where we highlighted our usual programming.

3. Budget. How will this celebration be funded? The size and scale of any event is determined by financial support. The bulk of our funding was provided by our Friends of the Library, whose sponsorship was acknowledged on a free book bag that was passed out at the event. The San Jose Redevelopment Agency provided some additional funding, and local merchants provided cake. Various performing groups were willing to participate, and library volunteers assisted with logistics.

4. Scheduling. Ideally, planning should begin several months prior to the event. City officials, in particular, have very busy schedules and should be booked far in advance. If special performers, photographers, or caterers are being employed, contracts will need to be signed and approved. Time lines, action items, and deadlines should be shared and published so that important details don't get overlooked. Our group used a Google Docs online spreadsheet that was easily accessible to all committee members and enabled us to track our progress.

5. Promotion and Marketing. This critical component will greatly contribute to the event's success. Marketing materials should be attractive, professional, and comprehensive. Once our fifth anniversary graphic had been created, our team worked on collateral items such as bookmarks, invitations, banners, and a website presence. We developed press releases, fact sheets, and radio blurbs for the local media and distributed fliers at the library branches and local schools. An online guest book was established so that patrons could share their comments and congratulations. One patron's appreciative online comment mentioned that he proposed to his girlfriend in the library, her favorite place in the downtown area.

6. Logistics. There can never be enough double-checking on details. Some things to consider:

- Will there be a need for a sound or projection system, and is there power close by?
- Who will set up the system and make sure it is working on the day of the event?
- Will there need to be security or emergency personnel on-site or on call?
- In the event of bad weather, what is the backup plan?
- Will there be a stage, podium, and additional chairs for the audience?
- Who is responsible for setup, and is there a diagram to follow?
- Will guest speakers need to be picked up, or are they responsible for their own transportation?
- What kind of decorations or flowers will need to be ordered or set up on the day of the event?
- Do any certificates, plaques, or programs need to be produced or ordered?
- Who will be handling introductions and master of ceremony responsibilities?
- Who will prepare a script or any pertinent background information?

- How will time management be handled?
- Are additional restroom facilities available?
- Does additional custodial help need to be scheduled?
- Do the event planners need to have cell phones or walkie-talkies?

If these tasks are discussed beforehand, the event should run far more smoothly. Our anniversary celebration was well attended and brought renewed attention and interest to the library. Typically, patrons would comment that they couldn't believe five years had passed. The library has become so deeply embedded and appreciated by its users that it feels like it has always been there. This celebration was a nice reminder of how libraries contribute to and invigorate their communities.

6
READING MATTERS IN MENTOR
Library Services at the Pools and Beaches on Ohio's North Coast
Lynn Hawkins

HERE ON the North Coast we make the most of summer, because the prevailing weather in northeast Ohio is often gray. July 2006 brought a string of beautiful days, and we bemoaned a dramatic drop in traffic and program attendance at the Mentor Public Library. I wondered about the possibility of taking storytime on the road by taking library services to the pools. Our patrons were there—maybe we should be, too! The city of Mentor operates three outdoor swimming pools. Civic Center Waterpark is an Olympic-sized pool on the government campus at city hall; Eleanor B. Garfield Pool is located about two blocks from the Mentor Public Library and adjacent to the Garfield Museum; and Morton Pool and Spraypark is in the Mentor Headlands area, several blocks from the Headlands Branch Library. Our Children's Services Department enthusiastically supported the idea of following our patrons to the pools, despite the fact that we were operating on reduced service hours and with reduced staff after a painful levy loss. We faced another levy campaign in the fall and were aggressively marketing library services. Civic Center Waterpark attracts around 2,000 swimmers a day during the hot summer months, and the prospect of having a library presence at such a busy venue was extremely attractive. We placed a call to the city's superintendent of recreation and proposed to read aloud to kids during the "all clear" pool break at 3:00 p.m. He responded enthusiastically to our proposal. We chose Wednesday because it is one of the busiest days at the pools, weather permitting.

"MORE BOOKS, MORE BOOKS!"

We necessarily started small due to our reduced staffing. Our pool debut took place at Garfield Pool because it is close to the library. The program is simple: one of our children's associates arrives at the pool shortly before 3:00 p.m. and sets up shop in a designated shady spot. We try to locate close to the concession stand in order to accommodate those multitaskers who like a little snack with their stories. Costumes on the part of our staff are optional. When the whistle blows for the 3:00 p.m. pool break, the pool staff advertise the storytime over the public-address system. Kids and some parents make their way over to our staff with their towels and snacks, and they are a happy and interested bunch. Our staff wear big hats and library logo shirts. They have lots of enthusiasm for the program.

The first storytimes drew just a handful of kids and curious parents. We had started late in the summer, but we agreed with the city that the program had potential and we planned for an expansion in 2007. We now provide Storytime @ the Pools at all three city pools on Wednesday afternoons all summer long, and each session attracts crowds of over eighty kids during the pools' break time. The city advertises the program in citywide Parks and Recreation mailings and on Mentor Channel 12, the city's television channel. We advertise in our fliers and our newsletter. There is something really great about the visual of a group of dripping-wet kids chanting, "More books, more books!" The program has raised our profile in the community and exposed a new audience to our storytimes.

MENTOR READS

In 2006 district test scores in our schools were not as high as they could be. The discussion among area educators and parents citywide included the question of how to keep kids reading over the summer. Inspired by the success of our Storytime @ the Pools collaboration, the superintendent of recreation approached the Mentor Public Library with a new program proposal. He suggested that the library provide free, gently used books that have been canceled from our collection for the three city pools. The program is called Mentor Reads. The library has purchased an extra-large basket for each site, and our outreach coordinator culls through our canceled children's books and donations for picture books and easy readers, labeling each with a big blue Mentor Reads sticker. The stickers instruct borrowers that they may either keep the book or return it to any city pool. A library staffer periodically checks the baskets over the summer months for restocking purposes. My daughter is a longtime Civic Center staffer, and she observed that the books were an instant hit with the kids, some of whom she said come from financially poor families and "have *nothing*, Mom." She said they were thrilled to be able to keep a book. Here in Mentor it is easy to forget that there are families out there that are really struggling financially, and the Mentor Reads program is a reminder of how valuable our services can be in nontraditional venues. We have expanded the program to provide canceled magazines and paperbacks for "pool moms," which they love; new life for our old items!

HITTING THE BEACH WITH LIBRARY LOOT

What seemed like a natural next step was to target the two beaches in our community, Overlook Beach Park and Headlands Beach. We approached Lake Hospital

Systems, our local hospital, to partner with us on our Beach Reads program and asked the hospital to provide sunscreen samples. We also arranged for sunscreen donations from the American Cancer Society, which added a small flier on safe sun exposure. The Beach Reads program advertises library services through the distribution of bags that hold a gently used paperback, the library newsletter, and sunscreen. The paperbacks are donated or are canceled from our collection. On Friday afternoons during the summer months, two of our staff walk the beaches and hand out bags to delighted adult beachgoers. Staff reported that they really liked to see the surprised smiles of folks at receiving "free" books. The bags are clear plastic handle bags with our logo imprinted on them, so our staff can see the contents. Many people are happy to tell us what they like to read, and our staff obligingly looks through the bags for a particular genre to match a requester's reading interest. We had originally hoped to borrow a golf cart from the city golf course and drive down the beach with our loot. The city was happy to loan the golf cart, but the Ohio Department of Natural Resources doesn't want librarians driving on its beaches. So our Outreach Department staffers brave the hot sand on foot. Next summer our staff along with volunteers plan to "storm the beaches" as part of an in-service session for our staff on the topic of outreach services. Our beaches and pools attract many people from outside the community, but one of the great things about Ohio public libraries is that any resident in the state can obtain a card at any public library in the state. We are happy to promote reading to community members and visitors alike!

7

SMALL GRANTS CAN HAVE BIG REWARDS

Chelsea Dinsmore

THERE IS an attitude, common to many institutions, that small grants just aren't worth it. They take time to prepare and submit, and then they take time to administer. Many business officers will tell you that anything under a thousand dollars and you hardly break even, and really, who would be interested in less than $10,000 anyway? I was unaware of this commonsense approach to grants when I put in my first proposal. It wasn't all that small, and I have since applied for smaller amounts, but I have found these to be entirely worth the effort. Small grants offer a unique opportunity to build relationships, network, and advertise.

WOW; OR, WHAT CAN YOU GET FOR $150?

When a group of University of Florida (UF) librarians wanted to try a new approach to orientation programs, we had to find monies to cover refreshments and prizes. The UF Libraries are state funded, and state funds cannot generally be used for giveaways and consumables. We found out about a mini-grant program run by the UF Dean of Students Office to support "Weeks of Welcome" programming (WOW) for freshmen and other new students. We applied for a grant and received $150, which bought a dozen sand pails for pirate loot and inflatable alligator floats (Go Gators!) for prizes, in addition to other prizes and decorations. More important, our events appeared on a calendar poster that was sent to every entering freshman and all faculty and staff. Moreover, it put the library on the dean of students' radar as an active campus participant for future events.

LET'S TALK ABOUT PARTNERSHIPS!

In 2005 I applied for an American Library Association and Nextbook Let's Talk about It: Jewish Literature, Identity and Imagination program grant because it seemed appropriate for our institution. For a seven-page narrative application form, you could receive $1,500 (at the time). You were encouraged to include letters of support, however, and partnerships also rated highly on the grading scale. The county library district was running an earlier iteration of the program, and I sought advice and a letter from their project manager. I also sought support and partnership from the UF Center for Jewish Studies (CJS) and Hillel at UF. The CJS agreed to partner with us and offered to provide refreshments as their part of the deal. Hillel gave us free use of their lovely new library space (the main UF library was undergoing renovation at the time) and a deep discount on their catering rates. With such solid community support, our proposal was successful. This also meant that our programs went up on the Hillel calendar of events and out in the CJS newsletter to alums and supporters. Hillel also began publishing a student newspaper at about the same time we ran this program and gave us a good deal on a series of ads.

In 2007 I applied for another two rounds of the Let's Talk program. Grant awards now totaled $5,000. This time I partnered with the public library but still asked for letters of support from the CJS and Hillel, who obliged and also gave us the same advertising assistance as before. This time the public library also put us on their calendar of events and provided a special-events blurb on their website. Putting the packet together the second time was much easier because I knew what was needed and I already knew who to call on for letters and help.

ON THE FRONT LINES

In 2008 I saw a call for applications for an American Library Association/Public Broadcasting Service pilot grant program. The grant amount in question was only five hundred dollars, but it involved screening episodes of PBS's *Frontline World* program on the topic of social entrepreneurship. The University of Florida had recently set up a new certificate program on social entrepreneurship, and several DVDs of the program came with the grant. I worked to set up a partnership with the public library, and I found a faculty member who is passionate about "social e." I also discovered that the Dean of Students Office runs a program to encourage students to get involved in their local communities, which fit in with the goals of the grant perfectly. The program had a very short deadline, a very short program window, and an equally short reporting window. I used the grant money for refreshments (because nothing pulls in students like free food), as well as two series of DVDs on the topic of social entrepreneurship and community involvement for the library. Because I already knew people in the public library and the Dean of Students Office, I only had to build one new relationship to pull off this grant.

CONCLUSION

Small grants are annoying to administer. I routinely offer my business office chocolate, by way of apology, when there has been some paperwork snafu or confusion over one of my small checks. However, I believe that the benefits to my library far outweigh the inconvenience. The networks I have built make it easier to obtain support for larger projects down the road. I have built up trust with local colleagues who know I will follow through on projects and offer my support to their efforts in return. This becomes my contribution to meeting an institutional goal of internal and external collaboration.

8

USING A DIGITIZATION PROJECT TO PRODUCE A BOOK FOR COMMUNITY OUTREACH

John R. Burch Jr.

CAMPBELLSVILLE UNIVERSITY marked its centennial in 2007. To celebrate this momentous event in the institution's history, University Archivist Tim Hooper and I wrote a photographic history, entitled *Campbellsville University*, that was published by Arcadia Publishing as a volume in its Campus History Series. Since its publication, the book has proven to be a much more effective community outreach tool than we ever envisioned.

Besides the stated purpose of the book, we did have a number of goals that led us to initially propose undertaking the project to our administration:

1. We saw the book project as a means to inventory the photographic images housed in the A. B. Colvin Baptist Collection and Archives Room in Campbellsville University's Montgomery Library.

2. The book project promised to allow us to experiment with various digitization technologies that the project necessitated we obtain. After the completion of the book, we could then use the equipment and skills gained to digitize other collections housed in the archives.

3. We wanted to show our appreciation of the administration's support of the library, especially because they had just established an archival facility as part of a recently completed renovation of our main library. Thus, we decided to donate all of our royalties to Campbellsville University.

As we began to inventory the existing photograph collections housed in the archives, it quickly became obvious that we did not have enough photographs to adequately capture Campbellsville University's history. This was not a surprising development, considering that it took the university more than ninety-five years to establish an archival facility to preserve its history. To address this problem, we began scouring the campus for photographs that existed but had not been placed in the archives. We found the greatest number of images in two offices, Public Relations and the Sports Information Department. The photographs and negatives were primarily stored in plastic tubs, file cabinets, and closets. The rooms in which they were stored were not climate controlled, and thus obvious deterioration could be observed by the naked eye. When the individuals in charge of the photographs discovered that we wanted to add their images to the archives' photograph collection, they graciously allowed us to digitize all of their work. Furthermore, they committed to sending us photographs in the future. If we had not needed photographs for the book, we probably would not have established an ongoing partnership with the two departments on campus that regularly took photographs of events around campus. Thanks to these partnerships, our photograph collection was more than doubled and continues to grow.

Once we had enough images to work with, we found another problem. We did not know the identity of many of the people that were pictured. We made educated guesses as to when the pictures were taken and then located people who were on campus during the respective periods and asked them for help. Many people gave us their time and knowledge generously. After hearing of our interest in preserving Campbellsville University's history, some of these individuals even donated materials to the archives that we did not know had even existed.

In compiling the book, we opted for a chronological presentation. This allowed us to divide the book up into sections capturing the school in its various phases of existence: an academy with a normal school attached for teacher education, a junior college, a senior college, and a university with a range of graduate programs. Within each section, there were an abundance of pictures of buildings, longtime faculty members, top administrators, and trustees. These were apparently the types of pictures that tended to be preserved by the institution. Hooper and I had to make a conscious effort to remember to include images of everyday student life. After looking at photographic histories prepared by other educational institutions, it was apparent that it is fairly common to forget the ordinary students and the flavor of everyday life on campus as one chronicles the evolution of an educational institution.

With the publication of the book, we thought we had marked the effective end of the project. Our goals had been achieved, and we had produced a work that Hooper and I, as well as the Campbellsville University administration, were proud of. It quickly became apparent that we had underestimated the value of the book project. In producing the book, we had forged new partnerships with several campus departments and constituencies. With the publication of the book, partnership opportunities within our region quickly emerged.

Although our book focused on the history of Campbellsville University, it was also a record of the development of Campbellsville, Kentucky. As the book began circulating in the community, people began to approach the library staff with questions about our holdings concerning the local area and offers of materials we might be interested in. This allowed us to engage local people in conversations about the availability of other forms of media, such as audio and video, that chronicled our service area's history, which we were also seeking to preserve. Hooper constantly demonstrated our digitization equipment to interested parties, which allowed people to see how they could help us collaboratively build a collection that would be available for use by the general public. The influx of materials in more formats than we anticipated led to the acquisition of even more digitization equipment so that we could adequately preserve what has been donated to the archives. Despite the costs of the software and hardware needed as the initial book project evolved into the development of a community photographic collection, we encountered no difficulties in securing funding from our administration because they were hearing from people around the community about the value of the work that was being done in the archives.

The partnerships formed through the book project and its aftermath will continue to be a major focus for the Montgomery Library for the foreseeable future. Partnerships with local historical societies are in discussion phases, and we anticipate digitizing their photographic collections within the next couple of years. The digitization project that is currently taking up the majority of our time is a partnership with our local newspaper, which is described elsewhere in this volume. Because our archives staff consists of two full-time people, assisted by work-study students, it is easy to envision that the partnerships that have already been developed with the community have the potential to keep them busy for at least the next five years.

9

USING PILOT PROJECTS FOR OUTREACH

Chelsea Dinsmore

LIBRARIANS AT the University of Florida (UF) Libraries were disappointed with dropping attendance numbers at traditional orientation sessions. In early 2004 the main campus library, Library West, was closed for badly needed renovations and expansion. Library West, one of nine campus libraries, serves the Humanities and Social Science programs, and the next thirty months brought a steady stream of irritated letters to the editor of the campus newspaper. Students, especially graduate students, complained that they had not been given enough notice of the closing; they blamed the library for not somehow compensating for the lost study space and workstations in the library; and they complained again that the reopening date was "too vague." As the reopening approached, however, we noticed the fact that orientation attendance numbers were in the single digits. We had two entering classes who had never had access to Library West, and they clearly felt no need for those services.

WHAT TO DO

The traditional classroom orientation session was not enticing students. Over the past several years a number of smaller colleges had had good luck with highly interactive programs loosely based on the idea of Dinner and a Mystery. Admittedly, many of these schools had small freshman classes, around five hundred or so, and could more or less make it mandatory for new students to attend, but the important part is that students were coming to the programs, having fun, and leaving with the belief that the library is an approachable space with helpful people. When a colleague brought the idea of trying something along these lines at UF to the newly formed Public Relations and Marketing Committee, we decided to run a pilot project and give it a try. However, there were two things we had to accomplish. First, we had to find funds and donations to cover refreshments and prizes, because regular library money cannot be spent on these things, and second, we had to figure out a way to adapt a program designed for small college libraries to an institution with an incoming freshman class of 6,500.

HOW WE DID IT

Our group approached several local merchants and bookstores and came up with a good collection of prizes, as well as plenty of donated pizza and ice cream. We were hoping for about twenty-five students at each event and decided free food would be a good draw. The UF Dean of Students Office runs a Weeks of Welcome (WOW) program every fall semester. Any group running a program geared for new students can have their program put on the WOW calendar. More important for us, the office offers mini-grants to help fund such programs. The librarians applied for $230 and received $150. This money covered the cost of decorations, which could mostly be reused, as well as additional prizes from the dollar stores. The office also offered to loan us some extra-fancy blow-up palm trees for one of our themes.

In possession of funds to pursue our programs, we planned a series of three scavenger hunts, each to be repeated twice. The first program was a sort of pilot for the pilot, to see just how many things could go wrong. The Library Survivor and Pirates @ the Library events were run at the Marston Science Library (MSL) and were straightforward scavenger hunts. The teams were given a list of things to find. A pilot run of Murder in the Stacks was done just before Library West reopened, so it served as a sneak peek for a lucky few students. This event had the added element of a mystery to solve from the clues found. We planned for about twenty-five students at each event, to be split into five teams of five. Prizes would be awarded to the two fastest teams, and everybody's name went into a hat for additional prize drawings. The blow-up alligators were by far the most popular prize.

The goal of the planners was for each student to leave the program knowing how to use the library catalog, use library databases, find a book on reserve, access e-reserves, and ask for help. In addition, we hoped that by meeting library faculty and staff under casual circumstances, and thus putting a face to the idea of "the librarian," the students would feel more inclined to include the library on their list of research resources.

We ran Library Survivor at the MSL, at the beginning of Summer B (our second summer semester), to see how many things could go wrong. We tried two different time slots—a weekend afternoon and a weekday evening—when the library was closed, so we wouldn't disturb any actual patrons. We learned a lot with this program. For example, it is important to ask the library administration if it is okay to run an after-hours program, and it is equally important that you recruit somebody who knows how to run the building lights and security systems to help with the program. Also, free pizza is a really good draw. Despite heavy summer storms, we had about fifteen students attend the first evening session and nine students at the afternoon session.

Pirates @ the Library and Murder in the Stacks both went fairly smoothly. We learned the importance of switching the order of clues given to the teams so that physical clues weren't being sought at the same time. One of the mystery program events was run when there were patrons in the library, so we had to warn staff not to be too concerned by any screaming they might hear. We had enlisted the help of the University Police Department to bring a police car up to the front of the library and string crime scene tape. That went over really well with students and participants; however, some people passing by were disturbed, and after the tragedies on other campuses the following year we cut that part from the script.

CONCLUSIONS

Overall, none of these programs reached a great many students. Attendance ranged from nine to twenty-seven. By the final program, some instructors teaching first-year experience classes had heard about it and attended to see and then asked us to do special programs for their classes. Unfortunately, we did not have the staff available at the time to run extra rounds. These programs were run by librarians who volunteered their time and students workers who were bribed with pizza.

The students had a good time, and all of our surveys came back with positive responses. Murder in the Stacks has evolved into Mystery in the Stacks and has run for its third year. It is now run by Library West librarians and staff who dress up in great costumes and have a lot of fun planning it. They still get small grants from the Dean of Students Office as part of the WOW events to cover expenses. The science library did not choose to continue the program, largely due to lack of faculty and staff time to pursue it at the time. These programs did not translate into an effective means of reaching large numbers of our entering freshmen. They worked really well for specific groups, whether self-selected through an open invitation or as programs for a class group. Despite the limited number of students reached, the goals for teaching and fun were definitely met.

PART II
Senior Outreach in Practice

BEYOND THE CAMPUS

Information Literacy Instruction for the Senior Community

Susan M. Frey

SINCE 2004 instruction librarians at Indiana State University (ISU) have traveled to a local retirement community to teach information and computer literacy as part of ISU's Bits 'n' Bytes program. Our reasons for initiating this outreach program were to align library initiatives and activities with those of the university. Part of ISU's mission is the development of collaborative partnerships with educational, business, social service, cultural, and government concerns that contribute to the academic mission of ISU and directly benefit the community. ISU is so committed to outreach that in 2006 the Carnegie Foundation placed the university in the Curricular Engagement and Outreach category.

The Bits 'n' Bytes program was also created in response to the local senior community's regular use of library electronic resources. As is the case with other Indiana state-supported libraries, the Reference and Instruction Department at the ISU Library provides a significant amount of reference assistance and individualized instructional services to a growing community of university alumni and emeriti, as well as the senior community at large. We hoped our creation of this outreach program would enhance our ability to serve this diverse population of users.

In the summer of 2004 the ISU Library set up a computer lab at the Westminster Village Retirement Community, a private, nonprofit facility offering both assisted and independent living apartments for seniors. We installed eight Gateway 1400 PCs with Windows XP platform and hardwired them to an Internet DSL line, two DeskJet printers, and a wireless hub. Due to an upgrade, this hardware was redundant in our library, and so we were able to use it for our outreach program. In addition to the lab, we were also able to utilize the retirement community's large-screen media room for lectures.

Once the lab was assembled in a room off of one of the retirement community's lounges, we developed the content and method of instruction. Each one-hour instruction session began with a fifteen-minute lecture in the media room on the various navigational features of computers, and then the class would move to the computer lab for hands-on practice. Using the semester as the guiding time period, we developed a thirteen-week syllabus of classes that met once a week. Each weekly lesson focused on a different topic, with the first four classes devoted to introductory topics such as computer basics, e-mail, and word processing. Many of the classes thereafter focused more narrowly on specific Internet sites or methods of finding information on the Internet.

At first, we assigned one librarian to develop and teach all the lessons. But after a year we realized that it would be more inclusive and offer more variety if we were to ask all the instruction librarians to take it in turns to teach a session. And so the role of the librarian managing this program evolved from teacher to that of teacher/ coordinator. At the beginning of the semester, the program coordinator would ask the instruction librarians what topics they would like to teach and what dates they preferred. A semester schedule would then be produced and sent to the retirement community for them to advertise. Each librarian would create her own handouts and lesson plans for one to two sessions per semester. By having subject experts teach to their specialties, program content became more robust. For instance, our government documents librarian has taught sessions on finding medical information on government sites, while our science librarian has used the Internet to teach seniors about nutrition. With the addition of these subject-specific instruction sessions, the coordinator focused on teaching basic and intermediate computer skills.

In the third year of the program we realized that Bits 'n' Bytes could offer our university students opportunity for growth, and so we worked with ISU faculty to open up the program as a field site for a student enrolled in a freshman social work course. After a few interviews with faculty, we arranged for an undergraduate who was enrolled in an Introduction to Social Work class to serve as an intern in the program. Our undergraduate volunteered as a teaching assistant to satisfy the course's thirty-hour volunteer requirement. While our intern worked with us we built a rich, diverse community made up of teacher-librarians, Westminster residents, and an ISU student. For us, our intern's presence has reinforced our belief that building community in the classroom greatly enhances learning for everyone. Our seniors certainly expressed interest in working again with another undergraduate intern. We are enthusiastic about this new component of the program and plan to develop it further.

Our experiences with outreach to the senior community have benefited us greatly. In these times of tight budgets and staffing shortfalls, some might call for a reduction of or a moratorium on outreach programs in academe. But the process of developing and managing the Bits 'n' Bytes program has demonstrated to us that information literacy instruction can and should extend beyond campus walls and into the local community. The program has grown in ways that we did not initially predict. What started out as an educational outreach program meant to build goodwill grew into a field site for one of our undergraduates and helped us to build community in the classroom. The program also afforded us the opportunity to work as a team to develop a mini-curriculum that showcases the best our instruction librarians have to offer, and has allowed us to teach on topics that are important to the senior community. As we continue with the Bits 'n' Bytes program, we hope that we will see further opportunities for growth and enrichment.

11

MEMOIR WRITING FOR OLDER ADULT GROUPS

Mark Donnelly

A GREAT contribution one generation can make to the next is to pass on its stories. Much of this is passed down orally, but having a written record helps preserve our history. Writing can clarify an event for the participant and for future readers. It can also generate a sense of pride in the writer as he or she reflects on a past event or accomplishment.

I am a published writer in addition to being a librarian. In summer 2006 I approached my library supervisor, Loida Garcia-Febo, about holding a memoir-writing workshop for older adults. This would be part of my ongoing work as an outreach librarian with the Special Services unit of Queens Library in Queens, New York. Loida was open to the idea, so I contacted Deborah Hoffer, then program manager of the Bayside Senior Center in suburban northeast Queens, to see if there would be interest in the project at her center.

Debbie was enthusiastic and began to recruit prospective members. We agreed to hold eight weekly sessions in the fall and early winter that I would run. We started that October with about eight seniors. As the weeks went on and the initial curiosity of some folks wore off, we settled in with a core group of four: two men and two women, ranging in age from the late fifties to mid-seventies. One man was Chinese, the other Italian. One woman was Filipino, the other Irish American.

Hometowns and seasons were prominent topics over the eight weeks. We produced the publication *Memories of the Mind: The Bayside Memoir Writers Project, 2006–2007*, in spring 2007 through the Graphics unit of the Marketing and Communications Department at Queens Library. Along with their favorite two pieces of writing from the class, members submitted childhood and young adult photographs of themselves. I also tapped the archives of Queens Library's Long Island Division for historic photographs of Bayside. The cover photograph was of a neighborhood street and store dating back to 1949. Copies of the publication were made part of the collections at both Bayside Library and the Long Island Division and were provided to the Bayside Senior Center.

My supervisor suggested I also target another section of Queens for a memoir workshop. Over the years, I had done nostalgia and educational programs with the Theodora G. Jackson Adult Center in Jamaica in central Queens. This center's seniors are predominantly African American and Hispanic. I approached Cynthia Ellington, Jackson's program manager, with the idea for a memoir workshop, which she liked, as did Tracy Reaves, the director. We started to recruit writers at a Guess Whose Photograph That Is program in August 2006, where seniors brought in photographs of themselves from earlier days. It was a lot of fun and opened the door for conversations about the past.

Per Cynthia's suggestion, the Jackson group met once a month, beginning that fall. The key person Cynthia recruited around was Kathleen Freeman, unofficial poet-in-residence, who wrote new poems for special functions at the center. I conducted the monthly workshops, and, as was true with my experience in Bayside, I developed a bond with the writers that went deeper than other programs I had done.

The Jackson group also went through ebbs and flows, but we ended up with eight writers in their sixties and seventies. Their work made up the final publication, *Memories in Poetry and Prose: The Jackson Senior Writers Project, 2006–2007*, also produced by the Queens Library's Marketing and Communications Department. Copies of the publication went to the Central Library in Jamaica, the Long Island Division, and the Jackson Center.

The two men in the Jackson group came on board toward the end of the project. They attended our public reading at the center and were eager to contribute pieces. Clifton Rutherford read his essay "My First Suit" about the suit he'd had as a fifteen-year-old in Westmoreland, Jamaica, West Indies. The three-piece "Knickerbocker" style consisted of a jacket, vest, and short pants with "a buckle and a strap below the knees."

> It was made in the United States of America. This suit was made to be worn in countries with colder climates, such as the United States, England, and Russia . . . Observers looked at the suit with two questions in mind: How is he going to wear this suit in this hot country? Where did he get this suit? In 1945, my father, a farmer, was recruited to the United States as a farm worker. He worked on a farm in Delaware. He worked for six months and returned. After his contract ended, he bought me the three-piece suit.

I have used the published memoir pieces by writers at the Jackson and Bayside centers when starting other memoir groups. In October 2008 I was doing an introductory lesson on memoir writing in the Adult Learning Center at Rochdale Village Library in Queens. To illustrate the theme of fall as a topic, I chose from the Bayside group publication a memoir by Connie Mallillin. Connie grew up in the Philippines and moved to New York City as a young woman. I read her entire essay "Remembering Fall" to the adult students in Rochdale. Here is an excerpt in which she describes her early days in Manhattan.

> As I left the church (Our Lady of Perpetual Help), I leapt for joy and headed east to the nearest park—Central Park. I could not help but stare in wonder at the sight of the multi-colored leaves falling down from the branches of the trees. There was a group of joggers that passed me by. They were scantily-clad in skinny tops and itty-bitty shorts; not like me dressed in woolen socks, thick navy blue sweat suit and heavy sweater.

After I finished reading Connie's piece to the group, I asked them to talk about their own memories of fall. Roy Hendricks described harvesttime on the family farm where he grew up in North Carolina in the 1940s. He talked of bringing in the corn and of preparing and storing food for the winter: canning various fruits and vegetables, freezing and packing beef, even freezing and packing fish they'd caught in the river. He came alive telling this story about a place he had intentionally left behind at age nineteen to come to New York City. He spoke in detail and with fondness for farm life. When I asked the class to then write down as best they could what they'd stated aloud, Roy retained those same wondrous details. He later read it proudly and told us how inspired he'd been by hearing Connie's piece. We do have the power to inspire others with our writing!

Here are some suggestions for running a memoir workshop with older adults.

A memoir is based on personal experience. Some topics that a writer can look at in getting started with creating a memoir could be

- favorite person or one who had a great deal of influence on the writer
- social events—places the writer went to dance, parties
- school
- the writer's home or neighborhood
- seasons and the memories associated with them
- holidays
- favorite actor, movie, or play
- favorite song
- favorite photograph
- experience(s) that brought about a change in the writer's life

Writing exercises on these or other topics can begin with discussions. Writers who are just starting out need not be intimidated by length. A short paragraph describing a favorite coat, dress, or meeting spot can capture the magic of a time gone by. On the other hand, maybe a memory is not a happy one yet still has a very powerful hold on the person. Writing about it can be cathartic.

The participants in a writing group for older adults should feel comfortable. It is up to the writer to decide what he or she wants to put down on paper. Only the individual knows how far he or she wants to delve into a subject. People who have lived through the Great Depression, World War II, immigration, or prejudice have certainly seen hard times, even if they were not directly affected themselves.

The leader of a writing group should encourage a supportive atmosphere in which people feel safe to talk. They can share memories in conversation on a particular topic as a warm-up activity. Then people can begin to write about that topic or whatever they choose. Freedom should be uppermost in the group, but writers should also be sensitive to the feelings of others. Offensive language can be *offensive*!

LOGISTICS

- Decide how often the group will meet, the location and time, the length of each session, and the total number of sessions. This may evolve, depending on the group.

- Supply paper (pads), pens, and pencils for group members.
- Make sure the room is properly lighted, with enough tables and chairs to accommodate members comfortably.

People should also be encouraged to write away from class, as time with the group is limited each week. A spark in class can be pursued at home. People can come back the following week and read aloud what they have written. Provide opportunities for workshop participants to share and respond to each other's writing. If someone is afraid to read his or her own work, the leader or another class member can offer to do so.

Comments about another's work should be positive, emphasizing the strengths of a piece. If comments start to become negative, the leader should step in. He can make it a rule that only he will respond to the work and only he can make suggestions as to ways to take the piece further.

PUBLICATION

An end goal can be the publication of selections from work produced inside or outside of class.

- Copies of the publication should be kept on file at the center. Your group is recording social and cultural history. Be proud of this!
- Have the leader (or another designated person) take responsibility for the collection of submissions. In starting off on a small scale, why not let each person pick out his or her favorite piece of writing for publication by the host center?
- Proofreading—spelling, punctuation, and grammar—is important when putting something down for publication. Proofreading by another eye is important. In addition, the writers themselves should have the opportunity to review their typed work before final publication.
- The personal level of spelling, grammar, and punctuation skills should not intimidate someone from joining a group.
- Drop the distinction between amateurs and professionals. We all have memories and our unique perspectives on the past. We all have something to contribute as writers!

A publication party can be the culmination of the workshop, where each member has the opportunity to read or have his or her work read to the invited audience. Each writer should get a copy of the publication, which can be as simple as typed sheets and a cover that are stapled together. The writers can decide on a publication title and even contribute artwork. Encourage other adults at the center to submit artwork based on the writings. An announcement can be made during the prepublication proofing stages to spur on this collaborative process. This gives more people a chance to be involved in center activities. Once a core group of writers and even artists is established at the center, it will be easier to hold a "second semester" class.

12

OUTREACH TO THE SENIOR COMMUNITY
One Library's Activities
Bob Blanchard

WHETHER IT is participating at a special event or providing ongoing services, the Des Plaines Public Library partners with the community's senior population in many ways.

Des Plaines is a northwest suburb of Chicago and, like other suburbs in the area, has a significant senior population. According to the 2000 U.S. Census, 17.2 percent of the city's population was age 65 and over. In addition to those 10,105 people, 5,756 residents were between the ages of 55 and 64.

One way the library serves this population is through at least two annual events—a regional Senior Celebration, sponsored by several entities, and the Senior Housing and Resource Fair, sponsored by the city of Des Plaines and the Des Plaines Community Senior Center.

The Senior Celebration is a huge gathering that honors the contributions seniors make to their communities. The twentieth annual event in 2008 attracted 2,500 attendees, who interacted with vendors, health screeners, and service providers. For several years, the library has staffed the city of Des Plaines–sponsored table for about ninety minutes at each celebration, and it has not had to pay for table space because of its affiliation with the city.

At the Senior Housing and Resource Fair, space has also been provided free of charge because of the library's not-for-profit status. But when it comes to profiting in a different way, older people and the library both benefit immensely.

As a rule of thumb, seniors like to pick up "freebies," including pens, pencils, rulers—and information. At any senior event, the library provides copies of its latest quarterly newsletter, fliers for upcoming programs, and brochures detailing its services for older people and its assistive technology for persons with disabilities.

The library's representative may also bring the following materials:

- applications for the free federal Talking Books program
- applications for the free Chicagoland Radio Information Service program, which broadcasts readings of local newspapers and other shows
- copies of the latest Low-Vision Fair's resource guide, which includes contact information about assistive technology vendors and service agencies (The library helps plan and host the annual event with several nearby libraries.)
- a portable magnifying machine from the library's circulating assistive technology collection
- mobile library schedules (The bookmobile has made regular stops at the Frisbie Senior Center for years.)
- a supply of his or her business cards

This checklist is a handy reminder of what seniors may want or need from the library.

The library's participation in these gatherings brings benefits in terms of good public relations. By being at such events, the library gives the correct impression that it serves seniors in many ways. The information given may boost attendance at library programs, including movies, dramatic presentations, and musical performances. In addition, the library may spark "eureka" moments for some seniors, such as informing them that most of the library's assistive technology may be checked out.

The library also helps the senior community with ongoing services and a varied lineup of programs.

For patrons who cannot physically come to the library or bookmobile, the library comes to them through its homebound delivery service. These patrons may check out everything available to library visitors, including books, CDs, audiobooks, and DVDs. Items are distributed on a two- or four-week rotation, and there are no fines for overdue materials.

The library serves the reading needs of seniors at nursing homes and senior living centers with deposit collections that include about fifty to one hundred items. The collections are at the facilities for a month and are then picked up and replaced with new selections. Again, there are no late fines, but institutions must pay for lost items.

The library has also held quarterly book discussions at a senior living center. Even if some participants have not read the book, they may enjoy talking about the book's themes and how they relate to their lives. *Water for Elephants* by Sara Gruen, *Suite Française* by Irène Némirovsky, and *Atonement* by Ian McEwan resonated with some attendees. After these programs, people who have not read the book may ask for copies.

Creating strong partnerships with senior-related institutions is the key to success. If the activities director at a facility shows enthusiasm for deposit collections or book discussions, the results include a smooth collaboration between library and facility and good turnouts at on-site programs. Activities personnel who lack a strong affinity for library services may keep shoddy borrowing records and risk temporary suspension of such services for their facilities.

For older persons who are more mobile, a librarian leads a bimonthly book discussion at the local senior center. The discussions have attracted nine to fourteen participants. Titles discussed in 2008 included *A Walk in the Woods* by Bill Bryson, *The Namesake* by Jhumpa Lahiri, and *The Pull of the Moon* by Elizabeth Berg.

The library's Adult Services staff also make presentations at senior gatherings. A senior residence's low-vision support group learned about the library's assistive technology, and a church group was introduced to the library's senior services. Some people were entertained by a Remembering School Days program. For this event, library staff used a Bi-Folkal Kit, which includes practically everything needed to lead a discussion and spur residents' memories. These fun kits, created by Bi-Folkal Productions of Madison, Wisconsin, cover a variety of topics, including "Remembering Music" and "Remembering the Fifties."

As the senior population changes, programming and services for this significant population will change to meet their needs. Many seniors attend the library's free computer classes, and some enjoy bowling with the Wii game system. The Des Plaines Public Library also has been considering forming a support group for persons with limited eyesight. Libraries must and will develop new events and services to satisfy seniors' ever-changing needs and wants.

13

SÍ SE PUEDE! / YES WE CAN!

Meryle Leonard

FOR MANY years, library staff members of the Public Library of Charlotte and Mecklenburg County, North Carolina, have offered programs to senior adults who do not have access to their local library. Film, storytelling, and craft programs have been part of a curriculum enjoyed by older adults at senior homes, community centers, and churches. With the changing demographics of our society, our programs have to be designed to be innovative and reflect the diversity of our community.

Sí Se Puede! is a library outreach program designed for seniors who speak Spanish and English as a new language. Seniors participate in biweekly literacy programs that are designed to educate, entertain, and enrich the lives of the participants. With the use of surveys and interviews, participants share their interest with library staff members who in turn develop programs based on the information they have received. The length of each program is 60–90 minutes, and programs have twenty to forty participants. At the beginning of the program, each participant receives a copy of the local Spanish-language newspaper. Specific biweekly programs include the following.

Remembering When. Participants use their senses to evoke memories as they share their experiences with their peers. Items may include smelling and tasting a mango, listening to a folktale or song, or even playing musical instruments. Participants are recorded so that they can enjoy the experience long after the program ends. In order for participants to enjoy a meaningful experience, the group should not be larger than twenty senior adults. Each participant will have the opportunity to become familiar with an object and share a memory. This program is designed to encourage seniors to use intellectual skills associated with productive aging. The facilitator shares the objective of the program and introduces items to the group, one object at a time. Group members take turns sharing memories and stories. If you have a large group, you are encouraged to limit sharing time to two or three minutes. It is important to be knowledgeable about the capacity of your group before introducing this program activity.

Beginning, Middle, and End. Your seniors will enjoy this mildly competitive literacy game. Divide your audience into three or four groups. Take a short, one-page story and divide it into three or four readable sections. Give each group the complete divided story. The object of the game is for the group to put the story together in the correct order. When each group has finished with the story puzzles, the correct story is read out loud by a member of each group. The group that puts the story in the correct order is declared the winner. Three to four stories can be used during the program time. If prizes are given out, we recommend that all participants receive a prize. Spanish-language newspaper articles are good sources for the short stories.

Shutterbug Club. Let your seniors tell stories of friendship and community through digital pictures. Shooting, viewing, and sharing are the object of this program. Facilitators will need enough digital cameras so that a group of four or five participants will share one camera, though one camera per participant is preferred. Participants in this program will be able to demonstrate basic care and use of a digital camera, including how to download, share, and store photographs. In the first 60–90-minute session, demonstrate digital cameras 101: turning the camera on, using the camera in automatic, focusing, self-timing, light, viewing pictures on the camera, and the correct way to handle a camera. Allow the participants to take plenty of pictures. Participants should also view their photos as a group and get constructive feedback regarding their technique in the first session. The second session should include downloading pictures onto a computer, and this session should be repeated as necessary. In the final session, seniors will learn how to print and store pictures on websites such as Snapfish and Flickr. Volunteers are encouraged to assist with this program. Supplies needed for this program are digital cameras, photo cards, a computer, projector, screen, printer, and photo paper.

Telling Our Stories. What do you get when you mix a roomful of seniors with a roomful of children? You get the opportunity to bridge the gap between the generations and have an exciting learning experience. This program lasts approximately two hours, and you would need to plan in advance to coordinate transportation for either group. Invite a local after-school group or classroom to your senior center. It is important to create an introductory atmosphere with food, music, and pictures that represent different generations and cultures. After 30–45 minutes of socializing, each group has the opportunity to share information related to the following questions. The result is a rich cultural learning experience.

- How do you celebrate your birthday?
- How do you celebrate holidays?
- Name your favorite foods.
- What type of toys or games did/do you play with?
- What kind of music do you listen to? Do you listen on iPods, CDs, or LPs?
- What country are you from or where were you born?
- What are/were your parents like?
- Talk about school.
- What items would you place in a time capsule?

- What was your career, or what you would like to be when you grow up?
- What are your hobbies?
- What would you do with a million dollars?
- What is/was in fashion? Did/do you have to wear school uniforms?
- Discuss your pets.
- What did/do you watch on television?
- What is/was your favorite sport?
- What did/do you do for fun?
- Do you use a computer, and why do you use it?

This program is designed for participants, young and old, who speak Spanish. It can be adapted to the audience as necessary. The sharing experience can be done in small groups or with all the participants at one time. You can also encourage a continual education experience by matching youth and seniors for pen pals. Use facility, agency, or school addresses instead of personal addresses for the participants in this project.

14
WHAT BOOMERS WANT
The Future of Outreach

Ellen Mehling

THE OLDEST baby boomers are now at or approaching retirement. Boomers, in part because of their sheer numbers (76–78 million by most counts), have transformed each stage of life as they've passed through it, and their retirement and aging will be no different. Boomers won't want the same kind of retirement as previous generations did, and libraries will need to address the needs of boomers, and respect their concerns and priorities, in order to keep or attract them as library patrons. Staff members should know that offering boomers the usual senior outreach programming is likely to be ineffective.

Baby boomers (also known as "flower children," "the Me generation," or "the sixties generation")

- were born between 1946 and 1964
- their numbers have given them immense buying power
- value self-reliance and self-expression; many are former or current activists
- have a history of influencing or changing American society to meet their needs
- will live longer than their predecessors and will be more physically active
- are used to abundance, unlike their Depression-era parents (and perhaps their children, too)
- are often financially independent, but many won't be

- have a youthful outlook: many feel, and behave and look, younger than they are
- retain and value the idealism of their youth
- are often "sandwiched": providing for the needs of their parents *and* their children

Common experiences that have shaped boomers include

- TV—they are the first generation to grow up with television; watching the same shows had a unifying effect on boomers all over the country
- the establishment of the national highway system and car culture
- the threat of thermonuclear annihilation ("duck and cover" drills)
- the election of John F. Kennedy, "Camelot," the assassination of Kennedy
- the "space race"
- other assassinations of leaders, including Robert F. Kennedy and Martin Luther King Jr.
- the Pill and the sexual revolution
- the Vietnam War
- Lyndon Johnson's "War on Poverty"
- Beatlemania
- the civil rights movement
- the women's liberation movement
- Watergate

Priorities and preferences of older boomers include the following:

- many want to remain in their current homes as they age rather than any other kind of living arrangement (retirement community, nursing home, etc.)
- they value their time; for some, it is worth more than money
- they want work (however that is defined, pre- or post-"retirement," full- or part-time, for pay or as a volunteer) to be meaningful
- many see retirement as the beginning of a new stage of life and intend to remain as physically, socially, and civically active as they've always been
- they want and expect to continue pursuing their usual interests and activities
- they support causes they believe in (which could include libraries)
- they are unlikely to be interested in traditional "senior center" activities

Some boomer interests include

- wellness/health
- financial planning
- computer classes and other classes
- spirituality
- travel
- social/civic engagement

- physical fitness
- genealogy
- arts and culture

When planning services and programs for boomers, it is wise to avoid

- inadvertently insulting them with "aging hippie" or other negative images/ references to growing older, even in jest
- any stereotypical depictions of post-retirement life: routine, predictability, inactivity (for example, rocking chairs, bingo at the senior center, etc.)
- any words/phrases in promotional materials such as "aging," "elder," "elderly," "seniors," "senior citizens," and so on; boomers do not think these words apply to them and are not likely to respond positively to such language ("mature" and "older" *may* be better choices, but that remains to be seen)

To appeal to boomers, libraries should

- market outreach and other programs to boomers' interests and lifestyle rather than to their age group
- promote the library as inclusive for all ages and as a social meeting space for boomers (with dedicated space for them if possible)
- ask for their input and participation in planning (some ideas: advisory boards, surveys/questionnaires, volunteers, consultants; one of the goals of outreach should be to get input from boomers in the community who are, perhaps, not coming in to the library). Demonstrate that the library values their participation and, for those who do volunteer, make every effort to give assignments that are meaningful to them; some may prefer teaching/training or working on discrete projects rather than repeated ongoing tasks.
- partner with local community/church/social services organizations and groups to reach boomers and offer programs that are relevant and interesting to them

AN INTERESTING INITIATIVE

"California: Transforming Life after 50" was a training institute in Pasadena in November 2007, held in conjunction with the California State Library, Libraries for the Future, and the California Library Association. Among the outcomes of this initiative were grants for twenty-four libraries to implement new programs and practices targeted to boomers, including the formation of dedicated spaces in the libraries just for boomers, guidelines for making the most of boomer volunteers' knowledge and skills, and classes to introduce boomers to new technology.

SOURCES

Croker, Richard. *The Boomer Century, 1946–2046: How America's Most Influential Generation Changed Everything.* New York and Boston: Springboard, 2007.

Flint, Suzanne. "Transforming Life after 50 in California—Update." October 17, 2008. http://lifelonglibraries.wordpress.com/2008/10/17/transforming-life-after-50-in-california-update (accessed October 25, 2008).

Green, Brent. *Marketing to Leading-Edge Baby Boomers: Perceptions, Principles, Practices, Predictions.* Ithaca, NY: Paramount Market Publishing, 2005.

Overly, Nanette. "Baby Boomers Seeking a Different Retirement Lifestyle—at Home." SeniorJournal.com (2007). http://seniorjournal.com/NEWS/Boomers/2007/7-03-08-BabyBoomersSeeking.htm (accessed October 25, 2008).

Schull, Diantha. "Library Services for a New Age: Transforming Libraries into Centers for Boomer Learning and Community." October 7, 2008. http://lifelonglibraries.wordpress.com/2008/10/07/library-services-for-a-new-age-transforming-libraries-into-centers-for-boomer-learning-and-community (accessed October 25, 2008).

PART III
Youth Outreach in Practice

BETTER THAN ONE
Collaborative Outreach for Homeschooled Teens

Catherine Fraser Riehle

PREPARING MIDDLE school and high school students for research in post-secondary education is essential, and academic librarians can and should partner with public librarians to ease transitions to higher education and to assist students in becoming lifelong learners. This chapter will describe a collaborative program for homeschooling families developed by librarians at a university library, a community college library, and a public library.

THE COLLABORATORS

In recent years, the Purdue University Libraries have made concentrated efforts to reach out to the local community. To help extend and promote libraries' resources and services, they hired me, the libraries' first instructional outreach librarian, to partner with and provide new services and programs for groups in the community. The Tippecanoe County Public Library (TCPL) has a strong tradition of providing outreach services and innovative young adult programming in the community. The downtown branch's young adult librarian hosts a variety of events throughout the year for patrons primarily twelve years and older. Lafayette's Ivy Tech Community Campus Library is a joint effort between Ivy Tech Community College and TCPL, providing for the information needs of the general public as well as students and faculty. Their Virtual Library provides access to online databases and virtual reference, and the library's college librarian provides a variety of instructional services.

THE PROGRAM

Planning and Marketing. The three collaborators—Purdue's instructional outreach librarian, TCPL's young adult librarian, and Ivy Tech's college librarian—met and communicated via e-mail to plan logistics and content for the program. We developed programmatic goals and learning objectives based on standards of the American Association of School Libraries. We focused the content on skills important for research in secondary and post-secondary education, including topic development, database searching, and citing and evaluating sources, among others. Our group also used the Texas Information Literacy Tutorial (TILT) as a guide for content and as a way to provide learning opportunities outside of the library by assigning relevant TILT modules for each in-person session. To market the program, we created fliers for distribution and posting at the libraries. The public library also submitted a press release to our local media venues. Costs for the program were minimal and included purchasing folders and printing costs for handouts and fliers. We used donated items and "leftovers" from past programs as giveaways for participants. We invited teenagers twelve and older from the local community, as well as their parents, and stressed that the program, though geared toward homeschooling families, was available to anyone interested. We required preregistration for planning purposes.

The Content: Search It. Find It. Use It. The program included three interactive sessions in three different libraries: a public library, a community college library, and a university library. Learners were introduced to primary research and information literacy skills, including how to find, ethically use, and evaluate information. In the first session, the young adult librarian utilized her sense of humor to engage participants' questioning minds, even accomplishing the unimaginable as teen participants got excited about the Dewey decimal system. Participants developed research topics using brainstorming techniques and encyclopedias, learned Boolean basics, and were exposed to the wide range of information sources available in the digital information age. In the second session, at Ivy Tech, the college librarian shared his extensive experience with thoughtful and engaging examples, as he explained the utility and primary search functions of research databases. Learners performed searches on their research topics in a variety of databases available through the community college. In the third and final session at the Purdue University Libraries, I illustrated the importance of information ethics, covering primary information evaluation criteria and demonstrating practical tips on how to avoid plagiarism. With the aid of visual and engaging "real-life" examples, learners left able to articulate how to identify inaccurate, biased, or misleading information. Participants in this three-part program were all given a folder full of relevant handouts compiled by the librarians, as well as blank paper for taking notes. Participants were also invited to attend a tour of each of the libraries, to learn more about the spaces and services available. Because of this collaboration, learners were exposed to different libraries as well as the relevance of these spaces and skills to different aspects of their learning and social lives. This partnership proved particularly valuable for homeschooled learners, who do not benefit from a school library or media center.

Feedback and Plans for the Future. The feedback received from post-program evaluations was overwhelmingly positive. Learners were grateful, reported that they learned relevant and useful information, and were eager for more programs in the future. The most common suggestion for change was to expand the program by offering longer or additional sessions. As the librarians plan for another program, we will include evening sessions instead of afternoon ones so fewer parents have conflicts with work. We will also add an additional in-person session.

CONCLUSIONS

These programs were made possible by the dedicated collaboration of three librarians. These sorts of partnerships between different types of librarians are critical in providing effective services to our communities, especially when preparing young people to succeed in post-secondary education. This type of targeted outreach raises the awareness and appreciation of library resources as well as stressing the importance of research and information literacy skills.

16

CHILDREN'S INITIATIVE

Establishing a Successful Partnership with a Local Public School System

Vera Gubnitskaia

BACKGROUND

The Orange County Library System (OCLS) serves an urban community of over one million residents. The Orange County Public Schools system (OCPS) is the eleventh-largest school district in the nation and the fourth-largest district in Florida. In 1998 the state of Florida implemented the Florida Comprehensive Assessment Test (FCAT), which requires that students in grades 3 through 10 attain certain scores before being promoted to the next grade. The FCAT has often been a source of anxiety for students, parents, teachers, and school administrators. Orange County schools have been working hard on improving children's FCAT scores. Despite significant progress, there are still some concerns because many children score below their grade level. Another concern is the funding of the public schools' media centers. Studies have demonstrated that well-staffed, well-stocked libraries drive up reading scores. Consequently, it was noted that students at schools with inadequate media centers have lower standardized test scores.

Recognizing these concerns, the OCLS made a decision to partner with the OCPS to create a synergistic effect for the children in our community. This is how the idea of the Children's Initiative came to life.

GOALS AND OBJECTIVES

Each elementary school in the county was assigned a library liaison. The goals of the Children's Initiative were to encourage each student to have a library card, to promote library services that support education, and to develop a strong partnership with the Orange County Public Schools district. In order to achieve these goals, library liaisons were to conduct the following annual activities:

- establish or renew contacts with the Orange County elementary schools
- facilitate library card campaigns
- attend school functions, such as open house, a family reading night, or a science fair in order to promote library services
- participate in faculty and parents' meetings
- visit schools to promote summer reading programs

A Children's Initiative internal website was developed to provide support to library liaisons. It contains time lines for each activity, a list of staff with their adopted schools, frequently asked questions, tips from colleagues, and results of library card campaigns. The site also includes schools' contact information, driving directions, and testing calendars. A program coordinator updates the website throughout the school year.

LICENSE TO LEARN CONTEST

Two annual License to Learn Library Card Contests are a part of the Children's Initiative. Teachers are encouraged to achieve 100 percent classroom participation by verifying that each of their students has a library card. Contests are conducted in the following manner. Elementary school teachers receive packets containing

- library card applications in English, Spanish, and Haitian-Creole to reflect the multiethnic population of the county
- contest posters
- an instructions sheet
- an entry form
- a manila envelope to return completed entries
- fliers, bookmarks, and newsletters promoting library programs, materials, and services
- letters to teachers and principals informing them about the contest and encouraging their participation

Teachers are asked to

- promote the contest to their class
- send home library card applications with students who don't already have cards (Students return completed applications to their teachers.)
- fill out contest entry forms
- mail or deliver card applications and entry forms to the library

After processing applications, we mail library cards directly to the students. Each teacher with 100 percent of the students with library cards is entered into a grand prize drawing. Rewards include a visit from the library mascot Squirt and a storyteller, plus a prize for the classroom of the winning teacher. As a reward for participation, every teacher who submits an application receives a special gift.

LIBRARY HONOR ROLL

In 2006 we added the "Honor Roll" concept to encourage a greater number of schools to participate in the Children's Initiative. To qualify for the Honor Roll, a school needs to enter at least one library card contest during the current academic year and satisfy at least one of the following requirements:

- invite library staff to come to the school's events
- place a link to the library on the school's website
- display the library's promotional materials
- make other strong efforts to promote the library through a variety of means

The library recognizes Honor Roll schools by sending them award certificates, displaying posters with their names at all library locations, and notifying the school board of their achievements.

The addition of the Honor Roll improved schools' participation levels in the Children's Initiative. Recognition, particularly when it is visible to peers, has proven effective. Being on the Honor Roll clearly is an accomplishment for which the principals want to strive. At the end of the 2005/2006 academic year, 47 schools were nominated and placed on the Honor Roll list. In the 2006/2007 school year, that number increased to 57, and in 2007/2008 to 64.

RESULTS

The Children's Initiative allowed us to increase the number of library card registrations. A special registration code was created allowing us to evaluate the impact of the program. Registration numbers resulting from the initiative's activities increased from 592 in 2004 to 3,018 in 2007.

As a result of the Children's Initiative, we strengthened our ties to the Orange County Public Schools system. More and more, school staff, parents, and students view the library as a partner in education. Having a stable liaison for each school allows us to personalize library service and even custom-fit it for each individual school.

SUGGESTIONS

The Children's Initiative and its activities can be replicated by other public libraries. Here is an outline of the steps a library can take to plan, market, and implement a successful liaison initiative with local schools.

1. Designate a project coordinator who will evaluate the needs, outline goals and objectives, and prepare a plan for the success of the initiative.

2. Obtain the most current list of the local elementary schools in your community.

3. Establish contacts within the school system to help obtain and disseminate necessary information.

4. Assign a liaison to each school.

5. Conduct an annual evaluation by collecting statistics and feedback from library liaisons and schools' contacts.

6. Make annual adjustments to goals, objectives, and planning as necessary.

The Children's Initiative is an efficient way for any library to streamline its work with the area's school system, increase its visibility within the school system and the whole community, and become a true partner in education.

17

HUNDREDS OF HIGH SCHOOL STUDENTS STUDY AT THE LIBRARY

Tiffany Auxier

THE NEED

High school students are busy with friends, sports and clubs, homework, dating, driving lessons, applying to college, and the list goes on. It's presumed that they use computers at home and purchase their own reading and entertainment materials, then visit the library as a last resort. With the social and physical changes they are experiencing, teens are sensitive to others' opinions, seek acceptance from peers or from adults while asserting their independence, have both an abundance and lack of energy, and simply want respect.[1] Many public institutions and businesses cast a suspicious eye on teens, while lamenting the loss when they go elsewhere. Teens may return to the library during college breaks or later when they have their own children, but how can we demonstrate what we have to offer them now?

Each January and June, our area's high school students have shortened school days from the weekend before final exams through their conclusion. Over 150 students per day arrive at the Hinsdale (IL) Public Library in need of study space, school supplies, computers, and research databases.

Our 30,000-square-foot library has approximately 600 visitors per day and seating for 115 in the public spaces on three floors. It was challenging to manage the library as students competed for space and staff time with other patrons. While we received complaints about noise, crowding, and messiness, staff saw this as an opportunity to develop a new service. We could do better than allowing students to study in the stacks or watching as other patrons found refuge in the quiet reading room or left.

THE PROPOSAL

A committee, headed by the young adult librarian, was formed to develop a program for finals week. The proposal was endorsed by the management team and presented to the entire staff, many of whom quickly volunteered to help. Our goals were to

- provide superior customer service to all patrons
- provide a quality program to an underserved group
- show respect for teens' needs, giving them freedom tempered with clear expectations, as they balance focusing on their tests with socializing[2]
- assist students with reference and study needs
- market other materials, services, and programs to students
- get instant feedback and suggestions for other offerings
- build upon the positive exchange to create "raving fans" who will visit again and recommend the library to fellow students[3]
- develop a successful program that could become a model for other libraries

THE SPACE

An informal space usage survey helped us to determine which seating areas could be used for the program. Accommodating as many students as possible, while having space for other patrons, was necessary for success. The following space designations were made:

- two public meeting rooms reserved for group study by high school students, which added seventy more seats
- four study rooms for small groups or independent study; reservations taken, but open to all patrons
- quiet reading room for silent study; open to all patrons
- an outside patio with wireless access

The public seating areas remained available to all patrons, including the overflow of students, provided other patrons were not disturbed.

THE STAFF

An additional service desk was placed near the group study rooms so a staff member could supervise and assist the students. A desk schedule with two- to four-hour shifts was shared by all public-service staff, with the majority taken by the young adult librarian. The duties were to assist teens with reference and computer searches, manage the space and walk the library, refill snacks and supplies, keep statistics, collect patron comments, and provide structure and behavior reminders as needed.

THE SNACKS AND SUPPLIES

In order to make students' studying go smoothly and lessen their need to bring in food or borrow from friends, the staff developed a budget for snacks and supplies. In addition to bottled water, we purchased a variety of pretzels, crackers, and marshmallow crispy treats. School supplies included pens and pencils, paper and note cards, calculators, and highlighters.

THE ADVERTISING

Our advertising for this service had two purposes. First, we needed to inform students, parents, and teachers about the program. Second, we had to inform our other patrons to expect some limited access and increased activity. Our advertising included

- half-page advertisements in the high school newspaper
- a posting to a local website hosted by residents
- press releases and newspaper articles
- cable channel
- library newsletter and e-newsletter
- library website (home page and young adults blog)
- in-house signs

THE RESPONSE AND CONCLUSIONS

In the two years since the inception of this service, attendance has grown from approximately 500 to 750 students per semester. Thankful comments from students and other patrons outnumbered disciplinary situations, such as noise.

- An impressed grandfather said, "Reminds me of DePaul's library."
- A parent said, "It's so nice that you are reaching out. This is a good atmosphere for them."
- A high schooler studying said, "Food! Really? Thank you so much."

At the conclusion of each finals week, the young adult librarian wrote a letter to the local high schools' principals relating how pleased we are to serve their students, the positive comments made by other patrons, and how well behaved and respectful the students have been.

The library has observed tangible benefits from this program and developed additional outreach services:

- increase in high school students' use of the library, particularly computers, study rooms, and required reading materials
- exposed students and parents to the teen lounge, our young adult area
- positive interdepartmental cooperation, including a better understanding of teens' needs and a larger awareness of managing service to all patrons

- addition of an online tutoring service to our website, which will assist students with test preparation, review college essays, and help with other homework needs
- launched a successful Student Film Festival

The Hinsdale Public Library could have been overwhelmed by the idea of that many students in the building. We could have implemented rules to discourage them. Instead, the library welcomed students and provided a structured but flexible environment. In doing so, staff were better able to serve all patrons, and in turn patrons of all ages, including the Library Board of Trustees, congratulated us on supporting these important members of the community.

NOTES

1. Patrick Jones and Joel Shoemaker, *Do It Right! Best Practices for Serving Young Adults in School and Public Libraries* (New York: Neal-Schuman, 2001), 1–6.
2. Sheryl Feinstein, "The Teenage Brain, Under Construction," *VOYA* 31 (2008): 122.
3. Jones and Shoemaker, *Do It Right!* 102.

18

REACHING OUT TO CREATE OUTREACH PROGRAMS AMONG TEEN LIBRARY PATRONS

Maryann Mori

ONE OF the best ways to increase outreach among teen library patrons at public libraries is to meet the teens where they are. That directive can mean either meeting teens where they are physically (as in another place) or meeting them where they are with their interests and abilities. As a former teen specialist librarian and current outreach services coordinator, I have known the benefits of creating outreach programs both off-site and on-site in a variety of ways and settings. One such program involved services to pregnant or parenting teens, while another service involved allowing teens to develop their own talents and interests by creating and leading library-sponsored programs.

When I became the teen specialist librarian for the Evansville (IN) Vanderburgh Public Library, I began searching for ways to simultaneously develop the teen program and outreach opportunities. One day I noticed a flier on the library's community bulletin board about an organization dedicated to teens. Not recognizing the name of this particular organization, I contacted its director to set up a meeting in order to discuss possible collaborations. Over coffee, the director shared her program and its focus (a newly established support group to help pregnant or parenting teens), and I shared mine (a developing teen program to promote literacy, reading, and socialization in a library setting). Suddenly, the proverbial lightbulb lit. Why not provide early childhood literacy programs to the teen parents and their babies? Why not incorporate the Every Child Ready to Read (ECRR) initiative among these teen parents?

Among my library experiences, I had worked in the Children's Department of a large central library, and I had also completed the ECRR training sessions. As the teen librarian, however, I had originally thought my days of storytime presentations were over. It had never occurred to me, prior to my meeting with the pregnant teen group's director, to reimplement those storytimes for a teen audience. I suggested my idea to this director, and she was thrilled with the concept. There was only one problem: she could not transport her students to the library. That's when I realized I had an opportunity to meet both my goals—those of serving teens and expanding outreach.

Since that first meeting with that particular director, I have expanded outreach among pregnant and parenting teen groups within the service areas of the Evansville Vanderburgh Public Library and the Des Moines Public Library. I have conducted numerous early childhood literacy programs for these groups, which always yield the same results: babies appreciate and respond positively to the experience, and teen parents gain a better understanding of the importance of reading to their children. In fact, many of these teens have previously struggled with reading, and by reading books to their babies these teen parents begin to redevelop and improve their own reading skills.

Over the course of my experience in working with these groups, I have developed the following suggestions for creating a similar program:

Learn the names of the schools and organizations that provide services to pregnant or parenting teens. Many of these organizations offer childhood development classes or parenting classes. Library storytime programs—especially ones that are developed around the ECRR initiative—fit nicely into these types of classes. Consider contacting organizations such as local schools, YWCA, and youth shelters.

Make a phone call or send an e-mail to request a meeting with the director of the organization. Be sure to stress the ways the library can provide early childhood literacy programs and complement the organization's goals.

Schedule a minimum of four sessions with the group. Teen parents have often been shuffled from one home or social agency to another, and as a result these teens are often leery of trusting anyone. After two sessions, you will likely have gained the teens' trust, and you'll still have two remaining sessions in which to build a positive relationship.

Use the sessions to present concepts such as the importance of reading to babies, an introduction to children's literature (including how to choose books for babies and toddlers), and implementation of literacy activities (ECRR's six prereading skills). Each session should include audience participation in an actual storytime and discussions of child development concepts pertaining to learning how to read.

Talk to the teens as adults, but don't forget they are still teens. Teens do not want to hear fancy jargon. They will, however, respond well when you tell them the honest benefits they and their babies will gain through reading.

Make sure you are educating the parents along with the babies. When you conduct a storytime program, the major focus and intended audience is the group of babies. However, take time to address the parents by saying things like, "And from that rhyme, baby is going to learn about . . ." or "How many of you have read this book to your baby? What was his/her response?"

Inform the teen parents about other library resources that can benefit them. For instance, mention parenting books, other programs (such as storytimes or teen events), public access computers, GED or job-hunting resources, and the fact that library events, services, and resources are free.

Do not give up. Depending on the composition of the group, your first few visits may make you feel as if you are wasting your time. However, the teens are often paying closer attention than you may realize.

I have letters of testimony from directors of pregnant/parenting teen groups who verify that they have seen an improvement in their students' attitudes toward reading after participating in my sessions. I have similar letters from fellow children's librarians who have seen the teen parents visit the library with babies in tow in order to check out board books for their children—after they have been convinced of reading's importance through my presentations. And I have heard from the teens themselves about how much they have enjoyed sharing children's books with their babies. These teen parents have also expressed enthusiasm at discovering the library's collection of teen literature. It is exciting and professionally fulfilling to know that this kind of outreach has a dual reward.

19

REACHING OUT TO STUDENT ATHLETES, TWO STUDENTS AT A TIME

Maureen Brunsdale

STUDENT ATHLETES are driven to succeed and motivated to excel. However, they are often overlooked when it comes to library services. Illinois State University's Milner Library—like all academic libraries—strives to provide services to the entire university population, including our student athletes with our Milner to Go program.

Illinois State University (ISU) is a medium-sized institution located in the heart of Illinois at Normal. The fact that the town is named Normal points to ISU's rich history of providing teacher-preparation education. Today, the university and its library provide support to roughly 20,000 students pursuing their studies in 35 disciplines. Providing outstanding library service drives a budget of nearly $7 million, a staff of 100, and a collection of 1.6 million.

There are myriad sports offerings for students to participate in on this campus, both intramural and intercollegiate. For the purposes of this project, we focused on athletes involved with intercollegiate sports and, more specifically, those of our athletes involved with National Collegiate Athletic Association Division I sports. While the coaching staff helps students excel in their chosen sports, the university's Academic Assistance Unit located in the Karin Bone Athletic Study Center (ASC) helps student athletes succeed off the field. The unit does this in part by working with various campus academic support personnel and by utilizing a database that tracks each individual athlete's academic performance. Through years of compiling data, the staff have been able to create a matrix of study-hour guidelines. When a student athlete arrives at the ASC, he scans his identification card, and in return the database identifies how many hours he has spent at the ASC each week. Students, staff, and coaches can easily determine if each student is reaching his allotted study hours for each week.

The library's Milner to Go program began simply. Five years ago I made note of my desire to do outreach to student athletes as part of my next year's goals. Four years ago, through my involvement with our Public Relations Committee, personnel contacts within the Athletic Study Center were identified. Three years ago, the Milner Library started providing outreach reference services there. The program started with a handful of library faculty and staff volunteers who agreed to leave the library to visit the ASC for two hours every Monday evening, holidays and breaks excluded. Mondays were suggested by the director of the ASC because that was the night of heaviest traffic at their facility.

Reference transaction statistics were not kept for the first two years, but it was generally agreed that the services we provided were both well received and appreciated. The service was wanted and needed, but because of massive reorganization of the Milner Library, the personnel needed to provide the service dwindled throughout the spring semester of 2008. At the same time, the reference coordinator was approached by a senior honors student desirous of eventually pursuing a master's degree in library science. She divulged that she wanted to eventually become an academic librarian but had little idea of what that entailed. She also wanted to complete a senior honors project, and because she was specifically interested in library outreach activities, she and I were paired.

During that semester, I worked with the honors student to assess her knowledge of library services and general database-searching strategies. Her search strategies were good and her communication skills were excellent. While having her shadow me during one of my shifts at the ASC, I was able to see firsthand how dramatically different students relate to one another versus how they relate to a seasoned library professional. A potential solution to the library's staffing problem in the ASC began to present itself.

In speaking further with our honors student, and after doing some additional research into our honors program and into various service organizations on campus, I learned that a similar "service learning" component resides in each entity. Put differently, each entity requires members to do some form of community outreach or service.

At the start of the 2008 fall semester, a small group—composed of the library instruction coordinator, the reference coordinator, the honors student, and myself— met to discuss our strategy for bringing library services to the ASC. We agreed that it would be a worthwhile experiment to use students as the Milner Library's ambassadors to the center. We tasked the honors student with reaching out to her honors student peers. She did so by working with the honors program on campus and by contacting the fraternities on campus. The response was minimal, however, and the program was eliminated at the end of the fall 2008 semester. However, the Milner Library maintains a "train-the-trainer" model for the graduate assistants who work as tutors in the ASC.

But working with the three students has been an educationally fulfilling and fun experience. The students seemed energized at the prospects of helping athletes succeed in the classroom. They have been very willing to undertake special library training, where we focus on simple reference-interviewing techniques and basic database and online catalog-searching strategies. They understand that if they field a question outside of their skill set or comfort zone, they will refer the athlete to a professional. We've made it easy for the volunteering students to do so by designing small tear-off sheets, about the size of a prescription pad, which list all librarians by name and identify their subject areas, instant-messaging screen names, phone numbers, and e-mail addresses.

The student athletes have similarly responded well. While group statistics were not kept for previous semesters, I personally never handled more than four questions in an evening shift. During the first week offering this student-to-student service at the ASC, the volunteering honors student was asked five questions. That is a small number in relation to the number of questions we field at the reference desk, but working with students to reach out to student athletes seems to have created a winning situation for the honors students, the Milner Library, and the student athletes.

20
TEEN THEATER AT THE PUBLIC LIBRARY

Licia Slimon

AS THE new teen services librarian at Whitehall Public Library in Pittsburgh, I introduced myself to the eight teens at our first Teen Advisory Group (TAG) meeting. I began to describe my expectations for TAG, but their glazed expressions made me pause and ask, "So what do *you* want to do?"

Justin's hand shot up. "Put on a play!"

Miranda chimed in, "For little kids!"

Everyone nodded enthusiastically.

We spent the rest of the meeting discussing what to perform and decided on *Alice in Wonderland.*

At our next weekly meeting the teens spent the last hour poring over different versions of *Alice in Wonderland* and writing their script. While we were preparing for the play, we lengthened our meetings because we didn't want to affect other TAG activities. That year, along with putting on three plays, we organized movies, bake sales, and a Library Lock-in.

For this first production we kept props to a minimum. We used the existing arrangement of the children's room to stage the play. The librarian's desk became the rabbit hole to disappear behind and emerge into Wonderland. We staged the Mad Hatter's tea party at the children's craft tables.

Although I had no prior experience in theater, my background in filmmaking and literature gave me a frame of reference. I volunteered to narrate and play the part of Alice's older sister. In this way I could get a measure of the group's strengths and weaknesses to determine how I could be most useful to them.

It also helped to get their families on board. Rachel's mother found costumes and the tea set at a local Goodwill store. Abbie and her mom organized the craft activity, and Justin's family baked cookies.

Dramatic productions can be a great way to build self-esteem in teens. Due to health problems, the girl who played Alice did not initially mix well with the others. However, she threw herself into the role. Her unorthodox interpretation of Alice's lines brought a delightful originality to the performance.

After the success of our first play, the teens wanted to do something bigger. They decided to perform their next play on the larger stage in the library's community room.

This time we teamed up with the Children's Department on a fairy-tale program for children and grandparents. The teens chose *Rapunzel.* They built the garden and Rapunzel's tower and wrote their own script (adding a feckless younger brother for comic relief). The Children's Department staff organized crafts and snacks.

I helped block out scenes and coached the teens in simple stage etiquette:

"Sam, your back is to the audience again—turn around!"

Although I perused websites and books for acting tips, I found that viewing rehearsals as a member of the audience was most helpful:

"Matt, try again slowly and clearly: 'It's getting dark and I fear we will lose our way!'"

Gradually, they began to "own" their parts. Abbie's natural elegance and flowing locks were the right match for the lead role. In the spirit of cross-gender casting, Courtney chose to play the prince. Her gallantry and physical energy brought the character to life.

After *Rapunzel* the teens were fired up to try something really ambitious. The production of *Charlie and the Chocolate Factory* began in August and was not complete until the following January. We divvied up the elaborate set so that each person was responsible for a major prop—for example, the Big Gum Machine went to Abbie. Our library had minimal storage space, so the teens had to store their set pieces at home. We were also burdened by the piles of candy we'd collected.

We spent so much time on set construction that we ran out of time to promote the play. We tried to do it all—crafts and refreshments—without assistance from the Children's Department staff. Turnout was lower than expected, and that was a disappointment for the teens after their huge effort.

What I learned is to keep it simple. Focus on fostering camaraderie, creative self-expression, and community-building skills. Avoid pitfalls, like complicated productions and unwieldy sets. Work with an experienced partner like the Children's Department staff that can provide a ready-made audience and professional assistance.

Our theater group filled a void left by the big school productions. Although the teens enjoyed participating in those plays, they never got major speaking parts in them. Additionally, homeschoolers like Rachel or parochial students like Justin didn't have the opportunity to participate at all. Furthermore, teens were understandably reluctant to perform in front of their school peers. At the beginning, the TAG members felt more comfortable performing for a "friendly" audience of children and grandparents in a public library setting. They wanted more opportunities for dramatic expression, and they found it at the public library: not only were they able to play major roles in smaller productions, but they got to try other aspects of stage production like set design and scriptwriting.

Moreover, as their confidence grew the teens were motivated to test their limits and tackle new challenges. At our last TAG meeting, Courtney and Rachel proposed putting on a romantic comedy they'd cowritten to be performed—gulp!—at the high school.

"We'll have auditions!" Courtney cried, waving the script. "I'll ask the guys from my church group!"

I began to offer words of caution, but I saw their hopeful, determined faces and reached out my hand instead. "Show me the script!"

Note: Teens' names have been changed to protect their privacy.

21

TEENS WILL RESPOND

Maryann Mori

ALTHOUGH "OUTREACH" is often interpreted to mean going "out" or away from the building for off-site presentations, it does not always have to mean that. Outreach is a way of "reaching out" to the people we serve at the library. When that kind of outreach begins within the walls of the library, it will have far-reaching benefits to patrons, the community, and the library. Allowing teens themselves to create and lead programs at the library enables them to develop their interests and abilities in ways that make them better students, better leaders, and thereby better prepared to continue leading and serving in their adult lives.

One such example of this kind of outreach occurred with the group of *otaku* students at the Evansville Vanderburgh Public Library (EVPL) located in Indiana. *Otaku* is a Japanese word that can best be translated as "geek"—in a good way. *Otaku* specifically are those people who have a great interest in things Japanese, particularly in Japanese comics (manga and anime). When I assumed the position as teen specialist librarian at EVPL, there was a small group of *otaku* (approximately ten of them) who had been meeting semiregularly to watch anime at the library. Although I had a keen interest in and knowledge of Japanese culture, I was not overly familiar with anime or manga—certainly not knowledgeable enough to do any kind of programming pertaining to it. Early in my job, I met with the main *otaku*, a rather quiet fifteen-year-old student who had an amazing wealth of knowledge about anime and manga. I told him I believed there were a lot more students who shared his interests, and I wanted him to spearhead a special group. With my guidance, this student put together a schedule of programs. He named the newly formed group Otaku Anonymous, and attendance at this library-sponsored club rapidly grew from ten students to fifty students and expanded from meetings once a month to ones on every other Saturday.

Soon other students were asking how they could assist with the meetings and other library programs. Teens assumed the roles of leaders for a large library-sponsored gaming program and later created a spin-off from that program to develop a board game program. Another group of teens from Otaku Anonymous developed a readers' theater and presented stories to children at library branch locations. This group was also invited to present at the local children's museum. Building on that concept, other *otaku* created a visual arts club where the students wrote, acted, filmed, and edited their own movies. Of course, by this time there were more than just *otaku* students involved in the activities, and what had originally started as a group of ten teens became a group of a hundred students.

The library became known as the "cool" place to hang out for area teens and offered programs for teens multiple times each week. Even on those weekends when the library did not have any scheduled teen activities, the teens would still flock to the library just to "hang" with their friends. They were comfortable at the library, and they knew it was a welcoming place for them. People in the community began to take notice. The local civic theater contacted the library to discuss the possibility of collaborations with the teen visual arts and acting groups. Teachers were receptive to the teen librarian going into classrooms to conduct information literacy instruction. The local newspaper ran a positive front-page story about the large number of teens at the library. These students proved to be a good audience from which to glean additional ideas and input regarding collection development and future library events. Some of these students also served on a committee to help review and implement ideas for the library's new website design. They were instrumental in developing the teen pages of the new website.

The teens who participated in these library activities were a diverse group. Some of them were "advanced placement" students who were on the fast track toward college. Other teens, however, were high school dropouts or had been kicked out of school due to behavioral issues. Yet all of these students were able to find common ground and a place of acceptance at the library. They were able to use their talents in a way to serve their own interests as well as to expand into new areas and serve other groups. Two of these "dropouts" had the idea to present what they called "weird science" programs for kids. They wanted to present and talk about science experiments such as exploding volcanoes and dancing raisins to children in order to excite those kids about science. This idea became another teen-led program at EVPL.

As the teen specialist librarian, I had an opportunity to nominate one of the teens as "volunteer of the year"—an award sponsored by a local civic organization. I nominated the rather quiet fifteen-year-old *otaku*, who by this time had become a confident sixteen-year-old. He won. His mother later shared with me just how much the library had come to mean to her son—not only because of the programs offered there but also because of the opportunities he had received to become a leader. The teen's award included a $1,000 check for the library (which was used to further teen events and resources), although that was not the most valuable result. The mother said she had seen her son develop his self-confidence and leadership abilities in ways that amazed her—all because he had been given the chance to use his knowledge of anime and manga to start a library program. This same teen started asking me questions about what it would take for him to become a librarian. As he considered his future studies and career options, librarianship was at the forefront of his thoughts. By reaching out and meeting this teen and his friends where they were, the library's outreach efforts had expanded to affect many students of all ages. The love for the library that was developed among these teens will undoubtedly last into these students' adult lives.

Whether traveling to an off-site destination to provide programming to a specific group of teens or working within the physical library building to encourage the teens who are already there, libraries and their employees have an opportunity to reach out to teens and make a difference in ways that will keep those teens returning to and supporting the public library.

22

UPWARD BOUND OUTREACH TO TALENTED HIGH SCHOOL STUDENTS

Jamie Seeholzer

FOR MANY years, the Reference Department at the Main Library of Kent State University has made efforts to reach out to students enrolled in the university's branch of the Upward Bound program. Upward Bound is a federally funded program that seeks to provide opportunities for its participants to prepare for and succeed in college. Upward Bound programs serve high school students from low-income families; high school students from families in which neither parent holds a bachelor's degree; and low-income, first-generation military veterans who are preparing to enter post-secondary education.[1]

The Upward Bound program at Kent State has three tracks: the Classic program, Prep Academy, and Math/Science Center. Each track recruits talented students in targeted high schools in the northeast Ohio area and pays for them to attend a six-week-long college experience at the Kent campus of Kent State University. Students range in enrollment from the ninth through twelfth grades and must maintain GPAs above 2.5 to participate in the programs.[2] Around two hundred students are involved in the various Upward Bound tracks each summer.[3] Students take classes at the university and engage in a variety of social and community-building activities to help them develop their own goals.

Regardless of track, the Upward Bound students take courses in common topics such as English. I was able to make connections with three instructors at Kent State teaching English courses and coordinate library instruction sessions for their students. One of the English instructors I worked with required her students to investigate a student group on campus they would be interested in joining and to write a paper about that group's involvement in the local community. She asked me to demonstrate a research database and talk a bit about finding service opportunities via the university's website. Her students were very engaged, perhaps because they were entering their senior year of high school and a majority of them had decided to attend Kent State upon graduation.

Another instructor wanted a significant library component to his English course. We coordinated four library sessions, and I provided instruction on using the library's catalog and avoiding plagiarism. He also requested a tour of the building and a session in our Special Collections and Archives. Working with one of our archivists, we created a session highlighting some of the rare books and primary sources available to students in the university's Special Collections. The students in this class were also high school seniors and expressed a high level of interest in learning about library materials.

The third English instructor asked for a two-day workshop for her students. The students in this course were assigned to write a paper about domestic violence issues in relation to a novel they were reading. I demonstrated a database for them, but these students expressed little enthusiasm for using it. They seemed more interested and comfortable with using some specialized encyclopedias I pulled for them about their topics. These students were in either the ninth or tenth grade at area high schools.

Success in these library sessions seemed to be tied to the age of the students participating. Two of my better instruction sessions were with the students entering their junior and senior years of high school. It seemed that these students saw a more pressing need for learning how to use the library resources I demonstrated to them, perhaps because they would be entering college soon, and some had plans to enroll at Kent State. Sessions with students in the ninth and tenth grades were a bit more difficult to manage. These students were often more boisterous and difficult to engage in the library material. I think that might have to do with their excitement at being away from home, on a college campus with their peers, for an extended period of time.

Students enrolled in the Math/Science track were also a bit problematic to connect with. I think these problems arose from the instructors' vagueness about what they wanted their students to accomplish from the library instruction. I worked with two instructors coordinating sessions in this group. One instructor with a group of ninth and tenth graders was adamant about the students not using any of the library's online resources, including our research databases, for their assignment about famous mathematicians from ethnic backgrounds. For this assignment, I was able to pull a variety of encyclopedias about great figures of various ethnicities and several reference books about famous mathematicians throughout history. Once the students had identified a mathematician, I was able to pull books for them from our general stacks about that person.

The other Math/Science instructor had an assignment for her students that required them to investigate the impact of a natural or man-made disaster and devise a response on the effect of such a disaster. This instructor requested a workshop session about using research databases. The students in this course were either in eleventh or twelfth grade, but as opposed to the students of similar age in the English courses, these students did not express interest in learning about library resources. It could be that this distinction arose from the time of day. The workshop time for this class came at the end of their school day on campus, making them, I assume, a bit eager to return to socializing together outside of the classroom.

There were some consistent stumbling blocks to my outreach efforts with the Upward Bound students. Time was the biggest issue. The students in each track were living in residence halls on campus, most without computers. The students did not seem to have enough time to draft and write out their assignments. I attempted to work around these problems by giving the students time to work on their assignments during the library session while I circulated and provided help as needed. We ran into another roadblock when it was discovered that the students had not been granted borrowing privileges from the library, due to a lack of communication between the Upward Bound registration office and library circulation staff. We worked around this issue by holding relevant books for the students at the reference desk for them to use in the library on their own time.

Outreach to the Upward Bound program is an important part of the library's mission in that we have the opportunity to highlight our resources to potential students. In addition, coordinating outreach efforts with Upward Bound provides the library with the chance to make connections with the faculty, staff, and community members who make the Upward Bound experience possible.

NOTES

1. U.S. Department of Education, "Upward Bound Program," www.ed.gov/programs/trioupbound/index.html.
2. Kent State University, "What Is UB Prep?" http://explore.kent.edu/ub/prep.html.
3. Kent State University, "Upward Bound Classic," http://explore.kent.edu/ub/classic.html.

PART IV
Correctional Facility Outreach

FREEDOM READERS IN A JUVENILE CORRECTIONAL FACILITY

Felicia A. Smith

THE UNIVERSITY of Notre Dame mantra is: "To be a force for good in the world." To that end, Felicia A. Smith, Notre Dame's outreach librarian, created the Freedom Readers Literacy Outreach Program at the Juvenile Justice Center (JJC), which is a juvenile correctional facility. For purposes of this chapter, juveniles are defined as those seventeen and younger.

There were three main objectives for this initiative: to increase interest in

- reading
- writing
- critical thinking

We read *The Freedom Writers Diary: How a Teacher and 150 Teens Used Writing to Change Themselves and the World around Them.*[1] An additional goal was to motivate the students to become lifelong learners. Six sessions were scheduled, each lasting 1.5 hours, three days per week.

THE PROJECT'S SIX-SESSION OVERVIEW

The initial class consisted of distributing class materials, which were books, journals, syllabi, and markers. Special attention was paid to the facility's security measures. Pens, pencils with a metal band around the eraser, spiral notebooks, and hardcover books were prohibited. If the JJC provided the books, they would need to be locked away when not in class. Luckily, Notre Dame purchased the books, so each student could have a personal copy to take home with him.

The JJC director recommended *The Freedom Writers Diary* because of its relevant correlation to the inmates' lives. Unfortunately, after the first class I was asked not to discuss any topics dealing with race, gangs, sex, misogyny, drugs, violence, and so on. For the record, this is a book composed of the diaries of sexually active, teenage gang members of different races recording the violence, homelessness, racism, sexism, and overwhelming abuse they experienced.

Once the students have their books and a revised PG-rated syllabus I can teach my class, right? Wrong! There were incessant interruptions that occurred seemingly every ten minutes.

I decided to name the students at the JJC "the Freedom Readers" in honor of the "Freedom Writers." The Freedom Writers got the inspiration for their name from the group of racially diverse activists who rode buses into the South to fight segregation and who were called "Freedom Riders."[2]

CLASS ACTIVITIES

Session 1: Icebreakers. The first activities were designed to be fun, relaxing exercises forcing the students to talk. These focused on perceptions and provided insights about them. I explicitly stated the instructional purpose after each activity so the students would understand its value. It was important to end each day with a positive recap.

I used a Stroop effect chart that consists of different-colored fonts spelling out the names of colors.[3] For instance, the word "RED" would appear in a blue font. The students are supposed to say what color they see instead of reading the word. Very few can do it successfully on the first try, and everyone enjoyed distracting those who were attempting to read.

Session 2: Perception Is the Great Determinant. I used optical illusions and asked students to help other students see the images they saw but that the others did not see.[4] The purpose is best summarized by Stephen Covey's quote: "We see the world, not as it is, but as we are — or as we are conditioned to see it."

I included motivational, thought-provoking quotations corresponding to assigned readings. The quote that elicited the greatest discussion appears in Alice Walker's book *Possessing the Secret of Joy*: "The axe came into the forest and trees said the handle is one of us."

Session 3: Know Thyself. The students completed identity charts by writing multiple one-word descriptions of themselves. This provided a lot of information, which I could skim and absorb quickly.

After this introspective exercise, the students were required to look externally at their classmates. This was done with a scavenger hunt. The students wrote secret clues about themselves on index cards. I read the clues aloud and they wrote them down. Then they tried to match all the clues with the right people. I quickly assessed their writing levels, and the students also began bonding as a group. They thought critically about identifying who the person was and how their perceptions led them to formulate their conclusions.

Session 4: Get to Know Me—Hokey Pokey. I wrote statements on the front of index cards, and if that statement applied to them they had to perform the activity written on the back of the card. A sample statement is "What colleges are you interested in?" This allowed me to gather more information about the students in order to personalize my lesson plans. To keep them engaged, I included funny questions such as "Do you know who Angelina Jolie's baby's daddy is?" They all did and they all laughed. On the back were silly actions like "Try to lick your own elbow" or "Pat your head and rub your stomach at the same time." I conducted this exercise similar to the "Hokey Pokey," a group dance activity. Social workers came into the room just to observe and laugh.

Session 5: Debates and Definitions. In the teacher's handout for *The Freedom Writers Diary*, there is an activity called Take a Stand. The class members stand on one side of a controversial statement and have to persuade people to come over to their side.

I added what I called Flip the Script. Before we started debating the merits of the case, I switched groups so the students were forced to argue the opposite of what they believed. The purpose was to help them think critically by taking opposing perspectives into consideration.

An engaging way to learn definitions was the Word Find and Define activity, listing terms to be located inside of a grid. I also included definitions with each term.

Session 6: Change Affirmation. The students wrote entries in journals every day. I included discussion topics for reading, such as

How do I see myself?

How do I believe others see me?

How does the way we see ourselves affect how others see us?

What masks do you wear?

How is the person you show the world different from your real self?

We learn from both positive and negative influences (people). Think of someone you use as an example of what you do not want to become!

The final and undoubtedly the most successful activity was the Change Affirmation Form, which included the following:

- Describe who you used to be, where you were headed.
- Describe something you wish you hadn't seen/heard.
- Describe a goal you want to achieve.
- Describe someone who hurt you that you choose to forgive.
- Describe a dream big and bold enough for your future.

The form ends with a declaration, "I will change for the better, starting now!" I was flabbergasted by the raw honesty and the deeply personal nature of some of the responses. One student even showed me a bullet wound literally one inch away from his heart that almost shattered his spine.

CONCLUSION

An important focus of preprogram planning consisted of written student evaluations on the last day of class. Unfortunately, this proved to be problematic as a result of the aforementioned interruptions. For example, on the first day of class I had twenty-one male students, but by the last day I had only four. I had seven girls on the last day, but only three were in class to complete the written evaluations. Of those three girls, one had just arrived that day. I never finished the second week with the second group of male students. But as a result of verbal feedback, the JJC director requested that I offer this program again.

In conclusion, I encourage librarians to be the vanguard of combating inequitable literacy levels, because we are uniquely positioned to stem arrested development among juveniles by creating information-empowered youth. This chapter showcases one concrete example of how librarians can directly address social issues in an underserved demographic.

My final advice for the students was that they should continue to be Freedom Readers and use information to get the appropriate knowledge necessary to keep them free, physically and mentally. They were encouraged to read material that will empower them to inspire others.

My greatest desire for these students is to continue what I call "the Freedom Chain." Learning about the Freedom Riders inspired a new generation of Freedom Writers. Reading about the Freedom Writers inspired my class of Freedom Readers. Now it is the Freedom Readers' turn to inspire the next generation of "Freedom Learners." The quote I concluded my class with was by Thucydides: "The secret of happiness is freedom. The secret of freedom is courage."

NOTES

1. Freedom Writers with Erin Gruwell, *The Freedom Writers Diary: How a Teacher and 150 Teens Used Writing to Change Themselves and the World around Them* (New York: Doubleday, 1999).
2. Raymond Arsenault, *Freedom Riders: 1961 and the Struggle for Racial Justice* (Oxford: Oxford University Press, 2006).
3. The Stroop effect chart is explained at www.pbs.org/saf/1302/teaching/teaching2.htm.
4. One such optical illusion is at http://dragon.uml.edu/psych/illusion.html.

24

HAS YOUR PUBLIC LIBRARIAN BEEN TO PRISON?

Participation in Summer Reading Games

Glennor Shirley

STUDIES CONDUCTED by the National Center for Education Statistics in 2003 reported that a high percentage of the nation's two million prison inmates who reside in state and federal facilities had learning disabilities and a lower level of literacy than similar age groups living in households.[1] These prisoners, 95 percent of whom will eventually return to society, and who are parents to 1.5 million children, use prison libraries extensively to seek legal and family resource information. However, the majority of them do not use public libraries when they return to their communities. Aware of the benefits of collaboration, Maryland Correctional Education Libraries initiated an outreach program to extend reading opportunities to the children of prisoners and encourage the use of public libraries.

Recognizing the importance of family involvement in the literacy level of the children of prisoners, this writer and the correctional educational curriculum specialist initiated a family literacy program, Reading Is Fundamental (RIF), at the Maryland Correctional Institution at Jessup, a medium-security male prison. We conducted a program once a month where children and prisoners interacted in a variety of reading and educational activities and took part in the public library's summer reading games.

Our partners were the correctional education teaching staff, Reading Is Fundamental, and the Enoch Pratt Free Library (EPFL). The teachers prepared the inmates for the reading session, RIF provided the initial funding, and EPFL provided professional training and conducted story hours.

Teachers were concerned that inmates who read below grade level would be reluctant to display poor reading skills in front of their children. We purchased three set of identical titles, one set for the classroom so the teacher and inmate would practice, one set for the prison library so interested inmates would browse, and one set for the children to take home.

RIF's popularity at the Jessup facility was the springboard for this writer's launch of a similar program at the Maryland House of Corrections, a maximum-security male prison. Developing programs in a prison required the support of security staff who knew the quirks of the institution and could get necessary permissions. The prison librarian identified the volunteer activities coordinator as the person to help get the program implemented.

We presented a proposal that showed commitment to security and highlighted the program's incontrovertible benefits.

1. A family literacy program would serve as a control tool, since participation was limited to inmates without disciplinary infractions. Because family was important to inmates, prospective candidates were more likely to conform to institutional rules for an opportunity to be with their families.

2. Participants would improve their reading and comprehension skills, making them more likely to succeed and thus reducing recidivism when they reenter society.

3. The program would provide an opportunity for children and inmate parents to interact positively. This could lead to behavior modification and improved academic performance among the children.

4. The program would provide certificates that inmates value as evidence of positive activities during parole hearings.

5. A successful program would be good public relations for the prison.

After the proposal was approved, the librarian and the volunteer activities coordinator identified ten inmates to be trained as facilitators. Specialists from the Howard

County and Enoch Pratt Free Libraries helped us train the inmates in storytelling and program planning for appropriate age groups and conducted a session of Mother Goose on the Loose, with a brief discussion on brain development.

Visitors had to submit their name, social security number, birth date, and driver's license number before getting permission to enter the prison. We informed visiting librarians that they must provide a list of items they intended to bring and that the items would be examined by security on the day of the visit. We also gave them a list of prohibited items and the institution's dress code, encouraging them to omit clothing accessories that might set off the security alarm, thereby subjecting them to more intrusive searches.

During the first training sessions, the inmates were nervous, self-conscious, and clumsy as the librarians urged them to liven up the stories with movements. The public librarians provided books on storytelling techniques from their collection.

While the inmates were being trained, the prison librarian advertised the program in various sections of the prison. She interviewed each applicant, reminding him that it was not a regular prison visit but one with a focus on reading.

The security staff had the final say on visitors, children, and numbers of participants, as well as on eligible prisoners who would participate. Initially, they gave approval for participation of only children who were eight years old and under. We invited the warden and security chief to view the programs and hand out certificates, and then pointed out the benefits of having at-risk teens and preteens interacting with their parents. The prison administration later relaxed the age stipulation, particularly after inmates had also pointed out the mutual benefits. Expanding the age range made programming more challenging, but with suggestions from the EPFL staff we selected materials and activities that had universal appeal.

After three months of rehearsals, facilitators and inmates gathered in the visiting room for their first program. They decorated the walls with ALA READ posters and displayed children's books on tables that during regular prison visits would have been the barrier between inmate and visitor. Our family literacy program and books removed that barrier, as we got permission for the children to sit beside their parents during reading sessions.

The first event was poorly attended because it snowed. The small audience became a live rehearsal for the men who said they had never read to their children and that they were not familiar with any of the popular children's books on display. At the next reading event the EPFL children's librarian conducted the story hour, providing a model for inmates, caregivers, and the facilitators to interact with their children.

When this writer informed the facilitators that the prison library had no funds to purchase props like the public librarians possessed, they made their own from materials that they found around the institution. The EPFL librarian, seeing our collection of mostly donated children's books, offered a rotating deposit collection of children's materials. Every eight weeks she selected a variety of books and checked them out to the prison. The inmates never checked out these books. The facilitators explained that prisoners were sensitive and might feel we were insulting their intelligence by placing children's books in the library. We erected a large sign that read

"Family Literacy: Books to Read to and with Your Children." Although the men did not check out the books, we observed them browsing, some of them saying they were artists and liked the illustrations.

Each program had approximately sixty participants that included caregivers, children, inmates, and facilitators. We rotated groups every three months, encouraging every group to continue on their own after the formal session finished.

As public libraries planned the summer reading games, this writer encouraged family literacy participants to sign up for these either at their local libraries or through our prison program.

None of our children or caregivers had library cards. This writer worked with the EPFL children's specialist, who allowed us to take library cards into the prison. We urged the children and their caregivers to apply for library cards and return the application forms to their local library. The EPFL made special accommodations for our children to take part in the summer reading games. This involved more paperwork, but the enthusiasm of the prisoners made it worthwhile.

Each year for three years, about twenty children signed up in the prison for the summer reading games. We also gave the incarcerated adults the summer reading game board to mail or give to their family members, reminding them to visit the public library in their neighborhood. We had no way of tracking if the children visited the public library, but we kept track of those who signed up in the prison. The prisoners proudly brought in their children's finished game boards and mini-book reports, which we put on display in the prison library. We conducted summer reading graduation ceremonies and presented the children with prizes from EPFL and a certificate of participation. The EPFL specialist and the warden handed out the prizes, reminding the children of the benefits of using the library and informing them that the library could help with their homework assignments.

The family literacy and the summer reading games were firsts for the majority of the prisoners. One inmate said, "I did not know I could be silly with my child." Another said, "It couldn't get any righter than this." One of the inmate facilitators said the program gave him confidence to stand up and speak in front of a group.

"Has Your Public Librarian Been to Prison?" is the title this writer used to encourage public libraries to do more outreach to prisoners and their children. It was also the title of a program we presented in collaboration with the EPFL during the Maryland Library Association's annual conference and the American Library Association's annual conference.

NOTE

1. U.S. Department of Education, National Center for Education Statistics, *Literacy behind Bars: Results from the 2003 National Assessment of Adult Literacy Prison Survey*, May 2007.

25

HAS YOUR PUBLIC LIBRARIAN BEEN TO PRISON?

Participation in Shared Grant Projects

Glennor Shirley

EASTERN CORRECTIONAL Institution West (ECIW) is a medium-security male prison on Maryland's eastern shore. The prison librarian, June Brittingham, runs a variety of programs with community partners. One of the programs is a classical book discussion conducted by the students at Salisbury University, and the other is a summer reading grant in partnership with the local public library.

The Somerset County Library System (SCLS) as part of its outreach wrote a mini-grant that enabled inmates at ECIW to participate in the summer reading games for three years. The program was implemented as a modified form of the children's summer reading games, Blast Off to Reading, Readers Rule, and Race to Read.

The modified adult summer reading game included book reviews by each of the participants and prizes as incentives, depending on the number of book reviews submitted. At the end of the program, the prison library compiled the book reviews and shared them with other prison library users as a way of marketing titles. The summer reading program and the reviews helped to increase circulation and served to entice reluctant readers to try out new titles. Because many of the inmates have school-age children, this became an incentive for the prisoners to encourage their children to participate in the summer reading games in their local libraries. It meant prisoner and child would have something in common — the summer reading games.

At the end of each program, an awards ceremony was held. Librarians from the SCLS came inside the fence and presented the awards to the inmates. Participants received certificates, with the top readers/reviewers receiving additional prizes. During the three years of the program, 175 inmates reviewed 1,236 books.

The program was so successful that although there was no more funding from the SCLS, it continued for a fourth year and was even extended to a prerelease prison. In the prerelease unit, thirty men read and reviewed over 180 books, an impressive achievement since they worked all day and had much less time to read and write reviews.

The participants in these programs expressed gratitude that people actually cared enough to provide positive programs for them. One participant said the books made "new friends" for him; another felt that books could "take him anywhere." Yet another said that reading was his "stress buster."

A report of the program can be read on this writer's blog: http://prisonlibrarian.blogspot.com/2008/05/family-literacy-and-incarcerated-adults.html.

PART V
Special Collections

26

BREATHING LIFE INTO THE CIRCUS COLLECTION

Maureen Brunsdale

ONE OF the largest collections within Illinois State University's Special Collections and Rare Book Room in Milner Library is the Circus and Allied Arts Collection. Begun in 1955 by library director Eleanor Welch, the purpose of this collection was to document the important relationship that existed between the twin cities of Bloomington and Normal and circus acts throughout modern history. Bloomington was a winter training location for aerialists, and Normal, as the home of Illinois State University, claims the oldest collegiate circus in the United States. The staff of Milner Library's Special Collections have recently begun aggressively marketing its unique collection to both the campus and the community via partnerships with circus coaching staff and students, outreach to local media outlets, and collaboration with authors, artists, and editors as they begin to articulate the tremendous cultural impact that circuses have had on the United States.

THE BEGINNINGS OF A SPECIAL RELATIONSHIP

There exists a significant gap in Special Collections librarianship at the Milner Library. Between the late 1980s and mid-2007, duties affiliated with Special Collections were split among many librarians and a few staff whose major responsibilities were outside the area, both intellectually and physically. A wonderful circus curator has been employed throughout this period, but because of his full-time job outside the library he has worked within the department only three hours each week. Though his comprehensive knowledge of circus information and lore is nearly without peer, he has had no formal training in librarianship. The collection has grown through the generosity of circus enthusiasts and through the curator's hard work, but with so little time spent in the department and with such a tremendous amount of librarian turnover in it, the area suffered.

In July 2007 the library was in the midst of a massive structural reorganization, and the position of special collections librarian was left vacant after a faculty retirement. A librarian who had previously been a generalist librarian stepped forward to assume leadership responsibilities in the Special Collections and Rare Book Room—an area that hosts several distinct collections, including the Circus and Allied Arts Collection. After roughly six months of clearing out junk (the area had become a repository for cardboard boxes, scrap paper, and the like), the distinctive collections held within the room became more obvious, with the Circus and Allied Arts Collection being by far the most unique.

Meanwhile, every April the Gamma Phi Circus—the nation's oldest-running collegiate circus—performs. For its seventy-ninth year, they worked on bringing a trapeze show into their act. To accomplish this, the coach and students worked with Tony Steele, a seventy-one-year-old man who had been "flying" since he left his Boston home at the age of fifteen to join the circus.

Working with and through the circus curator, Special Collections was able to host a small, intimate luncheon between Special Collections and Gamma Phi Circus coaching staff before their first show. Additionally, we were able to host a much larger Question and Answer event within Special Collections after their dress rehearsal. A crowd of around one hundred attended and included a majority of the library faculty and staff as well as the Gamma Phi Circus performers, coaching staff, and volunteer staff.

OUTREACH TO LOCAL MEDIA OUTLETS

The special collections librarian has a long history of reaching out to the community. About ten years ago, she was part of writing the first press release for the Milner Library. In the intervening years the library has hired a full-time public relations librarian. Working with the public relations librarian has garnered many opportunities for Milner Library's Special Collections that perhaps otherwise would not have been a reality.

After a press release went to the local media outlets concerning the advent of a trapeze act with the famous Tony Steele in the college circus, a newspaper columnist picked up the story about the Q&A event in Special Collections and featured it in his front-page column in the newspaper's Community section. As a consequence, many community members—a good number of whom are themselves circus performer alumni—showed up at the event. The campus newspaper was also there, interviewing both the featured speaker and some of the performers. Illinois State University also employs its own media relations personnel. It was through contact with staff there that a podcast of the event was developed and launched. The campus newspaper's interview covered all areas included in Special Collections, but the focus was the Circus and Allied Arts Collection.

ARTISTS, AUTHORS, AND EDITORS—OH MY!

The fine arts librarian has been an important link between Special Collections and Illinois State University's School of Art. Visiting artists along with professors of art history and graphic design have used artifacts from our collection to highlight various artistic trends and designs. It is delightful to highlight all of our collections within Special Collections, but the Circus and Allied Arts Collection is one area that seems to spark more interest among both the arts faculty and their students than the other collections within the department.

A number of authors and editors have used the Circus and Allied Arts Collection. Most recently, Noel Daniel, editor of Taschen Press's *Circus, 1870–1950*, visited our collection and culled from it a number of images that were later used in that book. The book was formally released in August 2008. Taschen Press, Illinois State University's bookstore, and Milner Library's Special Collections collaborated to host a book launch for Taschen's *Circus* book in our library. Held on November 6, 2008, the launch drew members from the community and from various regional chapters of the Circus Fans Association and the Circus Historical Society. Members of the Gamma Phi Circus performed during the event, and Noel Daniel was on hand to autograph books that were available for purchase. This catered event was a highlight for both the department and library.

COLLABORATION IS KEY

Collaboration is the common thread for the outreach success that Special Collections has thus far enjoyed. Working with the circus curator, the public relations librarian, subject bibliographers, and the campus's media relations staff has proven to be vitally important as we work toward getting the word out about our collection's strengths. It's true that the circus has had an incredible cultural impact on our society, but without marketing and public relations efforts such as press releases, podcasts, interviews, special events, and a supporting network, that impact would remain unknown.

27

BRINGING HISTORY TO THE PEOPLE'S FINGERTIPS

University of Florida Digital Collections and Historical Florida Newspapers

Melissa Shoop

TRADITIONALLY, THE University of Florida has microfilmed in-house the community newspapers for all of Florida, but in 2005 a Library Services and Technology Act (LSTA) grant from the State Library and Archives of Florida (along with other grants and funding) made possible the transition from microfilm to a digital medium. The University of Florida Digital Collection (UFDC) now contains over three million pages, of which over half a million are Florida newspapers.

The UFDC's role in the National Digital Newspaper Program (NDNP): Florida Newspapers, 1900–1910, and the Ephemeral Cities Project shows how collaboration between communities, universities, and federal institutions such as the Library of Congress and the National Endowment for the Humanities (NEH) makes the valuable resource of local newspapers from across the state of Florida readily available for use by members of the community. The NDNP is a phased program and is a partnership between the Library of Congress and the NEH (more information can be found online at www.neh.gov/projects/ndnp.html). The Florida Newspapers project is also a collaborative effort between all of the libraries in the State University

System of Florida, the State Library and Archives of Florida, and the Florida Center for Library Automation.

The Ephemeral Cities Project is another instance of widespread partnering. The project is still in production because digital content for Gainesville, Key West, and Tampa is still being added, but the collaborative effort of the project is worth describing. First of all, the project is funded partly through the Institute of Museum and Library Services. Other partners include three universities, two public libraries, four museums, two public records offices, the Florida Center for Library Automation, and a number of Florida citizens whose private collections are an important part of the project. Additionally, the project utilizes digital collections already extant: UFDC, University of South Florida Digital Collections, the PALMM Collections (State Universities of Florida), the Florida Memory Project (State Library and Archives of Florida), the Heritage Collection (Alachua County Library District), the Mile Markers Project (Monroe County Public Library), and the Ancient Records Project (Alachua County Clerk of the Court). The effort to coordinate and build this collection is an exceptional testament to the strength of partnering.

Reading microfilm can be time-consuming, and the reading machines can be cumbersome for people to use; now, basic Internet skills put local history at the people's fingertips. Community members, public librarians, historians, and businesses all benefit from the Florida Newspapers and Ephemeral Cities projects because these digital collections are "open source," meaning they are free and available for anyone to use for any kind of project or research on a home, business, or library Internet connection. In fact, all of the UFDC's materials are open source, and each page has detailed citation information. This means that libraries in Florida no longer need to spend money to purchase reels of microfilmed newspapers, because the University of Florida has them online. The collection of digital newspapers will continue to grow so that, in time, microfilm readers will no longer be needed to read old newspapers, and precious funds will no longer be needed to purchase new readers or to repair old ones.

The UFDC also partners with public libraries to preserve their microfilm collections. One current project that was made possible by an LSTA grant awarded to the Hendry County Library Cooperative is the digitization of the *Clewiston News* (1928–45). This partnership preserves and simplifies access for Hendry County Library users while simultaneously helping to build the UFDC collection. The UFDC does all the work and hosts the content on university library servers. Even more helpful, the resource is easy to navigate using basic Internet-searching skills. Anyone can learn how to look up information in newspapers in the collection.

The University of Florida library system is a member of the Northeast Florida Library Information Network (NEFLIN). NEFLIN provides services to its members such as equipment loans, resource sharing, webcasts, and training. It is an easy and effective way to communicate across libraries and to network with other librarians. In February 2009 the UFDC held a workshop through NEFLIN's Internet conferencing tool to market the UFDC's digital collections and to teach librarians all across northeast Florida how they can use this resource. Web conferencing is a valuable tool for introducing and sharing online resources such as the UFDC. Marketing the digital collections to other librarians via web conferencing has proven an effective method of reaching the members of the community. People who perform genealogical and historical research find this resource particularly valuable, and their local librarian can now assist them better. No longer will folks need to whirl through reels of microfilm, hoping to land in the right date range to find an obituary or an article about a particular business. Now all one needs to do is to enter a name or word, and the UFDC will find all occurrences in the collection. The existence and continual building of digital collections save libraries and users alike valuable time and money, while demonstrating the power of vast partnering and preservation projects.

The reader can visit www.uflib.ufl.edu/ufdc/UFDC.aspx for more information about the UFDC, the projects described here, and other digital collections.

28

THEY DIDN'T TEACH ME *THIS* IN LIBRARY SCHOOL

Managing a Library Art Gallery

Karen Brodsky

IT SEEMS a natural fit to have artwork in libraries. At Sonoma State University Library, in Rohnert Park, California, we have committed to an art gallery in order to support the liberal arts and sciences mission of the university. The gallery's exhibits explore a diverse range of ideas, values, and intellectual and artistic expressions. In working with artists, curators, educators, and collectors from the community, we provide unique possibilities for supporting learning and discovery, and we give students, faculty, and community members yet another reason to visit our library.

OVERVIEW

The Jean and Charles Schulz Information Center opened in August 2000. The original building plans did not include a gallery, but, due to last-minute design changes and the creativity of the campus architect, a 1,200-square-foot gallery was placed directly across from the main entrance. I was asked to coordinate this new service because I had a background in marketing and programming, as well as a huge desire to make it work. I was also liaison to the Art Department, which includes the SSU Art Gallery. (I call it the "Other Gallery.")

As a new coordinator, it was obvious to me that because my degree was not in museum studies, it would be imperative for me to reach out to experts. A fantastic expert came in the person of the director of the SSU Art Gallery, who was more than generous with his time, expertise, and creativity. His art credentials are impressive, and he has been a strong partner since our first show.

We established a mission for our gallery immediately, desiring it to be an integral part of the library, not a stand-alone service. The mission we created is simply "to support the Liberal Arts and Sciences curriculum of the university." This mission let us collaborate with different campus departments and members of the community. Some of the planning principles we established were to display works of art by students and professional artists, to show selections from the university library's unique collections, and to explore the possibilities of traveling exhibitions. We established a principle to work closely with the "Other Gallery" on campus to ensure that our exhibits demonstrated and maintained aesthetic standards and professional quality. We also committed to have one student show per semester—which could be an exhibit of student work or an exhibition that students curate. The exhibits we have shown include "Thinking about Freedom: Works from the San Quentin Arts Program" and "Fresh Starts: Sonoma State Painting Students."

THE HOW-TOS: MARKETING, FUND-RAISING, IMPLEMENTATION, EVALUATION

Although each exhibit is its own unique experience with unique challenges, there are consistent aspects to every show.

Preplanning. Developing an outline and time line is essential. Even with the best planning, something can happen to thwart time lines. It is important to build in some wiggle room because deadlines will be missed, installations will be more complex than anticipated, and the show must go on (this is the reason I never plan receptions on the day an exhibit is scheduled to open).

Exhibition Design and Installation. Installation requirements are obviously dictated by the work to be exhibited, the gallery space, the budget, and the mission. Some of our limitations include three solid walls and one glass wall and an eight-foot ceiling that we can't hang anything from due to insulation.

Promotion and Publicity. For each exhibition we develop an announcement card, usually a 4 × 6 postcard with an image on the front and basic information on the back. These cards are sent to an on- and off-campus mailing list (bulk-mail rates, labeled by student assistants; not using a mail house allows us to cut costs and gives late-night student workers something to do). A press release, with follow-up calls, is always created. We have a presence on our library's website and an extensive e-mail list. We also do an "opening" or reception with light refreshments and no alcohol (supporting the alcohol-free policy on campus—and saving money).

Staffing. The responsibility for design and installation varies depending on the exhibit. These aspects have been handled by students, community artists, gallery or library staff, and me.

Financing (Budgets and Fund-Raising). There is no line item for the gallery in the library budget, so expenses come directly out of the library operating budget or from fund-raising. Even though we keep the costs of our exhibits to a minimum, there have been several occasions where we raised money. The exhibit dictates where we look for funding. Departments on campus, donors in the community, external grants, and even the student clubs have all helped cover costs. It is important to remember that the gallery is only one of many library services, and we don't ever want to compete with ourselves for donations. Because of this, we act very strategically when asking for support.

Evaluation. Assessing each exhibit and the program as a whole provides some intriguing challenges. It is very hard to get quantitative data. There is no counter on the gallery door, and I don't always hear from faculty who bring classes over, nor do I know how many students have written a paper on an exhibit or how many community members have recommended the exhibit to friends. But I can gather some qualitative data from students, faculty, and community feedback. I also get feedback from our public services staff stationed directly across from the gallery door and from the guest book. I also solicit opinions from artists about their experiences exhibiting in our gallery and from other curators who critique the presentation.

CONCLUSION

The gallery has added a fabulous dimension to the library's programs and departmental learning objectives. It is also another reason for the community to come to campus. Although we continually examine the program to ensure its fit with the library as a whole, we always conclude that we must find a way to continue to offer engaging exhibitions that support the liberal arts and sciences mission of our university. As the campus and community continue to provide so much positive feedback about coming to the library to visit our gallery, we feel it is meeting its mission.

PART VI
Using Local Media to Reach Out to the Community

29

LIGHTS, CAMERA, LIBRARIES

Nancy Kalikow Maxwell

TELEVISION REALLY does make you look ten pounds heavier. It also accentuates the bags under your eyes and exposes the wrinkles on your neck. I learned these cruel facts when the first episode of *Library Matters* aired on the local cable television station. Watching my televised crinkles, my own face cringed with regret. Why had I ever suggested that the library produce this show?

But the next day on campus, when three people told me they saw me talking about the library on TV, I decided the assault to my vanity was worth it. The library and I had earned our fifteen minutes of fame. As I discuss in this chapter, other librarians should consider using their local cable television network to promote their library's message. All it will cost is time, energy, and maybe a few trips to the gym.

The turn of events that led to my televised wrinkles was the acquisition of a local community access television station by my employer, Miami Dade College (MDC). With more than 100,000 students at eight campuses in Miami, Florida, MDC is the nation's largest institution of higher education. Formerly known as Miami-Dade Community College, MDC grants both two-year and four-year degrees. Minorities make up more than 85 percent of the student body, and the college graduates more African American and Hispanic students each year than any other college in the country.

One of the most prominent programs at the college is the School of Entertainment and Design Technology (SEDT), which trains students to enter the broadcasting industry. In 2008 SEDT added to its academic programs a college access television station, MDC TV. Operated entirely by a small professional staff and advanced television students, MDC TV produces and broadcasts shows in English, Spanish, and Haitian Creole. Unlike other college cable stations, MDC TV reaches beyond the campus and can be seen by more than 500,000 households throughout Miami-Dade County. A live streaming video website (www.mdc.edu/mdctv/) extends the viewership to anyone with Internet access.

When the college obtained the station, the new station director came to a campus management meeting with an open invitation: "Any of your departments that want to put on a show are more than welcome to contact me." The first two department managers to accept his offer were those of the entrepreneurial program and the library. Both of us had something to sell. I wanted to promote libraries and librarianship.

THE LIBRARY SHOW

The idea for a show about libraries was enthusiastically accepted. As we later learned, public access stations are in need of topics that appeal to a broad viewership, and libraries fit the bill perfectly. Librarians thinking of approaching their own local station to begin a library show should be similarly greeted.

A committee of library employees was quickly assembled to begin planning the show. Under the direction of the assistant library director, the group met weekly to decide the topic of each episode, the language of the program, and each episode's hosts and guests. The station's format required that each episode be half an hour long and include one host interviewing no more than two guests. Because of the abundance of Spanish speakers available, the committee decided to produce shows in both English and Spanish.

After several animated discussions, the committee decided to launch the series with two topics: "Is the Library Obsolete?" and "Librarians as Authors."

THREE, TWO, ONE—YOU'RE ON . . .

Selecting these topics was the easy part. The more difficult challenge was finding people willing to subject themselves to being videotaped for television. Responses to invitations ranged from "I don't think so" to "No way!" One librarian agreed to participate when he was approached at the reference desk. But by the time his shift ended, he had changed his mind. The reasons he cited for declining the invitation included being camera-shy, the aforementioned extra poundage, and an inability to "think on one's feet" because shows were recorded "live-to-tape."

The committee had better luck recruiting students, faculty, and employees from other departments. Ultimately, two librarians with broadcast experience were identified and agreed to participate. One had been a Spanish-language television news anchor before immigrating to this country, and the other had previously hosted a radio talk show.

Once the hosts and guests were in place, a list of questions for each segment was produced and a rehearsal was held. The do's and don'ts of wardrobe selection were explained (no busy patterns, solid white shirts, or revealing skirts), the studio was booked, and the first show was taped.

ADVANTAGES AND DISADVANTAGE OF A LIBRARY SHOW

Since its first episode aired, *Library Matters* has been a huge success. The library has become a star of sorts, with many people in the community being made aware not only of library services but also broader issues such as librarianship as a profession, the future of libraries, and the importance of the library as an institution of democracy.

The show has also afforded opportunities to partner with other departments on campus. Guests on the show have been or will soon include representatives from the History, Social Sciences, and Media Services departments, to name a few. *Library Matters* has also enabled us to reach out to the nearby university library and public library to provide them a platform by which to promote their own services.

On a personal note, I found the opportunity to produce and tape a television show invaluable. I admit that the taping was terrifying. Sitting in front of the cameras watching the floor manager count down the seconds with his fingers and giving me the "cue" was probably one of the most dreadful moments of my life. But the experience was also fascinating. I now watch television with a new understanding— and appreciation—of what it takes to produce a television show. Though I am not a fan of talk shows, I have a greater respect for the skills, talents, and time it takes to produce and host these shows.

The most serious drawback to the show proved to be the incredible amount of time required to plan and produce each episode. Identifying potential participants, compiling interview questions, arranging for rehearsals, and scheduling tapings all take an enormous amount of time and effort.

But despite the time commitment, the show has proven to be an excellent outreach avenue. I would urge other librarians—especially those who are skinny and wrinkle-free—to consider launching their very own library show on cable television.

30
PARTNERING WITH A LOCAL NEWSPAPER TO DIGITIZE HISTORICAL PHOTOGRAPHS

John R. Burch Jr.

ONE OUTGROWTH of the Campbellsville University book project that is described elsewhere in this volume was the development of a partnership between the staff of the A. B. Colvin Baptist Collection and Archives, Montgomery Library, Campbellsville University, and our local newspaper, the *Central Kentucky News-Journal*. The partnership was facilitated by Stan McKinney, who is a faculty member at Campbellsville University and a former employee of the *Central Kentucky News-Journal*.

Mr. McKinney initiated the partnership by asking Tim Hooper, the Campbellsville University archivist, if he was interested in possibly digitizing the more than 100,000 photographs that McKinney had taken while working for the newspaper. Interest was immediately expressed because much of McKinney's work involved events on our campus over several decades. Our enthusiasm was tempered by the fact that McKinney did not own the photographs. Fortunately, McKinney had also broached the subject with the publishers of the newspaper, and they were willing to discuss a possible collaboration.

While not getting into the details of the negotiations, the main issue that had to be overcome was copyright. The newspaper had invested money in its employee, cameras, film, and processing materials for nearly twenty years and thus was not prepared to just sign over its copyrights. We settled the issue by devising a means whereby the newspaper kept the copyright to all of the images but gave Campbellsville University permission to use any of the photographs involving the university's history free of charge.

We then determined that two copies of the image database would be constructed: one for the archives that would be available to the public and one for the newspaper. The two databases being constructed are fundamentally different. The database for the newspaper is being created with JPG files at a resolution of 300 dpi (dots per inch). This format was requested in order to maximize the number of images that could be stored on a DVD. The archival images are currently being saved as TIFF files with a minimum resolution of 4,000 dpi. The TIFF files, especially at the resolution that we are using, are very large files. The expense of all the hard-drive space required by TIFF files is far outweighed by their benefit. The beauty of a TIFF file is that it picks up details from the photo negatives that cannot be seen with the naked eye. By zooming in to the TIFF image, one can glean details that were not even apparent in developed photographs from the same negatives.

With the agreement signed by the respective parties, the next issue to be addressed was the compilation of the image database. Although it had become relatively easy for us to digitize photographs and negatives, we were neophytes at constructing a searchable image database. After researching possible solutions in the library literature, Tim Hooper embarked on a trip to visit archivists at the University of North Carolina, Duke University, and Appalachian State University to see how they addressed similar issues. He discovered that these types of institutions were constructing their own software to give them options beyond those offered through just metadata. Because our library only employs three librarians and four other staff members, we realistically did not have the ability or resources to even begin considering writing our own software. Fortunately for us, we blundered into some computer experts. Some gentlemen from MCRMedia Associates made an appointment to demonstrate a database of religious resources that they had developed. While our librarians found their product interesting, we were particularly intrigued by the underlying architecture of the software. Their software was not designed for a library market, but in our view it had the potential to be superior to most of the archive software that we had been considering. A partnership was formed for MCRMedia to develop a searchable database product that allowed us not only to archive and display all of our digital files but to do so in a manner that was secure and easy to use by the public.

The resulting product, which is currently being beta tested, is currently named DATmanager. It is a complete digital asset management system that is designed to enable archive employees to quickly digitize media files in most formats, including images, audio, video, animations, PowerPoint presentations, PDFs, HTML, XML, Flash/Flex SWFs, and DVDs. The files can be selectively filtered to allow access to ones that an archivist wants to share while keeping all other files secure. Metadata creation and extraction per file is customizable, thus allowing archivists to control and maintain their digital assets in a manner that conforms to their desired work flow.

These various partnerships have piqued the curiosity of individuals outside of our library's normal patron base. They have resulted in some interesting opportunities for the individuals involved in various aspects of this project. McKinney, Hooper, and I made a presentation at the 2009 Kentucky Press Association's annual meeting on the development of the Stan McKinney Central Kentucky News-Journal Digital Image Collection. We hope that sharing our experiences with others will lead some of the newspaper publishers in the state to initiate similar projects with educational or public institutions in their local communities. Hooper and I, along with our partners from MCRMedia Associates, are scheduled to make a presentation about DATmanager at the 2009 joint annual meeting of the Society of American Archivists and the Council of State Archivists. With the way this project has evolved since its inception, it would not surprise me in the slightest to see new opportunities emerge as we share what we have learned with others at these meetings.

PART VII
Success with Book Festivals

31

MICHIGAN READS! STATEWIDE OUTREACH PROJECT

Christine K. Heron

GETTING FAMILIES of young children to participate in library programs can be a challenge. They may lack time, transportation, and knowledge of library services. At the Genesee District Library we capitalized on a statewide program, Michigan Reads! to make new connections with adults who work or live with preschool-age children. We also used this program to promote early childhood literacy.

Have you participated in the One Book, One Community outreach program? Imagine setting a goal of reaching every child from age zero to five with one book. In the state of Michigan, our former state librarian dreamed of promoting early childhood literacy by using the guidelines from One Book, One Community. The planning for this program began in 2003 with the dedication of a team of several youth services librarians from around the state. After the first year, 2004, the program was hindered by the lack of funding and personnel changes at the state library. By 2006 a major financial sponsor, Target, was secured. Over the last five years other sponsors have been secured and personnel have stabilized at the state level, giving the program the stability to continue each year. The program has been a success, and libraries throughout the state can use it to outreach in the ways that fit their budgets and staffing.

The following books were the titles selected:

2008: *Raccoon Tune* by Nancy Shaw

2007: *Big Chickens* by Leslie Helakoski

2006: *Bed Hogs* by Kelly DiPucchio

2004: *Barnyard Song* by Rhonda Gowler Greene

At the Genesee District Library in Genesee County, Michigan, we utilized the program materials to outreach to communities in several ways.

In 2004 we mailed invitations to a training workshop to teachers and aides from preschools, Head Start programs, and day care centers throughout Genesee County. We reserved an auditorium and provided a demonstration of how to implement this program and the early childhood literacy components in their educational settings. The demonstration featured a storyteller, Carol Bakke, who showcased the story and embellished it with songs and finger plays. Samples of farm-themed crafts and other activities such as skits and puzzles were highlighted. The teachers and aides received continuing education credit for attending. In addition, our children's librarian contacted several preschool programs around the county and offered to do a special storytime to promote Michigan Reads! as well as early childhood literacy and our library system. Seven school districts participated over a four-week period. Each classroom received a complimentary copy of the book. Additionally, two branches in our library system hosted Rhonda Gowler Greene as she shared her children's books and stories from her life. The Library of Michigan kicked off the inaugural event with a special reading by Greene held in Lansing.

In 2006 our children's librarian took the book *Bed Hogs* on the road to several elementary schools to promote Michigan Reads! In *Bed Hogs*, onomatopoeia was used with the kindergarten and first-grade students to demonstrate phonological awareness. Our children's librarian also contacted the leaders of the local SKIP (Successful Kids Involve Parents) programs to promote the Michigan Reads! program. Brochures and fliers announcing special storytimes held at several of our branch libraries were distributed to the coordinators of the SKIP programs. Our storyteller, Carol Bakke, again did an excellent job adapting *Bed Hogs* in a fantastic storytime that demonstrated the components of early literacy. Each child participating in the SKIP program received a complimentary copy of the book from her SKIP coordinator. Every public library received a tool kit designed by children's services librarians that included tips on promoting the program and utilizing the book in storytimes and activities. Target was instrumental in funding the tool kits for the public libraries, schools, Head Start, and the Michigan School Readiness Program. The tool kits included a copy of the book, a resource guide with sample programs and activities to promote early literacy, a poster, bookmarks, and stickers.

In 2007, due to management changes within the Genesee District Library and it being a taxpayer funding year, we were unable to provide the kinds of programs we had in previous years. Due to the uncertainty of our funding, we recruited volunteers from each community. Each volunteer read *Big Chickens* to children who came to the library. Make-and-take crafts were provided to the participants. We promoted the Guest Reader Storytime to the SKIP programs, the local newspapers, and the elementary schools. To promote Michigan Reads! across the state, Target sponsored a free fun day called the Target Book Festival for families at Kensington Park in Milford. Children's authors and illustrators came to the festival to share their love of reading. Face painting, live entertainment, and storytelling were available during the all-day event. Entrance into the park was free. The Genesee District Library ran buses from the headquarters library to Kensington Park. This provided free transportation to our patrons.

In 2008 the Genesee District Library invited author Nancy Shaw to share her Michigan Reads! title *Raccoon Tune*. Two special storytimes featuring Shaw and her beloved raccoons were held at the Fenton Children's Center and the Flushing Area Library branch. Outreach to the community included contacting the SKIP coordinators and the local newspapers. Again, we used the Target-sponsored tool kits to embellish the storytime and promote the Michigan Reads! program within our branches. Outreach to patrons also included promoting the second annual Target Book Festival held at Kensington Park.

The following outreach activities were successful in promoting the Michigan Reads! program:

- training workshop
- forming a partnership with area SKIPs
- elementary classroom visits
- storytimes held at preschools
- program-themed tool kits
- complimentary books
- Target Book Festival held at Kensington Park

Using the One Book, One Community model allows librarians to promote reading by using an outreach model that incorporates community collaboration. The Michigan Reads! program outreaches to the zero-to-five-years demographic while reinforcing the components of early childhood literacy. It's a great way to get out of the building and into the community.

32

BOOKS THAT SHAPE OUR LIVES
A Community of Readers

Jan Siebold

THE IDEA came to me after Christopher, a first-grade student, came up to me during book selection time. He handed me a wrinkled piece of paper on which the words "Bread and Jam for Francis?" were written.

"Do you have this book?" Christopher asked.

I led him to the picture book "H" section where Russell Hoban's Frances series was located.

"I'm just curious. How did you hear about this book?" I asked.

As Christopher examined the book more closely he replied, "It was my mom's favorite when she was a little girl, and she wondered if you have it."

After my exchange with Christopher, I started to think about the wonderful gift his mother had given to him by sharing the information about a favorite childhood book. Not only had she passed along the title of a classic piece of children's literature, but she had imparted the idea that a favorite book could hold a place in her heart after all of those years. And chances are, the reading of that book to Christopher was a very special experience.

I decided that it would be interesting to find out what other childhood favorites were remembered by parents of my students. And why stop there? Wouldn't it be fun to solicit information from the community at large?

After some thought, I decided to call my project "Books That Shape Our Lives." The following week I sent a letter to the local newspaper and to our school district newsletter. In the letter I described the project and asked parents, teachers, staff, and community members to send me the names of their favorite childhood books. I also asked readers for testimonial statements about the impact of books on their lives.

I listed a variety of options for sending the information to me: mail, e-mail, voice mail, or in writing via a student. Apparently my letter struck a chord. The replies began to come almost immediately. The response to my request was overwhelming. In the next few weeks I received almost four hundred replies.

The display of readers' responses soon spilled over from the library bulletin board to the hallways of our school. I shared some of the replies with each library class, especially those replies that were written by relatives of any student in that class. Our principal featured some of the more eloquent responses over the PA system during morning announcements.

After reading dozens of replies, it occurred to me that many of the titles that were mentioned were still part of our library collection. I decided to use this information in the creation of an OPAC search activity for my upper elementary students. Students searched our catalog for the titles that we received and were excited whenever they "struck gold" by finding one that still existed in our collection.

The age range of the readers told a story in itself. Young parents of our primary students mentioned authors like Eric Carle, Judy Blume, and Shel Silverstein. A slightly older crowd named writers like Carolyn Keene, Ezra Jack Keats, Walter Farley, Robert McCloskey, and Beverly Cleary. Senior citizens from the community were all over the place with their answers, depending on the circumstances of their childhoods. Authors such as Dr. Seuss, E. B. White, and Laura Ingalls Wilder were mentioned over and over by members of every age group. Anna Sewell's *Black Beauty* was mentioned so many times that it inspired me to finally read the book.

The sharing of responses led to library class discussions of what makes a classic. We talked about "classics" versus "modern classics." Students examined the dictionary definition of the word and found phrases like "enduring," "memorable," and "standard of excellence." After discussing the definition, I asked students to explain in their own words what makes a book a classic. They were passionate in their answers.

"It's a book that appeals to everyone."

"It's something that touches your feelings."

"Once you start reading it, you don't want to stop until you're finished."

"It's a book that you can read again and again."

"It would make a good movie."

The next question that I posed to students was: "What are some current books that will probably become classics and why?" I asked them to use the criteria that they had listed to make their choices. From the responses that I heard, it is safe to say that J. K. Rowling's books will have a place on library shelves for many years to come. Having been a librarian for over thirty years, I know that some of the titles mentioned will eventually fade into oblivion. However, it was heartwarming to hear the students defend their favorites so fervently.

What struck me the most about the responses that I received was the depth of feeling that people conveyed in their messages.

"Books made me realize that I could make a difference in the world."

"Books took me through years of adolescent turmoil."

"Some of my best friends were found between the covers of a book."

"My books provided comfort and gave me ways to figure out the world."

"I don't remember the name of my favorite book, but it had beautiful illus-trations of animals, and more importantly it was *mine*."

Considering my own feelings about reading, I'm not sure why I was so surprised by the overwhelming and passionate responses that I received from members of my school and from local communities. I only know I am glad there are so many others who share my appreciation for books.

33

COLLABORATION CREATES A SUCCESSFUL REGIONAL LOW-VISION FAIR

Bob Blanchard

IN 2008 the collaboration of eight public libraries resulted in a successful fair for persons with low vision in the north and northwest suburbs of Chicago.

I'm an adult services librarian at Des Plaines Public Library, and also on the 2008 low-vision fair's planning committee were Nancy Brothers and Karina Guico of Morton Grove Public Library, Dodie Frisbie of Niles Public Library District, Cathy Thompson of Park Ridge Public Library, Gary Gustin of Skokie Public Library, Janet McIntyre and Kim Comerford of Glenview Public Library, Laura Fantom of Vernon Area Public Library District, and Joyce Voss of Arlington Heights Memorial Library.

Outreach staff from the libraries built on the proven idea that one large event is more effective and stands to attract more people than smaller events at individual libraries. The goal was to provide information and an opportunity to showcase the latest developments in technology and services. The rationale for creating one fair was based on logistical, practical, and experiential reasons, including

- Planning and organizing a fair involving multiple vendors and participants is difficult for one person representing a solitary library.
- The Chicago metropolitan area has many assistive technology vendors, as well as numerous service organizations that aid persons with limited

sight. By working with staff from other libraries, the group could more effi-
ciently screen and select exhibitors.

- One large venue for guest speakers is more convenient for the public.
- The first multilibrary fair, held in 2007 and planned by five of the eight
  libraries, was highly successful.

The 2007 fair's planning and success were heralded in an article written by Nancy
Brothers and myself. It appeared in the February 2008 issue of the Illinois Library
Association *Reporter*. Partly because of the article, the Glenview, Arlington Heights,
and Vernon Area libraries joined the planning committee for the 2008 fair.

The fair's potential reach was a big reason for having both large-scale events. The
number of sight-related problems in the area is increasing because of a large elderly
population and a quickly growing number of aging baby boomers.

For the 2007 fair, the main challenge in planning had been finding an accessible,
low-cost, central location large enough to accommodate the exhibitors and speakers.
This was not a challenge in 2008 because the fair was held in the same location,
the Niles Senior Center. The village of Niles is roughly in the middle of the areas
served. Its senior center includes a large hall and two sizable meeting rooms. Also,
the senior center is across the street from the Niles Public Library and was made
available at no cost. The senior center's staff were again very enthusiastic about hosting the fair.

One of the easier parts of planning was lining up assistive technology vendors
and representatives of service organizations. The committee members were familiar
with the area's vendors by virtue of purchasing devices and software for their own
libraries. Some representatives of the service organizations also were known to the
librarians by way of referrals and personal contact. In addition, the vendors and service representatives participated in the fair for free.

Of the fifteen exhibitors, nine were vendors and six were representatives of service agencies, including the area's Talking Books center and a local low-vision support group. The Niles Lions Club provided screening for diabetic retinopathy and
macular degeneration, and a representative of a nearby hospital screened participants for glaucoma. Information on services and devices offered by the libraries was
available, as were pamphlets from the Illinois Society to Prevent Blindness. The
village clerk of Morton Grove was on hand to register persons to vote and to inform
them about early voting in the state of Illinois.

The two guest speakers were Polly Abbott, manager of adult rehabilitation services at the Guild for the Blind, a nationwide organization based in Chicago, who
spoke about the top ten things a person should investigate when diagnosed with
vision loss; and Dr. Stephen Conti, a local ophthalmologist, who discussed low-
vision problems that older persons may face. After she spoke, Abbott stayed for the
remainder of the program, and Conti patiently and thoroughly answered questions
throughout his presentation.

Each library was responsible for getting the word out to its patrons by posting
and distributing fliers, asking houses of worship to include announcements in their
bulletins, publishing articles in the library's newsletter, and through word of mouth.

News releases were sent to local newspapers, and public-service announcements were sent to radio stations well before the fair.

Keeping in mind the library programming adage "If you feed them, they will come," the publicity included one important phrase: "Refreshments will be available."

The combined means of publicity worked well. Most of the attendees were from the eight communities, but an amazing number came from Chicago and other suburbs.

In general, the fair was viewed very favorably by the exhibitors and the public. One exhibitor said it was the best fair he had been to in years. Some attendees called the fair "wonderful" and "very professional."

To the planners, the fair was a success. The attendance was very good. No one person or library was overburdened in planning and executing the event. The libraries divided the costs, monetary and in-kind, for refreshments, freebies like lens cloths and magnifying strips, the printing of three hundred programs, and gifts for the speakers.

All eight libraries benefited from the event, in terms of public relations and getting out the word about the services they offer to persons with disabilities. The outstanding cooperation strengthened their bonds and also cemented the partnership between the Niles Public Library and the Niles Senior Center.

In October 2008 the group began discussing plans for the next fair. Would the fair be repeated in 2009? Absolutely. The hours will be changed from 9:00 a.m. to 12:30 p.m. to 10:00 a.m. to 1:00 p.m. The group will pursue grants to fund the fair, have a free raffle for an assistive device, and tweak the improvements made since the 2007 event. The group also made a major presentation of the ideas, goals, and outcomes of the 2008 fair to a regional group of outreach librarians in April 2009.

Vision fairs are a helpful public service. A joint venture involving neighboring libraries takes the burden of planning and orchestrating a small fair off the shoulders of one person and spreads it over the collective expertise and ideas of several people. The result is a larger and more wide-reaching event. The eight-library fair shows that libraries can successfully work together. Most of all, the benefits are great because all participants—the attendees, the exhibitors, and the libraries—gain something, whether it's information, customers, clients, patrons, or a reputation for serving persons with limited sight.

34
ONE COMMUNITY, ONE STORY

Florence M. Turcotte

ACADEMIC LIBRARIANS often get wrapped up in their own area of specialization and are sometimes accused of ignoring the "real world" around them. It's true that with limited resources, our first priority should be curriculum and faculty support activities. Nevertheless, as educators, one of our responsibilities is to teach our charges how to be good citizens in a democratic society. Reaching out to the local community not only sets a good example for the students, it also improves town-gown relations. If, as is the case here in Gainesville, Florida, a community of a little more than 100,000 is asked to cater to the needs of 50,000 college students, there should be some outreach done by the campus community that enriches the life of the surrounding community in return.

One such outreach activity is the One Community, One Story (OCOS) program. The idea for this collaboration came from the question: "What if the whole community read the same book, at the same time?" Based on the successful One City, One Story in Seattle, but with a hometown twist, the greater Gainesville community has been doing just that for the last seven years. For this literary endeavor, many groups within the greater metropolitan area combine their efforts to encourage everyone in the community to read the same book. Programs related to the book and its theme or themes are set up on and off campus. These include group reading events, book discussions, film showings, artistic exhibitions, and dramatic presentations. The school, academic, and county public libraries play an important role in not only making multiple copies of the book available but in hosting group discussions, author events, lectures, and exhibits. Local bookstores and libraries stock extra copies of the book and put up posters publicizing related events. A local author writes a column called "Novel Conversations" in the community newspaper and invites members of the community into the conversation by publishing their comments. Thus, the ways in which a story can be related across different genres by different artists are explored, and a community-wide dialogue is initiated.

Do you think an OCOS program would work in your community? Here's how to go about setting it up.

Identify Stakeholders, Allies, and Participating Institutions and Businesses. These might include the local public and academic librarians, especially those in charge of adult services or outreach. Don't forget local agencies that promote literacy, arts programs, and culture-related events.

Diversify! The best way to reach the most people with your program is to include lots of different activities. Not everyone is inclined to sit down and read the book you have chosen. Look for a stage adaptation that your local community theater could possibly stage. Better yet, adapt your book choice to one of their upcoming productions! It'll be a lot easier to fund your program if the theater stands to sell a lot more tickets because of the interest generated in the play.

Saturate the Market! Schedule your events reasonably close together so that people can read the book, attend one or more of the activities, and move on to the next project. Somewhere from two to six weeks is ideal. Otherwise people will forget the story or move on to something else, and your momentum will stall. Speaking of momentum . . .

Build Up the Suspense and Finish Strong! You will want to hold your biggest event near the end of the program. Author appearances, pageants, and outdoor presentations or celebrations are a good way to culminate your program and get people interested in next year's program.

Get Your Public Relations Team Involved. With so many ways that people learn about community events, you need to use different means to get the word out about your program. Posters, websites, news releases, community billboards (actual *and* virtual), and Facebook and other social networking venues are all ways to get as many folks interested and involved as possible. Put up your schedule of events in as many places as possible, and be sure to produce printed schedules that can be handed out as bookmarks at local libraries.

After seven years, the One Community, One Story program is still going strong here in Gainesville, and new opportunities arise for community partnerships each year. Here is the list of programs from past years, as well as the general themes explored:

2002: *Diary of Anne Frank* (Holocaust, diversity, tolerance)

2003: *Romeo and Juliet* (suicide, teen issues)

2004: *War of the Worlds* (science fiction, cultural clashes, role of the media in society)

2005: *Nickel and Dimed* (the working poor, homelessness)

2006: *Very Old Man with Enormous Wings* (magical realism, the supernatural, family)

2007: *The Chosen* (Jewish identity, parent-child relationships)

2008: *Midnight in the Garden of Good and Evil* (southern identity, mystery)

The One Community, One Story program is designed not only to encourage reading but to provide opportunities for the academic community to "give back" to the host college town and enrich the lives of all in this vibrant and creative community.

35
SOKY BOOK FEST
Uma Doraiswamy

THE SOUTHERN Kentucky Book Fest is the largest library event in the state of Kentucky and is jointly organized by Western Kentucky University (WKU) Libraries,

Bowling Green Public Library, and Barnes and Noble. The mission of this event is to promote literacy in the region and the state of Kentucky. It was started in 1999 and has been successfully organized every year since then. In 2008 the partners hosted the tenth SOKY Book Fest with lots of special anniversary celebrations. This great event brings authors from different genres and attracts a large crowd of children as well as adults from all walks of life, not only from the state of Kentucky but from the surrounding states as well. The success of this event is largely due to the efforts of the Book Fest Management Committee, with the help of many volunteers and sponsors.

Volunteering at the SOKY Book Fest was an eye-opening experience for me as a librarian and made me realize how librarians can make a difference in the community. My responsibility was to provide information at the information desk. We had two people serving at the information desk at a time. There were also volunteers to assist the authors at their respective desks and volunteers to introduce the speakers, while other volunteers performed miscellaneous duties. People came to the information desk asking for directions to the rooms and seeking information about the speakers. We handed out name tags to the authors and volunteers and directed people to the desks where they could get complimentary items. We had been provided walkie-talkies so that we could contact the people working at the convention center. As people came in we gave them handouts of the event and a few complimentary items.

Volunteering at the Book Fest was not just about helping the participants and attendees of the events; for me it was also a cultural exchange avenue. I got to speak with a few authors, and one of them wanted to know more about Kashmir, India.

Overall it was great to see the enthusiasm among the crowds. It was a busy atmosphere, with people continuously coming in wanting to educate their children, hear the authors speak, or buy books and get them signed by the authors. For many authors it was a publicity avenue; they displayed their books, spoke to children and adults, and also sold quite a number of their books. There were special activities for the kids, while adults could attend the speaking sessions of various authors. Mitch Albom, Harlan Coben, Marc Brown, Kathleen Ernst, and several others attended this year's event. Pat Conroy, Scott Turow, Rick Bragg, Ann B. Ross, Janette Oke, Chuck Barris, Floyd Cooper, Cassandra King, Sue Grafton, Sharon Creech, David Baldacci, Avi, Marsha Mason, Homer Hickam, Karen Robards, David Halberstam, John Carpenter, LeVar Burton, R. L. Stine, and Dick Schaap have attended past SOKY Book Fest events.

The Book Fest was a good publicity avenue for WKU Libraries and Bowling Green Public Library; their librarians could demonstrate that they don't just provide information sitting behind a computer but also get involved in the community and encourage literacy, reading, and social engagement. There were other sponsors such as the National Endowment for the Arts, the Institute of Museum and Library Services, and Arts Midwest to encourage this event and market themselves.

WKU Libraries also organized some pre-fest events such as One Campus–One Community–One Book, Books and Baskets, and Macy's Used Book Sale. An event to help cultivate literacy, One Campus–One Community–One Book is held at

WKU Libraries and brings together not only faculty and students of WKU but also other people from the area. An author is invited to discuss his or her book, and many free copies are given away. Books and Baskets is an event that encourages the donation of new or used children's books, again for literacy purposes. The proceeds from Macy's Used Book Sale go toward the SOKY Book Fest. There are other programs as well. Through 1Read, where middle school students are encouraged to pick one book and read it at the same time, SOKY Book Fest partners promote literacy among preteens and teens. Fall into Books is a new program for schools held during Children's Book Week in November, in which three authors are chosen to visit area schools.

To conclude, I was proud to be a part of the SOKY Book Fest event, where children and adults are exposed to different books and authors from the state of Kentucky.

36

UNIVERSITY OF FLORIDA'S GEORGE A. SMATHERS LIBRARIES AND THE COMMON READING PROGRAM

Melissa Shoop

THE UNIVERSITY of Florida (UF) Libraries in partnership with the Dean of Students Office, the Alachua County Library District, local authors, and various other community and campus organizations hold events in support of the university's Common Reading program.

The Common Reading program furthers the effort to make new students' university experience a more meaningful, unified, and intellectual one and is headed by the Dean of Students Office. The program begins with a committee comprising members of the community, university students, and faculty (including librarians) and staff from a wide variety of departments charged with selecting a book for the program. The committee reads many books and meets frequently in order to make their final selection. The committee chose *When the Rivers Run Dry: Water—The Defining Crisis of the Twenty-first Century* (2006) by Fred Pearce for the 2008/2009 academic school year. They typically choose books that are widely applicable across the university's curriculum, and course instructors are urged to integrate the Common Reading book and events into their syllabi.

New students receive a copy of the chosen book at their summer orientation. When they come to UF for the fall semester, they already have something in common with their peers: the experience of having read the same book at the same time. They can identify other new students as they walk across campus by the book in their hands, and they already begin to feel a sense of togetherness or community.

Events relating to the book held on campus and in Gainesville provide forums for students and community members to share in a common experience with regard to current issues that affect our daily lives, thereby helping to integrate the university campus with the community in Alachua County, Florida.

One goal of the university is to foster in students a sense of community, not only with their classmates but regionally and even globally. The University of Florida exists as a microcosm of a much larger global community of learning, and the two are intimately entwined. Students' university experience therefore must extend beyond the buildings on campus. Because part of the college experience is becoming part of a community, the Common Reading program capitalizes on the opportunity to integrate organizations around the campus and region because the topics discussed in the book are relevant to the students' and community's everyday life.

This year's book is particularly relevant because changes in the economy have caused people to rethink their use and waste of materials in order to live more "green." *When the Rivers Run Dry* shows students the global perspective and ramifications of wasteful water use.

Today's new students already have a "green" mentality when they start at university, as evidenced by their reusable stainless-steel water bottles, but they can now choose majors or minors with that green twist. In fact, a new major in sustainability studies will soon be offered. *When the Rivers Run Dry* is a timely choice for this generation of students.

The libraries at UF are particularly interested in helping to build a sense of community. The libraries take every opportunity to demonstrate that they are not just buildings full of books; a library is a body of knowledge contained by no walls, a place both physical and virtual where ideas are conceived and shared, and where that knowledge grows. Wherever there exists a potential for a learning experience, librarians will be found. Librarians will create these opportunities, too. It only makes sense that the library would be involved in a program surrounding a book and that it would help develop programming in support of intellectual development.

Two librarians (one from the university and one from the Alachua County Library District) serve on the committee that chooses the book. The libraries actively engage the book by creating displays in their branches across campus. For instance, a current display features supplemental reading material and local artifacts that pertain to the issues of water and water conservation. Every year a READ poster is created by the library featuring the book and author. Other READ posters are created to help market the dialogue about the book and related issues. This year two posters featured university personnel who care deeply about the topics covered by *When the Rivers Run Dry:* Dedee DeLongpre Johnston, the director of the Office of Sustainability, and Patricia Telles-Irvin, the vice president for student affairs. The posters display interconnectivity between entities and ideas on campus and in the community by advertising the partnership between the Common Reading program, the person featured and her affiliation, and the libraries.

The libraries at UF play an important role in learning experiences, and librarians are constantly on the lookout for opportunities to join forces with other departments, offices, and businesses. When the Dean of Students Office approached the libraries with the idea of bringing in local author Cynthia Barnett, who writes on topics apropos of *When the Rivers Run Dry*, we embraced the opportunity. The Alachua County Library District got involved, and the event was held at the public library. Holding "campus events" downtown brings together the college and the community. Citizens and students unite under one learning experience. Barnett was invited to speak about her book *Mirage: Florida and the Vanishing Water of the Eastern U.S.* (2007). The library created a READ poster featuring Barnett and *Mirage* that was displayed in each of the ten public library branches as well as university libraries. These posters appeal to the eye and to Floridians' sense of possession of water—Florida's aquifer is a point of geologic pride, besides the fact that the state is surrounded by water on three sides. How can our water be disappearing when it is all around us? This question brought members of the university and Alachua County communities together to listen to a speaker and then to discuss the issue of water and how it is disappearing in one common, intellectual experience.

The Common Reading program is an important part of the UF experience; likewise, it is very important to the libraries. When the author of the Common Reading book visits the campus for an evening talk and subsequent audience discussion, the libraries host the afternoon reception. Both events are free and open to the public (as are all other related events) and are wonderful opportunities for members of the community to attend campus functions. Members of the community are also welcome to visit library and Dean of Students Office websites to learn more about the book, related events, and to find companion books.

The reader can visit www.dso.ufl.edu/nsp/firstyearexperience/commonread/ for more information about the Common Reading program at UF.

PART VIII
Classroom Outreach

ACADEMIC CONNECTIONS
A College Librarian Reaches Out to a Middle School

Margaret Keys

MANY ACADEMIC librarians conduct outreach to high schools, but an argument can be made for outreaching to younger students. Middle school students are assigned research projects but are not always taught the skills needed to complete them. Whether this is due to lack of time in class or a shortage of librarians in schools, the result can be the use of inferior information resources. Case in point: Two years ago, my daughter showed me a website she was using for her sixth-grade report on ancient China. The site was maintained by a palm reader. She saw no problem with this. Sensing that these students are developing poor research habits, I began to formulate an outreach focused on information competency and library resources.

Outreach to a middle school makes sense for several reasons. First, many schools do not have funds for field trips, and many teachers do not think research instruction warrants one. It is easier to find one teacher willing to dedicate a day to a classroom visitor. Second, the majority of schools now have computer facilities adequate for on-site instruction, enabling us to take students virtually into our libraries. Third, outreach allows us to connect with students at a teachable moment. Working with teachers, we can identify a group of students likely to be most receptive to library instruction, and we can tailor the outreach to a specific assignment, giving students an immediate opportunity to apply what they learn.

Although I originally formulated my outreach as a public librarian, I did not fully develop and implement it until I was working half-time as an instruction librarian at California State University, Sacramento, and part-time at the American River College reference desk. The ultimate catalyst of the outreach was a requirement by my daughter's eighth-grade science teacher to obtain materials from a college library for a biographical report on a physicist. Picturing students and harried parents wandering around academic libraries trying to check out books with no campus library cards, I volunteered to spend the day at the school preparing students for this outing. I worked with five classes, making contact with 144 students on behalf of two higher learning institutions. Further, I was able to introduce the teacher to some electronic resources that have evolved since he graduated, updating his research teaching skills.

For the outreach, I prepared a handout covering the basics of visiting each library, including purchasing parking and copy cards. I created a cheat sheet of instructions for searching in library catalogs and Academic Search Premier, as well as a list of reference materials available in each library. We went over community users' library privileges, such as the ability to search catalogs remotely but databases from inside the libraries only. We discussed what types of materials to use for a biographical report, as opposed to a lengthy research paper. We went over Boolean searching (just the AND) and the definition of a periodical. I demonstrated how to locate, choose, print, and e-mail full-text articles. We covered Internet searching and how to determine website credibility. We touched on public library materials and remote access. Finally, I showed them two sites to help with MLA documentation.

At work, I e-mailed my colleagues to warn them of the onslaught of young community users, and I left a copy of their assignment and my handouts at the reference desk. To improve access, I also put potentially high-use items at the reference desk for a few days. These steps ensured that the librarians were prepared to accommodate students and parents.

Overall, this was a successful outreach: students were prepared for an assignment that the area's college librarians had no idea was coming. We were able to continue the outreach effort by providing excellent service inside the library. I have been asked to repeat the outreach next year. When I do, I will survey the students at the beginning and end of their project to determine whether they think the presentation helped them and in what ways. This event came together in three days and did not lend itself to adequate assessment, which is needed to identify future program modifications. One change we will make is to reserve the school's laptops for the day so that we can incorporate search practice into my presentation.

As with any outreach, the key to success is a positive partnership. Work closely with your contact to coordinate the outreach with a research project. Obtain that assignment and prepare a lesson plan around it. Unless you have worked with middle schoolers before, meet with the teacher who created the assignment to demonstrate your outreach. This will enable you to discuss the level of your presentation, reworking it together, if necessary, or perhaps expanding it to a two-day event. If students are not required to visit your library, then suggest the teacher give extra credit to those who do. Making yourself available for a few hours of follow-up e-mailed questions will help the teacher and students process what they've learned and maximize your library's value to them.

Middle school outreach is appropriate for public as well as academic librarians, for both institutions offer more materials than school libraries. By high school, many students will need to utilize databases and advanced materials to complete assignments. Anticipating this need and teaching students how to use our resources lights the path to our door, forging a bond that benefits the entire community.

38

INTEGRATING MANUSCRIPTS INTO THE MICHIGAN CURRICULUM THROUGH ARCHIVAL OUTREACH

Marian Matyn

AS ARCHIVIST of the Clarke Historical Library at Central Michigan University, I find that many people really have no idea of the breadth of materials and information available for research at our facility. Over the years, I have been approached with requests to present information about manuscripts and historical documents to public school teachers who are seeking to integrate a variety of manuscripts into their curriculum. The goals are designed to strengthen K–12 teachers' understanding of the early American and Michigan history they teach and to provide them with teaching tools to use in their classrooms. I love to present opportunities for using manuscripts and encouraging fellow educators to use the unique documents and insights preserved in an archival institution.

Teachers are constantly updating and learning new skills. Michigan's statewide Social Studies Standards require students to evaluate historic decisions and events and assess their implications and long-term consequences for themselves. Students assess the implications and consequences by developing critical thinking skills, including analysis and synthesis abilities, through their study of historical manuscripts in the classroom. Teachers must integrate the use of manuscripts into their classes, which is called text-based teaching. In Michigan, the evaluation test requiring this lesson format is the Michigan Education Assessment Process. These test scores are used to determine the teaching ability of teachers, the effectiveness of their curriculum, and the teaching methods of the district, as well as funding issues.

To meet the requirements for the teaching curriculum, it is necessary to understand how to use and how to find manuscripts. As an archivist, I can provide expertise and support to educators seeking good manuscript examples; I can give them ideas for getting students excited about using manuscripts; and I can show them how to introduce and integrate manuscripts into their curriculum so that it is not overwhelming. An archivist can assist in the structuring of an effective lesson plan that addresses key questions: what parts of the manuscripts should be highlighted to the students and why; what correlating information sources could be used for comparison to provide extra information; and what reference sources should be used.

DEFINITION: WHAT IS A MANUSCRIPT?

A manuscript is unique information with permanent, historical research value. A manuscript may also be called a historical record, a primary source, or archival material. Manuscripts have existed since ancient times, in many languages, in many formats: bone, stone, animal skin, papyrus, paper, metal, electronic, and film media. Examples of manuscripts include speeches, correspondence, maps, diaries, treaties, account books, original plans or drawings, census records, home movies, photograph albums, criminal case files, presidential papers, and membership records. An author researches a topic via a number of manuscripts, analyzes the information, and eventually writes and publishes an article, book, or newspaper. These published sources are called secondary sources. Manuscripts are primary sources waiting to be analyzed.

INTRODUCTION OF MANUSCRIPTS IN THE CLASSROOM

I approach requests for manuscript information by offering an overview of materials and topics using a variety of formats. I pull together a packet including photocopies of selected manuscripts, a copy of what the catalog record for each manuscript looks like (in order to demonstrate the description and subject headings that help find related materials), a brief list of important definitions to use while teaching about manuscripts, and a bibliography of online sources, as well as contact information for my institution. Using the examples, teachers see that a wide variety of topics and materials can and should be used to interest students who have an equally wide variety of interests. Trains, Native Americans, wars, teachers, women, students, and the development of local towns are just a few of the topics that can be discussed.

Historical facts allow a teacher to lead a classroom discussion that extends beyond the text. I like to use a Michigan general store's page from 1889 to illustrate the cost of items then compared to now, what was available in a general store in 1889 compared to what is available in today's stores, what people grew or raised at home for food and their basic survival, differences in vocabulary then and now, and basic math. For example, general stores sold globes. These globes were for oil lamps; they were not round things to understand the continents. Why did stores sell globes? People needed globes for their oil lamps to see at night because there was no electricity in 1889. This leads to a conversation about electricity—when it became widely available and how it changed people's work habits and evening activities. Suddenly, people could embroider or read at night without being next to an oil lamp or fireplace. People could play cards or checkers long after the sun set, or they could repair broken equipment. Electricity soon became a source not just of light but also of power, which again affected Americans' work and leisure habits.

Some people recorded in the general store's volume bartered for goods. For example, one man brought in enough feed and hay for the store owner's horses to eat all winter and then took home a variety of store goods in exchange. Throughout much of history, people used the barter system to exchange what they had for what they needed or wanted. Students will probably be shocked to learn that people survived for centuries without credit cards.

Other manuscript examples include a Civil War death notice, a lighthouse keeper's journal, and two diaries. One diary belonged to a Michigan girl in high school during the 1919–20 school year. According to her diary, the girl got in trouble for talking in class, hated her English teacher, had annoying younger siblings, and loved to drink soda pop and go to movies. Today's students can relate to her even though she walked everywhere and had no TV, computer, iPod, or tattoo. How much has the human condition really progressed emotionally over the centuries? The girl's feelings, recorded in her diary, are relevant, interesting, and personal to the students.

I believe that teachers will realize the advantages in integrating locally interesting manuscripts into their classes and will maybe even use some of their own family papers. I hope that by opening lines of communication to educators I will subsequently encourage historical thinking about and analysis and research of manuscripts. Archivists, like librarians, love to help people who want to learn more.

USING TOPICAL MANUSCRIPTS IN THE CLASSROOM

Another approach focuses on specific topical manuscripts to create an easily identifiable context for students. I have provided information to teachers for integrating various types of Civil War manuscripts, both national and Michigan specific, into their curriculum, utilizing a select group of these manuscripts that were diverse in both content and format. I like to have examples of relevant supporting documents and a brief list of the secondary sources, including some online reference sources regarding U.S. colored troops.

It can be helpful to begin by using simple, easy-to-read forms with a little bit of writing. Types of forms include muster-in, muster-out, enrollment, promotion, inspection, passes, transfers, equipment, formal memos and general orders, pensions, and pay orders. There are also myriad forms for Civil War–related organizations both during and after the war. Classroom discussions can examine what a few forms were used for, the information on the forms, and what it means. I also like to provide examples of widows' pensions, Native American records, discharge forms, and a few neatly written journals.

Students find personal documents interesting, which helps motivate their participation and interaction with the material and the educational process. Other examples of manuscripts I find compelling are newspaper articles and accompanying documents about specific people, including an item about a Michigan woman, Sarah Emma E. Edmonds, who disguised herself as a man to serve in the Civil War, and a Civil War steamer's log that noted when an exploration crew stopped a stagecoach and confiscated $1.2 million in Confederate notes.

We know that the history that is often taught represents the facts of the majority, leaving out the opinions and perspectives of the minority. This is a very important fact to teach students: history is more than facts and statistics about the majority. Until twenty years ago, the minority's perspective and experience were usually not included in history textbooks. History is the personal story of many individuals, who cried and rejoiced, failed algebra, loved their children, suffered, and did not always get along well with their neighbors. In other words, the people of the past could be very much like individuals today.

The cooperative efforts of an archivist and a teacher help to educate students by using the unique materials of manuscripts. I am gratified by the opportunity to use the manuscripts in my collection. It is important that the public, especially teachers who work with students and the students themselves, know about local archives and historical libraries, not only so the manuscripts in them are used but also so those manuscripts may serve as a resource providing insight and questions for students and teachers. People need to be involved in the role that archival repositories play in preserving and making available for research so many important manuscripts of common, everyday people who were and are the backbone of our nation.

USEFUL TIPS

Short and neat examples are best, or parts of a manuscript rather than a long manuscript.

Start with a printed form with a little bit of handwriting on it. Students today are used to computers. They are not used to trying to read handwriting, particularly if it is messy or stylized. They can quickly become frustrated and fatigued trying to interpret lots of handwriting and give up.

Something that relates to their hometown or a topic of particular interest to them or the class as a whole is a good option.

If the students cannot relate to one item presented in a class, try again. Encourage them to bring something they are interested in to class.

Encourage students to bring in a copy of a family manuscript, or a letter from grandpa during World War II or from a family member who served in Desert Storm. A family manuscript will have more meaning to a student and is more likely to keep his interest and encourage him to conduct additional research.

Have supporting materials—websites, images, maps—to show where the author of a particular manuscript lived and what life was like at that time. A good example is a local newspaper. Have the students create a list of questions to compare and contrast then and now: Who was the mayor? What did food cost and who sold it? What did people do for entertainment? Was the nation at war or in a time of peace? What was the town or county's population? Compare and analyze the information to discuss how much things have changed.

Discuss how to create a transcription of a family manuscript and why. Talk about how people make mistakes in writing because they are rushed, upset, or imperfectly educated. A written manuscript with all the words spelled correctly and written in perfect penmanship is rare. Some people make up words, use minimal or no punctuation, and even spell the same word, including their own name, several different ways on the same page.

39

PUBLIC SCHOOL TEACHER WORKSHOPS CONDUCTED BY THE UNIVERSITY OF ALABAMA AT BIRMINGHAM'S MERVYN H. STERNE LIBRARY

Delores Carlito

THE UNIVERSITY of Alabama at Birmingham (UAB) is located in an urban area with one-quarter of the state's population living within a twenty-five-mile radius. Twelve public school systems, along with many private schools, are in the Birmingham area. The Mervyn H. Sterne Library, the primary research library at the University of Alabama at Birmingham, is open to the public and frequently accommodates public school students as patrons.

The state of Alabama provides the Alabama Virtual Library, a collection of databases available to all Alabama citizens. No log-in is required for school use, although residents do need a password to access the library at home. The use of all databases at the Sterne Library is free, although off-campus use is limited to UAB students, faculty, and staff.

The Sterne Library has created a presence in the public schools by keeping in touch with area media specialists, technology coordinators, and teachers. At the beginning of each school year, the reference librarian for instruction and outreach and the reference librarian for education send a letter to area media specialists, principals, superintendents, curriculum specialists, curriculum resource coordinators, technology coordinators, and teachers who had previously sent students to the Sterne Library. These letters are reminders of our outreach services. From these letters, the librarians receive requests for attendance at in-service days (i.e., days devoted to professional training to help teachers and media specialists develop their skills). Librarians at the Sterne Library have participated in teacher, principal, and media specialists' in-service events through being exhibitors and through presentations and instruction.

WORKSHOPS

The librarians at the Sterne Library are recognized as specialists in researching and have therefore been invited to give workshops at many area public schools. When asked to speak to a group, we find out who the audience will be, how many will be in attendance, the overall theme of the day, and the available presentation technology. The content of the workshop varies depending on the request, but it is usually one of three types: informational, instructional, or inspirational. *Informational* workshops outline the services available at the Sterne Library for secondary schools. These workshops contain basic information about the library and our databases, services, and policies. Informational workshops also outline information about visiting UAB and what is required of group visits to the Sterne Library. *Instructional* workshops demonstrate new ways to use the material that is already available on the Alabama Virtual Library. These workshops explain the minutiae of research and the ways teachers and media specialists can use the Alabama Virtual Library in the classroom. *Inspirational* workshops present ways of using other tools. These workshops can be on locating web resources specific to a subject or on using freely available tools such as wikis, blogs, or podcasting.

EXHIBITING

If not asked to speak at a school meeting, an academic librarian can often attend the meeting as an exhibitor. The Sterne Library sets up an exhibit table with a display containing information about the library. Several librarians staff the table. As an exhibitor, we promote the services that we provide to secondary teachers.

STEPS TO SUCCESSFUL WORKSHOPS

1. Get to know area media specialists and teachers. School media specialists are the best way for an academic librarian to connect with schools and teachers.

2. Make yourself known. Invite yourself to in-service events if the schools do not invite you. If you get the opportunity to be an exhibitor, do that. Let school systems know that you are interested not only in your university's students but in their high school students.

3. Prepare for your audience. Find out what they need. If you will be speaking to language arts teachers, emphasize literature resources. If you are speaking to media specialists, show them how you can support the services they offer. For principals, show them how willing the library is to partner with their schools.

4. Provide handouts. Usually there is a great deal occurring during in-service days, so attendees cannot be expected to remember everything. Bring along sheets that describe your services and outline your rules for groups of students visiting the university. Bring business cards, but make sure your name and contact information are on everything you hand out. Attendees may pass along some of the materials, so you want to ensure that everyone knows how to get in touch with you.

5. Be excited and savvy. In-service days often occur in August when everyone is looking forward to the upcoming school year. Share in their excitement.

Attending teacher in-service days gives the Mervyn H. Sterne Library more exposure to area public schools so that we can partner with them and promote the library and the university. It is important to partner with area public school systems because their students will be ours soon. The best way to promote ourselves and to underscore our commitment to collaboration is to meet media specialists and teachers in the schools instead of being names on a letter.

40

SECONDARY CLASSROOM INSTRUCTION IN BIRMINGHAM

Delores Carlito

THE UNIVERSITY of Alabama at Birmingham (UAB) is located in an urban area. Twelve public school systems are in the Birmingham area, and one-quarter of the entire population of Alabama lives within a twenty-five-mile radius of UAB's Mervyn H. Sterne Library. As UAB's major academic research library, the Sterne Library is often the information portal of choice for supporting the needs of the university community, and that community includes not only those who are students, faculty, and staff but those who live in and visit the Birmingham area.

The Mervyn H. Sterne Library is committed to serving the community. We encourage visits from schools in order to promote information literacy, higher education, and the University of Alabama at Birmingham. We recognize the importance of the library in the development of responsible citizenship, local education, and culture, and we encourage students to develop research skills before admission to college. Therefore, we partner with local school systems to deliver research instruction to their students. Many of the students we see in high schools later become our university students.

Students feel more comfortable when they walk into an academic library and can recognize the face of a librarian, so we feel it is important to meet the students in person. Media specialists and teachers view the librarians at the Sterne Library as specialists in researching and another voice to promote information literacy to students.

In order to let the teachers know that we are available to speak to their classes, the reference librarian for instruction and outreach and the reference librarian for education send out letters of introduction to media specialists, principals, superintendents, curriculum specialists, curriculum resource coordinators, and teachers. We include in these letters a school library visit checklist, also available online. The checklist provides information on using the library, along with links to parking and eating at UAB.

We offer to conduct instruction at the Sterne Library or go to the schools. Occasionally, the teachers request a combination of the two.

INSTRUCTION AT THE LIBRARY

When a teacher requests instruction for her students at the library, it is usually not an easy task for her to accomplish; she must schedule a bus and get permission forms, and the students miss other classes. Therefore, it is important that the students use their time at the library wisely. Depending on the level and discipline of the class, checkout privileges may be given.

Before they arrive at the library, the librarian and teacher meet to discuss the assignment and topics. The librarian uses this meeting to determine the requirements for the students' papers, the number of students attending the session, and whether or not the teacher wants the students to have checkout privileges. Between the meeting and the session, the librarian creates a handout designed specifically for the students and their assignments.

On the day of instruction, the librarian meets the students at the front of the library to make them feel welcome. During instruction, the librarian includes strategies for forming and conducting a search in the local catalog and databases. The librarian also covers the layout of the library and instructions on how to locate materials organized by Library of Congress Subject Headings. For advanced placement, honors, and international baccalaureate classes, if possible, it is advantageous for students to meet the subject-specialist librarian so students will know two people to contact for help in the library.

The librarian provides plenty of handouts. Students can be overwhelmed by their first visit to a college library, so they need something to remind them of the steps to take when researching. They also need to know how to ask for help once they leave the library. The Sterne Library provides research help to all patrons online via e-mail and instant messaging, over the phone, and in person. The librarian emphasizes to students that many library services are not limited to UAB students.

After the session, the librarian is available to answer any questions. Often, the teacher includes an hour or two of research time in their field trip. Finally, the librarian thanks the teacher for bringing the class.

INSTRUCTION AT THE SCHOOLS

Sometimes it is difficult for teachers to organize a field trip to the library; there may be too many students or the logistics are too difficult. In these instances, the librarian may be asked to go to the school.

Before visiting the school, the teacher and librarian discuss the levels of the students and their assignments. The librarian makes sure that the teacher or media specialist has the appropriate audiovisual materials for instruction. The librarian can offer to spend all day at the school so that several classes can be covered in one visit. The librarian also determines whether to include university resources in the instruction or only material available to students in the public or school library. Based on this information, the librarian creates a handout specifically for the students, their assignments, and the materials available to them.

On the day of instruction, the librarian includes research strategies and appropriate research tools. If the students are to visit the college or university library, the librarian also instructs them in the use of Library of Congress Subject Headings. Again, handouts are important so that the students will be able to recall the information at a later time. The librarian welcomes students to use the university library and informs them of the various ways to obtain research assistance.

After the session, the teacher might want to set up a time for the students to visit the library on their own, such as a night or two during the week. During these nights the teacher must be at the library, and the librarian is available to answer students' questions.

Although students may receive the same information about researching from their media specialists and teachers, hearing it from another professional always helps. Coordination with area media specialists and teachers is important in developing the critical thinking skills of community students and, therefore, the community.

41

TEACHING AMERICAN HISTORY
Archivists Partnering with Public Schools

Sharon Carlson

ARCHIVISTS HAVE traditionally served scholarly audiences. Genealogists and public historians also make up a substantial number of their patrons. Traditionally, public school teachers and their students have been among the least represented user groups. The Western Michigan University (WMU) Archives and Regional History Collections partnered with public schools to increase access to students, particularly in middle and high schools. This chapter explores the topics, techniques, and resulting benefits to the students, teachers, and the archives.

In 2003 WMU received the first of three federally funded Teaching American History Grants. WMU's History Department partnered with the Kalamazoo Regional Educational Service Agency (KRESA) to train high school and middle school teachers through summer institutes. The Teaching American History Grants from the U.S. Department of Education have been awarded since 2001. Developed under the leadership of Senator Robert Byrd of West Virginia, the grants seek to improve the teaching of American history in public schools. Since their inception, more than a half-billion federal dollars have been awarded to school systems around the country to further this goal.[1]

Since the first grant implementation in 2004, twenty to twenty-five public school teachers in southwestern Michigan ranging from middle school to high school level have participated in this program annually. WMU's approach involves a summer program with two full weeks of content instruction and other activities to improve instruction and student learning in history. Several follow-up sessions and assignments in the fall also focus on these goals. Teachers may earn graduate credit or continuing education units for continuing teacher certification. The focus at the high school level has spanned both the nineteenth and twentieth centuries, with emphasis on the periods 1850–77 and 1968 to the present. Faculty from WMU's History Department provided content instruction. Collaboration with public historians from the Kalamazoo Valley Museum introduced participants to the use of artifacts in instruction.

In 2004 the archival component involved a morning session at the archives to introduce teachers to the types of resources available and to research strategies. Feedback provided by teachers at the conclusion of the first year's program indicated that participants wanted additional time at the archives. As a result, the sessions offered in 2005 and 2006 were expanded to include a morning of instruction by the archivist and an afternoon session of research with documents.

With the expansion of the archival instruction component, teachers spend the morning getting preliminary instruction in archival research. They learn about the types of archival materials available and how to analyze archival documents.

Document analysis involves examining documents for format, content, and bias. Documents supporting the themes presented in content sessions provide primary evidence of historical events. Because the WMU Archives and Regional History Collections focuses on a twelve-county area in southwestern Michigan, most of the documents also have connections to local history.

The afternoon research session allows teachers time to develop lesson plans based on the primary sources in the WMU Archives and Regional History Collections. In Michigan, high school teachers focus on the late nineteenth and twentieth centuries. High school teachers delved into materials documenting the Columbian Exposition, Dr. Martin Luther King Jr., and the history of technology in the twentieth century. One of the major assignments for high school teachers involved creating lesson plans. The lesson plans required the use of primary sources. Teachers were able to get copies of the archival materials and incorporate them into the plans. Many of these plans may be viewed at KRESA's website.[2] The focus of middle school instruction has spanned the period from 1789 through 1877. The archives provided primary source documents focusing on the development of midwestern agriculture and abolitionist movements in Michigan. For logistical purposes, the teachers have routinely been separated into two groups for most of their activities during the Teaching American History institutes. This has resulted in groups of nine to twelve teachers using the archives at any one time. However, anytime an archive is actively trying to serve twelve patrons, it can result in an atmosphere of controlled chaos—not one that is generally associated with an archive. Since the program has evolved, the following points have facilitated this process.

1. Begin by providing an overview of ground rules for using an archive.

2. Be prepared to handle beverage and break needs for people engaged in instruction and research for an entire day.

3. If possible, get research topics in advance so more materials may be readily available.

4. Be prepared for research topics to evolve.

5. Assign staff to specific tasks to facilitate work flow. The day will be spent retrieving collections, providing copies, or providing reference service. It can be very intensive because of the number of people involved.

6. Be patient. For many, this is their first experience researching primary sources in an archive.

The long-term benefit of participating in the Teaching American History program and working with advanced placement teachers is difficult to quantify. Several teachers participating in the Teaching American History program have maintained a relationship with the staff of the archives and made additional inquiries about its holdings. One teacher requested a program for other teachers not participating in the program in order to provide them with information about the archives' resources. It appears that teachers and students have become more comfortable with using archives and archival sources. Despite the introduction of archives and archival sources to teachers, the latter remain a vastly underrepresented patron group.

NOTES

1. See "Senator Robert C. Byrd, 2007 OAH Friend of History," *OAH Newsletter* 35 (May 2007).
2. See Kalamazoo Regional Educational Service Agency, "Teaching American History, 2004–2008," www.kresa.net/instructionalcenter/HSTAH/index.htm (accessed May 30, 2009).

42

A DIFFERENT KIND OF SCIENCE PROJECT
A Partnership between a Community College Library and a High School Media Center

Nancy Kalikow Maxwell

EVERYONE KNOWS about science fairs. Spelling bees are so popular they have been featured in books, movies, and Broadway productions. But have you ever heard of a library contest? Six lucky South Florida high school and college students not only know about such a contest but have earned college scholarships and an internship thanks to one.

Funded through a $168,000 grant from the U.S. Department of Agriculture, the library contest was a central component of Miami Dade College's Library Gateway Project (LGP). Intended to encourage high school and college students to pursue science careers, LGP goals included sponsoring the library contest; improving high school and college library resources; and providing faculty, librarian, and media specialist training in science resource instruction.

THE PARTNERSHIPS

The college/high school student library contest was the culmination of a two-year partnership between a community college and a public high school. Miami Dade College (MDC), the project administrator, is the nation's largest institution of higher education. With more than 100,000 students at eight campuses in Miami, Florida, MDC offers both two- and four-year degrees and graduates more African American and Hispanic students each year than any other college in the country. In the past few years, MDC's North Campus has distinguished itself in the area of science instruction and is currently constructing a multimillion-dollar science complex.

Coral Reef Senior High School was chosen as MDC's partner because it is the premier magnet high school for agriscience and engineering technology in Miami.

High school students in this specialized program study areas such as agronomy, horticulture, forestry, entomology, aquatics, environmental science, mechanical technology, and agricultural biotechnology.

The project also included a partnership between the science departments at each institution and their library or media center. Throughout the project, librarians, media specialists, and science instructors received training together and collaborated to create and implement the library contest.

As a precursor to the contest, more than twenty high school and college science faculty, media specialists, and librarians participated in a focus group on science resources. The group was asked to identify key library materials and research skills needed by high school and college students. Based on their recommendations, additional online and print resources were obtained. Training in the use of these and other resources was provided to a team of librarians, media specialists, and science teachers who traveled to the National Agricultural Library in Beltsville, Maryland. The library contest was unveiled at an all-day workshop on science library research that was held at MDC.

THE CONTEST

The library contest portion of the program was designed to encourage students to learn about the resources available in their own libraries. Contest entry forms required students to provide the following three responses.

1.   Name three online science databases offered at their school.

2.   Explain why library research is important when studying science.

3.   Explain how winning a scholarship or internship would help shape their future goals.

Entry forms were distributed to high school principals, high school science department chairs, and college science faculty. A panel of judges, which included science faculty and librarians, scored the responses and chose the winning entries. The top high school winners were awarded scholarships to MDC. The college student who was the grand prizewinner received a paid internship at the National Agricultural Library.

CONTEST CHALLENGES

The biggest challenge faced in sponsoring the library contest was the lack of entries. Who knew it would be so hard to give money away? Though the contest was publicized widely through the college and high school science departments, few students entered. After working with the college's scholarship office, it was learned that financial aid officials, too, often experience difficulty in finding awardees for certain programs.

Another challenge was that the financial award prizes—though generous—were not attractive incentives to the potential market. Coral Reef Senior High School is a premier science magnet high school, and its students aspire to attend prestigious Ivy League schools. Few of the students were planning to attend the local community college and thus did not need a scholarship to that institution. Likewise, the grand prize offered to college participants—a paid summer internship in a suburb of Washington, D.C.—did not fit into many students' summer plans because of school and work commitments.

PARTNERSHIP CHALLENGES

Scheduling proved to be the biggest challenge posed by the school/college partnership. Books purchased for the high school media center arrived over the summer when the school was closed. Scheduling meetings was difficult because the high school science teacher and media specialist could not leave the school during the day. As a result, most of the meetings were held at the high school media center, which presented its own set of difficulties. Lacking a separate meeting room, a large table in the middle of the library became our meeting location, and the media specialist was frequently interrupted by students.

PARTNERSHIP ADVANTAGES

Despite these challenges, the partnership offered substantial benefits. The collaboration between the science departments and the library or media center made science faculty aware of the resources available in their own library. Many science teachers remarked that before this project they did not realize the wealth of information available at their own institution. On the institutional level, the project was one small step toward attaining one educational reform recommended by national experts: aligning instruction from high school to college in order to enable subject content to develop seamlessly as the student advances in the educational system. By improving the high school media center's resources and library instruction, students should be better prepared to use their college library. And improvements to the college library's resources and instructional program will benefit students transferring to universities.

Of course, the students also benefited from the partnership by being given the opportunity to compete for college scholarships. Though the library contest did not generate the publicity of spelling bees, and no Broadway shows or movies resulted, the students who participated learned skills that will last a lifetime.

PART IX
Diversity Outreach

43
DÍA DE LOS NIÑOS / DÍA DE LOS LIBROS
Meryle Leonard

DÍA DE los Niños / Día de los Libros (Day of the Children / Day of the Books) is a program originated by author Pat Mora and her family to celebrate children, literacy, and culture. The Public Library of Charlotte and Mecklenburg County, North Carolina, has celebrated Día de los Niños for ten years and was a corecipient of the 2008 Mora Award. The object of our Día de los Niños program is to celebrate all children from all cultures through literacy and to promote the celebration of Día de los Niños throughout North Carolina. Día celebrations will be unique to each host site as it meets the needs of individual library systems, branches, and communities.

Listed below are some helpful steps in beginning or enhancing a Día de los Niños celebration.

1. Give Yourself a Head Start. Día de los Niños celebrations take place on April 30, with celebrations targeting the end of the month. Planning for Día de los Niños should begin in November of the previous year.

2. Form a Día de los Niños Committee. A committee can consist of library and community members. Recruit committee members that represent the dynamics of your community.

3. Create Your Día Plan. How will your library celebrate Día de los Niños? How will you advertise the program? How much funding will be needed for the celebration? Will you invite an author or illustrator? Will you collaborate with other community agencies such as schools, preschools, volunteers, cultural organizations, and media? Listed below are some Día de los Niños program ideas.

International storytelling: This is a family activity designed to introduce participants to different cultures and languages through storytelling. Secure a location that is conducive to storytelling. Call or send letters to international organizations or your local storytelling guild to recruit storytellers who can share international stories. Advertise your event in the local newspapers and radio station. If you are targeting your Latino community, advertise in the Spanish-language media. Plan your program for 60–90 minutes. The cost of the program will include the fee for the storytellers, advertisements, and refreshments if included in the program.

Celebrate Día de los Niños through books: This is an ideal program if you are just starting your celebration or if you want to add to your celebration. Set up a book display for the month of April. Display children's fiction and nonfiction books that highlight different cultures and customs.

Display flags or pictures that highlight the cultures in your book display.

Author/illustrator day: Invite an author or illustrator to visit your program. Planning for this program will include booking your author, traveling and lodging accommodations, and ordering books for a book sale and signing. You may consider collaborating with your local school system or another community organization to minimize the cost of this program.

Storytime: Enhance your traditional storytime with an international theme. Include stories and music celebrating different cultures in your toddler, preschool, and school-age storytime programs. Dedicate the month of April to Día de los Niños storytime programs. Encourage families to check out books for home reading by displaying book bundles. Your book bundles will be three to four books with the Día de los Niños theme, bundled together in an attractive tie ready for checkout! Use this opportunity to invite library patrons and volunteers to share stories, music, and artifacts about their culture.

Celebrity read-a-thon: Invite local celebrities, the mayor, councilpersons, principals, and librarians to read in your community. Arrange for television characters from your local public television station to be present at the reading. Contact your public television station about reserving costumes.

Día de los Niños crafts and fun: Children can create piñatas, books, paper flowers, and other crafts that represent different cultures. Plan crafts according to the age of the audience and create a budget for the supplies. Registration for craft programs is recommended.

Art and writing contest: Create a citywide art and/or writing contest. Create a theme based on celebrating cultures and books or design a theme around your Día de los Niños program. Establish your criteria and deadlines and advertise with your local school systems, parks and recreation department, and any media that reach children and parents. Recruit judges and plan a special reception to reveal the winners and a venue to display their work. The cost of this activity will be advertising the contest, prizes, and food for the reception.

Libraries often have a Día de los Niños daylong event. This is the event that is planned in November. Events can be planned for any length of time. Volunteers are recruited and assist with setup and cleanup, program activities, and directions and information. Volunteer recruiting should begin in November, allowing time to recruit bilingual volunteers. The celebration may include the activities listed above but can also include

Collaboration with local cultural agencies to provide dance, music, and puppet programs. The Public Library of Charlotte and Mecklenburg

County opened its Día celebration with dances from Latin American and Asian countries.

Government and community officials serve as chairmen for the event and officially proclaim April 30 as Día de los Niños.

During the daylong celebration, offer a variety of family workshops, which can include storytelling from around the world, drama, karate, and arts and crafts. Simply contact local businesses or refer to your arts and science council for local artists.

If your budget allows, consider including a book giveaway in your celebration. You can extend the Día de los Niños experience by providing age-appropriate books for families who attend the event. Contact your local bookstore for discounted or donated books.

4. Evaluate. The final step for any Día de los Niños celebration is evaluating the programs. Evaluate participants, volunteers, staff, and your committee as a way to analyze your Día program. Information from the evaluations will assist you in strengthening your Día program and understanding the needs of the community you serve.

Visit www.ala.org/ala/mgrps/divs/alsc/initiatives/diadelosninos/index.cfm for more information and resources for your Día de los Niños celebration.

44

DOCUMENTING THE EXPERIENCES OF AFRICAN AMERICANS, NATIVE AMERICANS, AND MEXICAN AMERICANS

Archivists Partnering with Oral Historians

Sharon Carlson

IN 2006 archivists, museum professionals, and educators in southwestern Michigan developed an oral history project to document communities less represented in the historical record. The Voice and Images project relied on interviewers versed in Spanish and Anishinabe and familiar with Mexican and Native American cultural norms. Interviews were combined with documentation to trace the history of African Americans, Native Americans, and Mexican Americans and the transformation of the greater Kalamazoo community from 1920 to 1980. The purposes of the project were (1) to provide a rich, well-documented history of an important, yet largely undocumented, dimension of Kalamazoo history; (2) to advance local, state, and twentieth-century history; and (3) to make that history accessible to educators, researchers, students, and the general public through establishing a new archival collection. This chapter explores the techniques and resulting benefits to the constituencies participating in this program.

Earlier oral history projects in the community sponsored by Western Michigan University and the Kalamazoo Valley Museum had been limited in scope. An oral history project conducted by the university in the 1970s had gathered some accounts of African American experiences. The Kalamazoo Valley Museum had collected histories by Mexican Americans during an earlier project. Neither had collected accounts by Native Americans. Each of the underrepresented groups also had unique circumstances, despite common experiences of home, work, recreation, education, religion, and community.

At the beginning of the project, two committees were established for the project. A steering committee provided an advisory role. This committee included members of the communities selected for the project because of their inside knowledge of the culture and their expertise. Several had affiliations to universities and colleges in the area and brought various disciplinary perspectives.

A working committee was responsible for much of the day-to-day activities of the project. Members of the working committee were interviewers and included six individuals from the Greater Kalamazoo area who were themselves African American, Mexican American, or Native American. Their age and experience ranged greatly and included an undergraduate student with prior experience conducting oral histories, a former newspaper reporter with a background in journalism, an author experienced in collecting Native American oral histories, and a museum professional.

The project was also aided by an outside trainer hired by the Kalamazoo Valley Museum. The trainer had significant experience in conducting and processing oral histories and provided a full day of instruction. Instruction focused on the ethical, legal, and logistical aspects of collecting oral histories.

POSITIVE OUTCOMES

Sixteen individuals were interviewed in the course of the project. From these interviews transcriptions were prepared. Translations were prepared for interviews conducted in Spanish. Although this may be a relatively small number, the interviews greatly expanded holdings at the Western Michigan University Archives and Regional History Collections. The gathering of Native American oral histories was especially significant because there were none prior to this project.

Relying on native speakers in the interviews with Mexican Americans and Native Americans was an invaluable part of the project. The interviewers also brought knowledge of cultural norms. The interviewer of several older Native Americans brought an offering of tobacco before the interview began. In several instances, interviewees were willing to talk to a person familiar with them or their culture where they may have felt uncomfortable talking to people outside of the community. The interviewers gained a confidence and rapport with their interviewees.

In addition to the collecting activities, a symposium to promote the project and engage others interested in oral history culminated the yearlong project. Several of the interviewers and interviewees participated in a panel discussion. Instruction for community members in oral history was provided. There were about thirty participants in this free symposium held at the Kalamazoo Valley Museum.

WHAT WE LEARNED

Despite successes, the project encountered pitfalls and was a learning experience for all involved. There were technological challenges and unrealistic expectations about what could be accomplished by relatively few people in a short period of time.

Digital recorders were selected for ease of migrating interviews to the Internet in the future. These were difficult for some of the interviewers who were used to cassette recorders. The interviews often had several stops and starts as people negotiated the equipment. We assumed that all participants would master the technology much more quickly. Interviewers agreed that practice sessions on the equipment should have been built into the project.

Because we selected digital recorders, we failed to anticipate difficulties that would occur with transcription. Several of the transcriptionists were used to working with traditional cassette recordings and also had to learn how to work with digital formats. We also made digital videos of the interviews. In the one instance where the digital recording failed, we were able get the voice recording off the video recording. Multiple copies or formats in this case saved an interview.

In some instances, the shared cultural experiences between the interviewer and interviewee presented some challenges that were not foreseen. Because of the cultural familiarity between interviewer and interviewee, sometimes interviewers failed to ask follow-up questions or questions that would set events in a broader context. Although the interviewers and interviewees fully understood the cultural significance of certain events or even words, people outside the community without that knowledge would have lost some of the meaning. Interviewers tried to fill in some of the gaps to the record after the project.

The original project proposed three interviews at different times for each participant. A few people were willing to meet twice. None of the participants was willing to participate in three interview sessions. About half committed to two interviews, and the remaining participants committed to one interview. These interviews were to be conducted over the summer months, and scheduling became a problem, especially with multiple interviews. The interviewing period took six months to complete. The transcription process also took longer because of the technological problems but also because of the delays in scheduling.

In addition to the oral history, the project also sought to collect videos of the interviews and make copies of related archival documents. We were ambitious and assumed that an interviewer could handle a digital recorder, video camera on a tripod, and possibly a scanner. In hindsight, having an assistant accompany the interviewer would have been very beneficial. The interviewer could have focused on the interviewing process without dealing with technology. Ultimately, staff scanned family photos or other documents after the interview at the museum or the archives.

The idea of interviewing individuals in their homes was attractive on many levels. Precious photos and artifacts would be nearby. It would increase the comfort level of interviewees and reduce travel. Most interviews were conducted in people's homes, but a few were not for various reasons. The museum served as a backup site for interviews. Ultimately, it had the advantage of providing more control over technology, background noise, lighting, and electrical capacity.

The interview recordings and transcripts have become part of the oral history collections of the Western Michigan University Archives and Regional History Collections. Several students have viewed the transcriptions for various classes. Portions of the oral histories or related documentation may be used in future Kalamazoo Valley Museum exhibits. There is also interest in presenting these collections on the Internet.

45

ETHIOPIA READS

Loriene Roy

ONE OF the most gratifying experiences of a career as a professor in professional librarian education is to see students pursue careers they find fulfilling. Even more satisfying is knowing when an alumnus is applying his or her education in making a difference in the world. One such student is Yohannes Gebregeorgis. Gebregeorgis was raised in Negelle Borena, a village in southern Ethiopia, where he had access to a school library staffed by literacy volunteers from the Peace Corps. At nineteen years old, he discovered leisure reading when a friend gave him a copy of a romance novel. In 1982 he sought political asylum in the United States. After completing an undergraduate degree from the University of Buffalo in 1989, he enrolled in the Graduate School of Library and Information Science (now the School of Information) at the University of Texas at Austin, where he received a master's degree in library science in 1991, completing a program of studies for a career in academic librarianship. After employment at a college library in Texas and several public libraries in California, he took a position at the San Francisco Public Library as a children's librarian. Inspired by the lack of children's books in Ethiopian languages, Gebregeorgis founded Ethiopia Reads in 1998 as a 501(c)(3) nonprofit organization. After two decades in the United States, he returned to Ethiopia in 2003 with a gift of 15,000 used children's books donated by his coworkers at the San Francisco Public Library. The original name for Ethiopia Reads was Ethiopian Books for Children and Educational Foundation.

MISSION AND SERVICES

The mission of Ethiopia Reads is to "create a reading culture" by placing books in the hands of Ethiopian children.[1] Literature about Ethiopia Reads provides data on the deep needs within Ethiopia: 72 percent of Ethiopian children do not attend school, and less than half (43 percent) of the general population is able to read. Gebregeorgis provided details on the status of school libraries: 99 percent of schools do not have libraries, and many classrooms lack even a single book. Ethiopia Reads fulfills its mission by establishing physical libraries (including a mobile donkey library), building collections, promoting reading through storytelling, and publishing. Gebregeorgis established the Shola Children's Library in the first floor of his house in Addis Ababa and recorded 40,000 visits during the first year of operation. He opened a second library, the Awassa Reading Center, two years later in 2005. The donkey bookmobile is a two-wheeled cart that Gebregeorgis uses to visit children living in rural settings. In 2007 Ethiopia Reads established the first five school libraries in Ethiopia.

Gebregeorgis contacted Jane Kurtz, a children's book author who had published a number of books about Ethiopia. Through her efforts, Gebregeorgis wrote and published *Silly Mammo*, the first bilingual children's book in English and the Ethiopian language, Amharic. Gebregeorgis dedicated income from the sale of this folktale to establishing a free public children's library in the capital city of Ethiopia, Addis Ababa.

By 2007 Ethiopia Reads had published eight children's books. Ethiopia Reads also provides much-needed employment for field staff in Ethiopia. Volunteers from the United States work with Ethiopian librarians and educators to provide training in literacy and library science to Ethiopian project staff.

Ethiopia Read's annual budget for 2007 was approximately $400,000, with half (56 percent) of the amount derived from individual donations and the remaining funds received from foundations (19 percent), special events (16 percent), and sales of books (9 percent). Each year the program organizes an Ethiopian Children's Book Week with events staged in Washington, D.C., as well as in Ethiopia. The 2007 Book Week theme was "Ethiopia Will Stretch Her Hands to Books" and included a launch of new books, a street march, the opening of a new library, a drawing competition, a distribution of 2,000 books to area schools, and dramatic performances of "The Emperor's New Clothes." A dozen children were recognized with Reader Awards.

The organization's website (www.ethiopiareads.org) provides more information about the Friends of Ethiopia Reads Partner Program and the International Board of Directors. Press and media about Ethiopia Reads are available on the website, including copies of *The Ethiopian Bee*, a newsletter featuring articles about library patrons, staff, visitors and visits, and statistics of library use.

RECOGNITION

Gebregeorgis is receiving recognition for his efforts at reaching out to children in his homeland of Ethiopia. In November 2008 he was declared a CNN Hero. Content about his work was featured on CNN.org. He and nine other CNN Heroes were recognized on a nationally televised program that aired on Thanksgiving evening 2008. He was the recipient of a 2008 ALA Presidential Citation on Innovation in International Librarianship. The text of the citation read:

American Library Association
presents this
Presidential Citation for International Innovation
in the year 2008
to
Ethiopia Reads

For the efforts of Yohannes Gebregeorgis in founding free children's libraries in Ethiopia, providing nearly 100,000 children in Addis Ababa with access to libraries;

For publishing bilingual books for children in both Amharic and English;

For establishing the first Donkey Mobile Library in Ethiopia;

For establishing an annual Ethiopia Children's Book Week;

For providing innovative library services to children—including free haircuts—that reflect community needs;

For serving as a true hero to children in Ethiopia and a shining example of commitment to literacy around the world.

Anaheim, California, June 2008
Loriene Roy
President
American Library Association

NOTE

1. Ethiopia Reads, "FAQs," www.ethiopiareads.org/faq.htm (accessed May 24, 2009).

46

HOMEWORK CLUB FOR ENGLISH LANGUAGE LEARNERS

Licia Slimon

WHEN I walked into Sharon Snee's English Language Learners' (ELL) class at Harrison Middle School to give a booktalk, I never expected to come away with the conviction to start a tutoring program. As a part-time teen services librarian at the Whitehall Public Library, I already had enough on my plate. But in class that day I met Adofo and the other students from Gambia, Sudan, Bosnia, and Afghanistan, many of whom had spent years in refugee camps before immigrating to the United States.

We had fun that day. I talked up Alice Mead's excellent *Girl from Kosovo* and read a chapter from *The Adventures of Captain Underpants* by Dav Pilkey. I had them give it a try. I was struck by how lively and imaginative they were and by how many of them struggled to read English at a third-grade level.

After meeting these students it hit me: as a teen it would be especially hard to assimilate to a new country, to "fit in," to catch up in language, not to mention academics. I noticed that many of the kids were embarrassed to read aloud in front of their peers. I wanted to do something to make the transition easier for them.

I had no experience tutoring or organizing outreach programs, but I did know that I needed help. Sharon Snee was willing. Her easygoing style belied a fierce devotion to her students. Over the past year ELL enrollments had exploded, and in this recent wave many of the children had little or no formal schooling. Although many of her students attended an after-school tutoring program, they needed additional help with literacy skills.

First I found people who were doing similar work. I visited the local immigration and literacy agencies: South Hills Interfaith Ministry (SHIM) and the Greater Pittsburgh Literacy Council (GPLC). Both have offices in Prospect Park, the large apartment complex where many of the immigrant families live. These agencies offer job training and literacy classes to adults, and day care and tutoring to children. However, due to budget cuts neither had a program just for teens.

Next I needed to learn the basics of tutoring, so I started volunteering with SHIM during my workday. Soon I was helping third graders with their math and spelling homework. In the meantime I discussed, mostly via e-mail, the idea of a Homework Club for teens with the librarians at nearby Baldwin Public Library and a teacher at GPLC.

Within a few weeks I'd recruited two tutors: Kristin at GPLC, and Gina, the new teen services librarian at the Baldwin Library. Baldwin's director agreed to host the program in the library's study room. Kristin helped me draft permission forms, and Snee distributed them among her students. Four sixth graders signed up immediately.

As all the pieces fell into place, I decided to act. I found a replacement for my position at SHIM, gave my third graders big hugs, and officially launched Homework Club on March 12, 2008. We would meet every Wednesday after the school bus dropped off the kids.

There was Adofo, a short, muscular boy with a fleeting smile. Conversation with him was always brief, but he had a calm, peaceful presence. Dominic was tall and lithe, the more outgoing of the two, and a better reader. And the girls, Sahar and Nafisa, were sly and conspiratorial one moment, exuberant and affectionate the next.

Kristin's gentle guidance was a good fit, especially with Dominic. Gina's unflappable manner kept us all grounded. I believe the 4:3 student-teacher ratio was essential to the program's success. However, one week Kristin and Gina had prior obligations, and I brought my husband along to fill in. I overlooked the rules at the beginning; it was so important for me not to lose momentum.

Initially, the kids ignored our focus on literacy. They'd "forget" their book reports and bring math assignments even though their math skills were already at or above grade level. So we slogged through fractions and integers, proportions and word problems. But by the third week Snee put pressure on them to bring their reading assignments. Thus began the true work of our mission.

Explaining to a teen from Gambia the cultural references in Carolyn Haywood's *Eddie and the Fire Engine*, a book about a small midwestern town in the 1950s, proved quite a challenge. One scene described a White Elephant Pond, and I had to reread it several times just to make sense of it (and I'm from a small midwestern town!).

Dominic, who once spent an hour watching a web video on how to perform knee surgery—"I can do that!"—managed better with his book about a veterinarian after I explained to him the concept of medical care for pets.

The girls egged on and competed with each other in spelling bees. One day we all pored over *American Girl* magazines to find new vocabulary words. I gave them the old copies to take home, hoping their parents wouldn't mind.

I also made mistakes.

By their nature, outreach programs often require the participation of more than one organization. In our case, Harrison Middle School, SHIM, GPLC, and two public libraries were initially involved. At first it was unclear to me how their functions would overlap and under whose jurisdiction my program would fall. I tended to plow ahead without informing everyone of my progress. And I broke a few rules. In the dark, frigid winter afternoons I drove the kids to and from the library, but driving kids around is a big no-no. My mistakes resulted in confusion over what I was doing and criticism over how I was doing it.

I did the only thing I knew to do: I went to the people in charge—SHIM's upper management, Whitehall's director, Baldwin's director—and apologized. They accepted my apology and were happy to help find solutions that would work for everyone.

After some discussion we agreed to move to an empty GPLC office. Whitehall and Baldwin libraries took over administration of the program. This transfer of responsibility gave us more leeway to develop and implement new ideas.

Building relationships and keeping folks informed are integral to successful outreach. A willingness to take chances, admit you're wrong, and try again are important, too! My commitment to the kids guided me through the rough spots.

With the pieces now in place, it was easy to start again this fall. Twice as many kids signed up this time. Luckily, I found two more tutors from GPLC. In Snee's class, a student's participation hinges on good behavior: "If you don't settle down you don't get to go!"

There was one time last spring when Adofo called his dad to get permission to stay an extra hour. We were both sweating from exertion: Adofo struggling to string the words into a narrative, me explaining how a scarecrow suddenly springs to life. It seemed like an impossible story for him to digest. Yet he labored away. I remember driving back that day feeling anxious—would he write a good report from his notes?—but also buoyant. And the hope and joy I felt for Adofo's life spilled over into my own.

47

IF I CAN READ, I CAN DO ANYTHING
A National Reading Club for Native Children

Loriene Roy

HISTORY

In 1998 Sarah Ann Long, director of the North Suburban Library Association in Illinois, was chosen president-elect of the American Library Association (ALA). She selected a presidential theme of "Libraries Build Community" and sought to express this outreach philosophy in initiatives she supported. She and I had met earlier in the year when she was campaigning at the Texas Library Association annual conference. She contacted me after her election, asking me to develop a demonstration project illustrating her commitment to librarians' support for community literacy. I suggested that we test an approach to support the role of librarians at tribal schools. With her approval, graduate students at the School of Information of the University of Texas at Austin and I visited Marty Lindsey, then the librarian at Rockpoint Community School in northern Arizona. We outlined a plan for supporting reading by American Indian students that was modeled along the lines of public library summer reading programs. Lindsey gave the program its title: "If I Can Read, I Can Do Anything," paraphrasing what she told each class of students visiting her library. We recruited a pilot site at the Laguna Elementary School in New Mexico, and in August 1998 we began our demonstration project. Ten years later, If I Can Read continues to serve nearly thirty schools in the United States. This chapter summarizes our services, lessons learned, and plans for the future.

SERVICES

Our initial plan for If I Can Read was to work with tribal librarians to develop reading promotional events such as local expressions of such national celebrations as Teen Read Week, Teen Tech Week, and National Library Week. We quickly revised our plans after accessing the quality and quantity of the library book collections: we determined that it was not possible to promote reading when children did not have new or appealing books. We focused our energies on creating a book flood at each site. Because we decided to expand the program to include other sites and felt that we could not replace the need for local support to build and refresh library collections, the book flood was defined as a donation of 1,000 books with the approximate value of $10,000. We paced the donations according to the librarian's ability to process and display new materials and to respond to any specific collection-building requests. Librarians chose to receive shipments of titles we selected or selected titles from lists sent for approval. Now, ten years later, we continue to receive requests from schools for donations of new books. Native students still need books.

During the pilot year we tested activities around the weekly themes of rodeo, sports, Native peoples, animals, and science fiction/fact. We learned that school calendars were busy, and it was a burden for the librarian to add additional events. We continued to support selected activities tested during the pilot year, including

- family reading nights
- storytelling, reading, and open microphone events featuring scary stories
- reading incentives such as foam visors and wristbands for distribution to students

In addition, we tried to respond to special requests. When one school asked us to purchase a pocket dictionary for each student, we held several fund-raisers and donated the honoraria from speaking engagements to cover this cost. Another school asked us to fund the relandscaping of the school grounds to prevent spring floods from damaging the library. We contacted several local foundations that answered this request. We supported the attendance of a librarian and several students at the 2002 ALA annual conference and continued to alert the schools about opportunities. We have hosted various visitors at schools, including members of Te Ropu Whakahau, the Maori in Libraries and Information Management organization from New Zealand. In 2008 we organized "A Gathering of Readers," an international event celebrating indigenous children's reading and culture during National Library Week. Participating schools contributed content on a website and their students received incentives, including LIVEStrong wristbands donated by the Lance Armstrong Foundation.

Our initial funding to test the If I Can Read project came from Sarah Ann Long's initial donation of $5,000 from her ALA presidential initiatives budget, along with support from the Four Directions Technology Innovation Grant from the U.S. Department of Education. The Tocker Foundation provided $129,000 in subsequent funding. These funds were dedicated to financial support for a graduate research associate, supplies, postage, and site visits. We received donations of new books from multiple sources including publishers, authors, and reviewing journals.

LESSONS LEARNED

The If I Can Read project still provides a useful service for children attending tribal schools. It helps elevate the role of the librarian and helps her stay informed about continuing education opportunities and activities sponsored by ALA. As a service learning program, it provides graduate students attending an ALA-accredited master's degree program with an opportunity to apply their growing expertise in appreciative environments. It helps students learn about cultures other than their own. The Graduate Research Association learns project management skills by planning and organizing events for If I Can Read. We learned to be flexible and serve as advisors rather than directors. There is a long tradition of outside researchers using temporary grant funding to conduct individual research or start projects in Indian country. Our promise is to offer long-standing contact and support for tribal school libraries while keeping a low burden on the site.

FUTURE PLANS

We still aim to be the national reading club for Native children. Although we currently work with some 30 schools in 12 states, there are over 150 additional schools that might benefit from our presence. Our dreams for the future include supporting Native-language revitalization efforts, hosting annual summer institutes for tribal school librarians, and assisting tribal school librarians in continuing their education through school librarian certification or master's degrees from ALA-accredited programs. We look forward to assisting Native children in acquiring a lifelong love of reading. We hope someday to expand this club to include Native children living in urban areas and attending schools away from their tribal homelands.

48

LAPTOP LITERACY

Language and Computer Literacy Services to Refugees in Burlington, Vermont

Barbara A. Shatara

NORTHERN VERMONT'S refugee and immigrant population has increased substantially in size and diversity in the last decade. In the same time period, federal funding for programs that assist new Americans with literacy services, such as the Vermont Refugee Resettlement Program and Vermont Adult Learning, have declined in recent years. Requests from these agencies and from our patrons inform our decisions regarding services and materials. In 2006 feedback regarding the need for computer training for refugees and immigrants shifted our focus to computer literacy. The Fletcher Free Library now offers free resources to aid the transition for refugees and immigrants into the Burlington community in a very different way.

Literacy services at the library include English classes for nonnative speakers (referred to as ESL), an English conversation group, citizenship classes, and books and audiovisual materials for improving grammar and pronunciation. As literacy continues to evolve beyond language competency, the newest need is for better understanding of technology and computer literacy skills. Library statistics show a significant rise in library usage by the city's most disadvantaged residents, particularly for computer access. The Fletcher Free Library's focus on computer literacy is a response to a gap in the community for just this service and is also inspired by anecdotal observations of refugees and immigrants who need extra assistance in the library's computer center.

Unfortunately, adult refugees and immigrants have fewer formal chances to improve their computer skills. Burlington's refugee population is at great risk of staying at or falling below the poverty line. Language barriers, educational disparity, limited affordable downtown housing, limited transportation options, racism, and unfamiliarity with city resources complicate the already difficult relocation process. Outreach to a population that is often unfamiliar with the services offered by community organizations is particularly necessary.

In 2006 the AmeriCorps VISTA position at the library was rewritten to reflect the changing nature of our literacy services. The position was renamed director of multimedia literacy services and charged with the task of developing a curriculum for ESL computer classes and finding resources to incorporate technology with English-language instruction. Amber Gaster, a recent graduate from Winona State University in Minnesota, was hired to select appropriate literacy resources, organize ESL and computer literacy courses, write grants to fund these projects, and increase public awareness of library services.

Working with community organizations representing new arrivals, including the Association of Africans Living in Vermont, the Somali Bantu Association, and the Vermont Refugee Resettlement Program (VRRP), a series of eight computer classes was organized to assist refugees and immigrants with little to no previous experience with computer use. This partnership allowed the library to make connections with a number of newly arrived refugees in Burlington and has assisted in bringing new patrons into the library. The classes introduced basic computer use and were designed to assist individuals in gaining the basics they need before entering a beginning-level computer course. The Fletcher Free Library offers a series of computer classes to the general public in the fall and spring of each year. The classes are open to all but do not have the staff to assist low English literacy students. A small grant from the Vermont Public Library Foundation funded the ESL computer literacy classes.

Classes were held at the library in cooperation with the Association of Africans Living in Vermont, who recruited students and provided transportation to the library. A mobile classroom with eight laptops was used for instruction. Amber Gaster assisted the instructor and an interpreter. Dependable transportation, having patience with latecomers, and engaging an instructor familiar with the nonnative English speakers proved key to the success of the class. A curriculum was planned for a more advanced course to be offered in 2009.

In addition to the computer literacy classes, two Rosetta Stone programs for building English literacy skills were purchased and marketed to ESL students in the area. Gaster visited the Franklin Square Public Housing community center and ESL classes at the VRRP to inform students of library resources, including the Rosetta Stone English-language-learning program. The visits built a bridge to the library from other social service agencies.

The Rosetta Stone language-learning software was chosen after consulting with library staff and market research. Rosetta Stone has been widely used for ESL programs. Rather than relying on memorization and translation, Rosetta Stone encourages the use of visual sense to acquire language, focusing on the strengths of the individual. Rosetta Stone also adapts to individual needs by allowing users to move at their own speed and repeat areas of difficulty. The program allows users to test their proficiency before moving on to more complicated lessons.

The software was installed on two computer laptops, available from Fletcher's circulation desk. As a language-learning tool, the laptops have several unique advantages. Although computer programming can easily be incorporated as a supplement to traditional classroom ESL teaching, it also stands alone as an effective tool for self-instruction. The flexibility of computer programming allows for a range of applications that encompass the entire spectrum of language acquisition—comprehension, pronunciation, vocabulary building, reading, writing, grammar, and syntax—and allows for specialized application to a variety of real-life situations. Furthermore, the ESL programming allows for interactive language learning at the convenience of individuals, in contrast to the rigidity of set class times.

Rosetta Stone proved quite popular. The laptops went out nearly every other day from the time they first began circulating in March 2007. The computers have been used frequently in ESL classes and tutoring programs by area service providers, and particularly by the VRRP. The latter's tutors have been instrumental in the success of the program by bringing their students to the library to use the computers during their tutoring sessions. Several tutors have mentioned that the use of the program has enhanced their tutoring sessions and has been a unique way to highlight topics that they wish to cover in their lesson plans.

A major focus in the promotion of Rosetta Stone has been on increasing access to the program for African refugee women. The computers have been used by women who bring their children to the library while they use the computers in the youth area, allowing them to focus on learning English while their children play in a safe environment. In coordination with the Burlington Housing Authority, which oversees low-income housing, the library makes the computers and a tutor available for an hour each week while children participate in a story and craft hour. The ability to access the computers in these ways has increased the value that parents see in the library, both for themselves and for their children.

49

THE LONG JOURNEY TO VERMONT
Immigration, Cultural Identity, and Book Discussions That Build Community

Barbara A. Shatara

THE LONG Journey is a six-week book and film discussion series that examines issues of acculturation, identity, and prejudice faced by immigrants and refugees in Vermont. The program ran for six years and has been very successful. Notably, it has cultivated friendships and thoughtful inquiry among a diverse community.

Once referred to as "the whitest state in the Union," Vermont conjures images of pastoral villages, covered bridges, and a population as homogeneous as the milk for which it is famous. Vermont is undeniably a small rural state, but its demographics reflect a growing diversity. Burlington, the state's largest city with just under 39,000 residents, has the largest concentration of foreign-born residents in the state. In the late nineteenth century, Irish and French Canadian descendants were joined by immigrants from eastern Europe, Lebanon, and Italy, creating a mosaic of enclaves. Few vestiges remain of these neighborhoods, but the immigrant population in Burlington still increases annually.

Today, over thirty different languages are spoken in Burlington schools. Immigrants from all over the world, more than a thousand from the African continent alone, require services to adjust to and thrive in their new home. As these new Americans become more established in their communities, maintaining their cultural identity becomes more important to them, especially among first-generation immigrants. Disparities in English-language proficiency between parents and their children alter traditional family dynamics. Building community among a disparate population is needed to buffer ethnic tensions. The Long Journey book and film discussion series was developed to address these issues.

Originally funded by a Libraries for the Future grant from the MetLife Foundation, the Long Journey series was organized by an AmeriCorps VISTA (A*VISTA) volunteer at the Fletcher Free Library, Burlington's only public library. Since 2000 this VISTA member's position, coordinator for outreach services to refugees and immigrants, has been responsible for evaluating and addressing the city's literacy needs. The Fletcher Free Library's Outreach Department consists of one full-time librarian and the VISTA member, who serves a one-year term. Each year, a new VISTA team member develops or revamps projects in response to the ever-changing immigrant population.

VISTA places talented college graduates in social service agencies working to alleviate poverty and improve the lives of low-income Americans. The agencies gain a full-time position at minimal cost, usually under $12,000. During their year of service, members are charged with the task of building organizational and financial resources to aid the work of the agency. On average, the Fletcher Free Library's coordinator raises $6,000 each year in grant monies, recruits five volunteers to assist with literacy initiatives, and strengthens cooperation between the library and regional organizations of service to refugees and immigrants.

Under VISTA Colleen Wright's direction, the Long Journey book discussion series brought together teenagers and parents from many different cultures to examine issues associated with immigration and assimilation. Discussions were led by authors, professionals working with refugees, and scholars. The book and film titles were chosen in consultation with youth librarians, professors from the Master's in Teaching a Second Language program at St. Michael's College, and a review of literature in the field. Marketing efforts targeted members of local Vietnamese, Bosnian, Tibetan, Russian, and Sudanese social organizations. Teens were recruited with the assistance of Burlington High School administrators and teachers. The University of Vermont's Linking Learning to Life office provided volunteer assistance and publicity on campus. Additional publicity included advertisements in local newspapers, posters, and word of mouth. The discussions meet on six consecutive Wednesday nights in the summer. Each series ends with a potluck held at a local park or at the library, depending on the weather. The first year proved so successful that MetLife funded the project for a second year, and it has remained one of the library's most popular programs.

Participants in the Long Journey mirror the region's changing demographics. Marketing efforts targeted teenagers and their parents, but college students and other interested adults also provided a wide range of insight and experience. A family from Tibet, a mother and daughter from Bosnia, college students from Vermont, "Lost Boys" from Sudan, and a domestic worker from Peru shared stories of their own immigration or contemplated the experiences of others.

The books and films discussed included *Zlata's Diary: A Child's Life in Wartime Sarajevo* by Zlata Filipovic; *Kiss the Dust* by Elizabeth Laird, featuring a Kurdish refugee family; and the films *Benjamin and His Brother*, about Sudanese refugees, and *Rebuilding the Temple: Cambodians in America*. In addition to funding multiple copies of the books in the series, publicity materials, and refreshments, the MetLife grant made possible author visits, such as those of Loung Ung, author of *First They Killed My Father: A Daughter of Cambodia Remembers*, and An Na, author of *A Step from Heaven*. The poignancy of the books and films aided conversation. And one cannot discount the effect food has on conversation. Across cultures, participants found that many immigration issues were universal, such as the trauma of leaving family members behind, transitioning to a country with very different social norms, and the frustrations faced by immigrants with advanced degrees in finding work appropriate to their training.

Most Long Journey participants have an intermediate or better level of English competency. It is not considered a literacy program in the traditional sense. The series was designed to improve cultural understanding among the residents of Burlington, build friendships across ethnicities, and facilitate dialogue between first-generation immigrants and their children. Feedback from participants has been overwhelmingly positive over the years. Evaluations completed by Colleen Wright helped to shape future programs. The series was suspended in 2007 to accommodate computer literacy initiatives, but we hope to reestablish the series in 2010.

50

OUTREACH TO THE RUSSIAN- SPEAKING COMMUNITY IN THE ARAPAHOE LIBRARY DISTRICT

Katya B. Dunatov

ARAPAHOE COUNTY is a 550,000-person suburban county in the Denver, Colorado, metropolitan area. The commitment of the Arapahoe Library District (ALD) to providing multicultural services has a long history. However, in the early 1990s this history got a new turn when our Glendale branch established services to refugees from the former Soviet Union in the form of a special collection, programs, staff, and other services in the Russian language.

The outreach to the Russian-speaking population at ALD is implemented in the first place through collection development, which is done by the Russian-language outreach librarian in close rapport with Russian-speaking patrons. Their requests are taken into consideration when purchasing decisions are made. Lists of newly arrived materials are published regularly in the three local Russian-language newspapers. Readers' advisory information about the winners of various Russian and international literature prizes is regularly delivered to (and eagerly anticipated by) the patrons, and the books by these authors are speedily purchased. A Russian Book Club that is well known in the community meets every month and discusses the latest and most popular books.

The Glendale branch, where ALD's Russian collection is housed, has five Russian-speaking patron services specialists (PSS) who, together with the Russian-language outreach librarian, offer reference services, teach classes, host programs, and provide technical assistance to Russian-speaking patrons.

In this age of rapidly growing digital communications and the digital divide between cultures, we consider outreach through marketing and technology as one of our most important tasks. Information on ALD events and programs is published in the Russian version of the ALD newsletter *Dewey*, as well as in the three local Russian-language papers. The Glendale Library has seventeen computers capable of supporting an Internet connection and equipped with Russian fonts and phonetic layouts, which allow for comfortable use of the fonts on the standard American keyboard. This also allow for easily switching between Russian and English fonts. Instructions on how to download such a layout on their home computer are offered to the public. Russian-speaking PSS staff teach computer classes in both English and Russian. The manuals used in these classes are translated into Russian and can be used by the patrons for future reference.

ALD Outreach Services, in cooperation with the Glendale Library's Russian-speaking staff and the Digital Services Department, are working on developing a

Russian page on the ALD website that would mirror the English-language information concerning ALD rules, regulations, and services offered. There is also work in progress on the "Annotated Guide for Russian Online and Local Resources." This guide will provide an annotated list of local Russian-language educational, cultural, religious, and other institutions and social services. It will also assist in getting information on such important issues as citizenship and naturalization and consular services from the countries of the former Soviet Union. The guide will also provide access to Russian online reference sources and the most authoritative Russian-language educational resources. The work on the content part of the three modules of the guide, concerning citizenship and naturalization, consular services, and Russian online reference resources, is completed, and while Digital Services is working on mounting the guide on the Web, the modules are being used by the PSS staff on the floor as Russian-language reference tools.

Our philosophy concerning programs for the Russian-speaking population is that we provide outreach to *all* generations of this population in order to preserve and maintain their language and culture. We offer programs for the elderly: author talks, mini-concerts, craft classes, and other activities, which are hosted in Russian or are translated into Russian. The Summer Reading Program for Adults is one of the most popular programs in the community. We also participate in the Denver Russian Festivals, where the Russian-speaking staff distribute information on the district's policies and programming, issues library cards to new patrons, and organizes book sales.

We take special care when offering programs for kids, because by doing so we are participating in bringing up a new generation of bilingual readers and patrons. Bilingual Storytime for babies and toddlers is hosted on a regular basis by the Russian-speaking PSS staff. Russian dance classes, taught by the Science, Arts, and Sport Center, take place on the library premises and attract both Russian- and English-speaking kids. Russian Folktales in English is a program targeting a very special audience of American families who adopted children from the countries of the former Soviet Union. The program is offered in English with a modicum of Russian language. It teaches appreciation of Russian folklore and familiarizes children and their parents with the basics of the Russian language.

Outreach through partnerships is yet another way to get to the Russian population. Partnership with the Spring Institute serves the purpose of delivering English-language classes to all our multicultural patrons, including Russian speakers. Partnership with Seniors, Inc. allows us to provide information services to Russian-speaking seniors and to maintain deposit collections at senior facilities. We also use Seniors, Inc. help to provide assistance to Russian-speaking seniors during the tax season. Partnership with Jewish Family Services allows us to offer weekly consultations on various topics for those who are newly arrived in the United States.

Outreach to the Russian-speaking population is an important part of ALD's efforts in the provision of equitable services to all patrons, as well as in serving the community by propagating multiculturalism.

51

OUTREACH TO NEWLY ENROLLED AFRICAN AMERICAN COLLEGE STUDENTS

Jamie Seeholzer

THE ACADEMIC STARS (STudents Achieving and Reaching Success) program at Kent State University was created by the university in 1990 to foster the development of talented African American students at the beginning of their college careers. The Academic STARS program is a "freshman-year transition and retention program" that begins with a seven-week summer program, according to the Kent State Student Multicultural Center. The summer program provides the students with opportunities to earn college credit that they can apply toward their freshman year and to gain some exposure to support services and resources on campus. The Kent State University Main Library has had a presence in the Academic STARS program for many years.

The Academic STARS summer program begins in July with an enrollment of about thirty students. STARS students have regularly scheduled classes Monday through Friday and time during the afternoons for a variety of workshops and cultural events. When I approached the director of the STARS program in the summer of 2008, the students had a free workshop time for two hours on Tuesdays that could be filled by the library. Working under the direction of Ken Burhanna, head of instructional services at the Main Library, I coordinated a series of four workshops for the students that would highlight some library services and give them a chance to learn about the variety of resources available to them as Kent State students.

Ken and I spent the first session of our workshop series highlighting resources available from the library's website and taking the students on a tour of the library building. At the end of the first day, the students were required to complete a set of self-paced skills modules created by Kent State librarians that teach students how to use the library's catalog, form a search strategy, evaluate websites, and search a basic database. During our second session, the students demonstrated their mastery of this material by using "clicker" assessment to answer quiz questions about accessing and using library services. We also used the second session of the workshop to build on skills learned in the modules. The students were divided into pairs to complete exercises on locating and analyzing results from a research database and the library's catalog.

During the third session, we introduced a problem-based library challenge and divided the students into teams to complete the assignment. The decision to use a problem-based learning activity was based on the idea that it would give the students a chance to practice their newfound library skills. We provided the students with most of the third session to begin their research. Setting the session up this way gave us the chance to circulate among the students and answer their questions about how to start researching. I divided the students into teams because I did not want the students to settle into their established cliques and not focus on the project. I was also careful to team the students who participated more in class with group members who wouldn't "carry their weight." The students were broken up into seven teams, with four to five members on each team.

Each team was given an open-ended question that required them to figure out an answer for themselves. Topics included: "Is the earth in danger of being hit by a near-earth object?" "Who is more likely to cheat on college exams, men or women?" and "Does money buy happiness?" The students were also assigned a librarian from within our Reference Department to assist them in their research.

In an effort to increase motivation in the students, we added a competition element to the assignment. Ken and I developed a rubric in order to evaluate the students, and we used that rubric in combination with peer reviews from the STARS students to determine the winning team. Each team member in the winning group would receive a ten-dollar gift certificate to the campus bookstore and an additional ten dollars added to their university identification cards.

On the final workshop day, the students presented the findings of their research in PowerPoint presentations. Many of the students incorporated brief movies and interactive activities into their presentations to highlight the range of materials they found. The presentation aspect of the assignment was a great opportunity to introduce the students to our Student Multimedia Studio within the library, where they could get help with adding multimedia elements to their presentations. The students showed great creativity in answering the problem-based questions and engaging their fellow students in thinking about the issues associated with each question.

The team that ended up winning the problem-based assignment competition was a group that faced a few obstacles. It was originally a group of four, but one student dropped out of the STARS program for unexplained reasons, and a second was forced to return home for a family emergency. With only two group members left, this team presented a compelling argument for their opinion on the problem-based assignment and won over their classmates.

One goal of mine for future outreach to STARS students is to focus on exposing these students to more resources available to them within the Main Library. Even though an increasing number of library resources are available online, the value of in-person instruction should not be lost. The students in this STARS class were able to see and use study spaces around the library and received in-person help with research databases and the library's catalog. Their final project gave them the chance to use the skills they had learned in previous library workshop sessions and the expertise of the librarian assigned to them, as well as the support of our multimedia staff, to create engaging and thoughtful presentations.

The Academic STARS students are an important population to reach out to. These students are responsible, mature, and academically focused. Providing a workshop series for them will hopefully give them a good foundation for starting their freshman year and for being aware of services available to them.

52

SERVING MULTICULTURAL PATRONS AT THE ARAPAHOE LIBRARY DISTRICT

Katya B. Dunatov

THE ARAPAHOE Library District (ALD) has long been in the forefront of providing services to new immigrants, refugees, and other multicultural populations in Arapahoe County and the state of Colorado. Its commitment to diversity is reflected in its objectives: "In response to the growing diversity in our communities with respect to age, ethnicity, race, means and family, ALD will acknowledge and respect diversity by incorporating variety in its services, facilities, outreach, programs and collections."[1]

In the early 1990s our Glendale branch established services to refugees from the former Soviet Union in the form of a special collection, programs, staff, and other services in the Russian language. As this population grew, so did the services. The U.S. State Department has long recognized our Glendale branch as exemplary in serving its Russian-speaking patrons. Our services to Spanish speakers evolved over the past several years as this population reached a sufficient threshold level in our community.

People working at ALD are deeply convinced that multicultural library services (MLS) benefit "minority" communities and individuals by helping them adjust to the way of life of the mainstream society by decreasing the sense of isolation, by providing vital survival information, and by enabling their democratic participation in the civil society. We completely agree with the IFLA statement that such services also benefit the *whole* community by providing to its members information about each other's respective cultures, languages, contributions to the society, values, and so on, with "the end result being increased understanding and communication."[2]

One of the most important goals for ALD is to develop cultural competency, to raise awareness of cultural differences between people and the benefits deriving from MLS on all levels, among the employees and the management, as well as in the community. And the creation of institutional policies is the most crucial step in this direction. For several months Outreach Services have been working on the development of ALD's Multicultural Library Services Plan, which will include an individual plan for each ALD department and branch, with specific actions related to programs, services, collections, staff, and marketing. The plan will systematize our efforts in offering MLS, determine the scope of these services, reveal any gaps in them, and outline what has to be done in the future.

Another important step toward developing cultural competency at ALD is staff training. A class on serving multicultural patrons, taught by the language librarians, is offered every six months through collaboration between Outreach Services and the Training and Staff Development Department. The class discusses cultural differences in general and cultural differences in library use in particular. It teaches how to understand multicultural patrons' expectations and how to create a welcoming environment for them, how to communicate successfully with patrons with limited English-language skills, how to help patrons with limited computer skills to deal with various digital environments, and many other things. The importance of using friendly mimics and body language, as well as such strategies as active listening, using paraphrasing when talking to a patron with limited English skills, "talking" patrons through the task while showing them how to use computer applications, and so on, is emphasized during the class. The ALD Special Populations Interest Group meets quarterly and enables professional and paraprofessional staff to share their experiences in providing library services to multicultural patrons and other types of special populations. The discussion continues on the web pages of the Special Populations Interest Group blog throughout the year.

Finally, outreach to multicultural populations is yet another step toward raising multicultural awareness both among the staff and in the community. Outreach is implemented first of all through collection development. Besides its main collection that includes titles in various languages, ALD has two special collections, Russian and Spanish, which are developed independently.

Developing multicultural information access points is an important part of outreaching to multicultural populations. A telephone service called Russian/Spanish Hunt Group makes it possible for a patron located at any ALD branch to immediately get help from a Spanish- or Russian-speaking staff member. ALD language librarians, in cooperation with Digital Services, are working on the development of Russian- and Spanish-language web pages that would not only mirror the information on library services, programs, and regulations on the main page but would also provide information on available Russian- and Spanish-language online and local resources. Information on programs and classes is presented to patrons in the monthly newsletter *Dewey* in three languages: English, Russian, and Spanish. The information on programming, together with lists of newly arrived materials (for the Russian titles only), is published in local Russian- and Spanish-language newspapers.

ALD's approach to outreach through programming is to provide programs that can educate ALD patrons of all backgrounds about various cultures of the world. Good examples of such programs are Culture Fest and Fiesta Latina, which take place in various branches of the district. At the same time, ALD considers crucial the development of "womb to tomb" program selection that would target *all* generations in Russian and Spanish populations and help these populations to maintain their indigenous cultures and languages.

Presenting educational opportunities to patrons with limited English skills is another ALD concern: computer classes teaching the skills vital in the contemporary world are provided in three languages (English, Spanish, and Russian), and teaching ESL classes is considered one of the major ways to outreach to the multicultural populations of the district. English Conversation circles are organized in several branches to assist patrons in English-language acquisition.

It should be added that teaching ESL classes represents another way of outreach, namely outreach through partnerships. Our partnership with the Spring Institute

(SI) is one good example of this: SI teachers teach at the ALD premises at Glendale and Sheridan public libraries and at Smokey Hill High School. The students receive not only ESL instruction but also regular library tours in the Glendale, Sheridan, and Smokey Hill libraries. Upon receiving a Western Union grant called "Immigrants' Integration: Libraries and ESL Classroom," SI and the ALD Outreach Services Department began working on incorporating library instruction into the curriculum of ESL classes. Another example is ALD's partnership with the Four Mile Family Resource Center, which results in the provision of such services as homework help offered in English and Spanish. The service also exists online and allows students in grades 3–12 to connect with an online tutor for live homework help in math, science, social studies, and English.

We at ALD strongly believe that developing cultural competence at all levels both in the library and in the community, implemented through the provision of institutional policies, training of the staff, and outreaching to multicultural populations, as well as educating the general population on multicultural issues, will allow us to fulfill our objectives and to comply with the ALA code of ethics, which states: "We provide the highest level of service to all library users through appropriate and usefully organized resources; equitable service policies; equitable access; and accurate, unbiased, and courteous responses to all requests."[3]

NOTES

1. Arapahoe Library District, "Our Vision, Values and Mission," www.arapahoelibraries.org/go2.cfm?pid=435&p1=10&p2=1.
2. IFLA, "Raison d'être for Multicultural Library Services," www.ifla.org/VII/s32/pub/s32Raison.pdf, p. 1.
3. American Library Association, "Code of Ethics of the American Library Association," www.ala.org/ala/aboutala/offices/oif/statementspols/codeofethics/codeethics.cfm.

PART X
Community Group Collaboration and Outreach

53

COMMUNITY GROUPS JOIN FORCES FOR FAMILY FUN

Tiffany Auxier

THE VARIETY of educational and entertainment offerings at the library and within its service area are often in direct competition. They may be for the same age group, be on the same topic, or be held at the same time or at a closer location. The likelihood that the library program is free may be the only difference.

Public-service organizations strive to maintain their base, attract new patrons, and fulfill their mission to enrich and educate. Yet we all struggle with similar barriers, such as small staff or budgets that cannot accommodate every new idea or request, and trying to engage families who have increasing demands on their time.

Collaboration between agencies can maximize the expertise and interests of staff members, share costs, attract a broader audience, and increase community awareness about each organization.

For a decade the Hinsdale Public Library has been a member of YES (Youth Enrichment Services), a group of fourteen community agencies that support the educational, recreational, and emotional life of youth. Members meet bimonthly to share news about their organizations. However, after a few years, we had not moved beyond passing out each other's fliers and occasionally cohosting programs. The YES website, developed with grant funds, was also languishing because all members did not have the staff to keep it updated. We had to either take a bold step in reaching out to our residents or discontinue formal meetings.

YES members knew that each group had something unique and important to share and did not want to disband. We conducted a survey of community-wide events and discovered that there were no large nonschool events between Christmas and spring break. Our event needed to introduce the community to all of our organizations, appeal to a wide age range, and not conflict with kids' sporting activities.

After brainstorming ideas, we decided to put our own twist on the traditional open house. Each member would have a table to promote its organization, play games with the kids, give away prizes, and create arts and crafts. There would also be scheduled performances, refreshments, free T-shirts and tote bags emblazoned with our names, balloons, fingerprinting by the police department, tattoos, and face painting. Participants could drop in or come for a specific show. Kids could play while parents learned about the many programs and services we offer.

Each YES member contributed to the event, based on their budgets, staffing, and contacts within the community. The planning for the first annual YES Family Fun Fest involved

1. Finding a location and creating a floor plan

   - A member offered its gymnasium and maintenance staff for setup and cleanup.

- We kept animals and activities that would create long lines away from each other to keep the event flowing.

2. Developing a budget and soliciting donations

- Several members had contacts at businesses and banks who contributed funds for prizes ranging from T-shirts and gift baskets to a bike and savings bonds.

- Three members booked and paid for performers such as balloon-making clowns, face painters, and a roaming juggler.

- A Chamber of Commerce member brought and staffed his popcorn machine at the event.

3. Schedule of activities

- Each member was responsible for the activities at its own table and any prize or candy giveaways.

- A local school chorus performed and drew a large audience.

- Other local arts or sports groups also performed, such as the Irish Dancers and a karate club.

4. Decorations

- A member knew a balloon artist who decorated the gym in exchange for passing out her business cards.

5. Advertising

- One member created, copied, and distributed the flier to all schools.

- Each organization included the event in its brochures.

6. Extra hands

- A member with an active volunteer program recruited high school students to assist at the event. They helped unload members' cars and set up their tables, decorate, cut out door prize tickets, staff the welcome booth with the T-shirts and tote bags, assist at the food tables, and clean up and load members' cars.

The first annual YES Family Fun Fest was held on a Sunday in March from 1:00 to 4:00 p.m. Over eight hundred children and adults attended and were thankful for the opportunity to have a fun, family-focused event just as they were awakening from the winter doldrums. YES members were excited to find a new avenue to promote our organizations and work as a team. We had a follow-up meeting to refine issues, such as space, the variety of performers, and offering more refreshments. Yet we were determined to continue, and we have made subtle changes to improve the program each year. To date, YES has hosted six successful Family Fun

Fests and has helped strengthen ties among community organizations, businesses, and schools.

Cooperative programs that resulted from the strong ties built by YES members include

- a villagewide Fall Festival was developed with three YES members at the helm
- young children read with trained therapy dogs and handlers at member libraries, organized by the Hinsdale Humane Society
- DARE (Drug Abuse Resistance Education) Lock-in: YES members attend a fifth-grade sleepover hosted by local police departments and prepare games and other activities
- librarians read at park district events for Christmas and Easter holidays and at the swimming pool in the summertime
- gaming programs were hosted by the library and the Youth Center
- a library-led historical fiction book discussion was held at the Historical Society
- the Hinsdale Center for the Arts sponsored arts education programs at the library
- the library created booklists for the Forest Preserve District's Earth Day celebration
- there was volunteer-sharing between organizations

The Hinsdale Public Library would like to thank YES members for their dedication to public service and for their continued support: the Clarendon Hills Public Library, Community House, Fullersburg Woods, Graue Mill and Museum, Hanson Center, Hinsdale Center for the Arts, Hinsdale Historical Society, Hinsdale Humane Society, Hinsdale Parks and Recreation Department, Hinsdale Police Department, Robert Crown Center for Health Education, School District 181, and the Youth Center.

54
CONNECTING WITH THE COMMUNITY
Partnering to Deliver a Storytime Outreach
Margaret Keys

WHEN I joined the Sacramento Public Library, I had the privilege of implementing an early literacy outreach grant written by my predecessor, Cara Randall. Funded by the Target Corporation, this $2,500 grant paid for program materials and free picture books for one hundred children attending free day care or preschool in the Arcade Library's service area. The grant stipulated that storytimes be conducted in Spanish and English, with parents attending. Although this is just one example of many possible outreach ideas, the process for organizing and delivering it can serve as a model for others working to connect with their communities.

Before seeking partnerships, it is critical to develop a clear outreach plan. First, identify the target audience and determine where they congregate. For children's programming, possible outreach locations include parks, community pools, recreation centers, schools, and day care centers. Once these elements are determined, prepare a summary of your outreach, including its goals and benefits, so that you are well prepared to make your pitch to community partners. You may only need to contact school principals or park district directors in order to coordinate an outreach. If your needs are greater or require funding, however, then you will need to cultivate other partnerships or seek grant money.

One place to start developing partnerships is at chamber of commerce, PTA, or other community meetings. To make contacts for my outreach, I attended the San Juan Unified School District's "First 5 California" grant committee meetings, which happened to be held in my branch library's community room. First 5 is a state commission supervising the development of education and child care programs for children five and under. The group meeting at the Arcade Library oversees school district programs that the grant helps support. Through these meetings, I met the district's social worker for the School Readiness First 5 program. She was instrumental in coordinating our outreach with four Head Start summer school classes, which parents attended on Fridays. Without this partnership, it is doubtful whether I could have delivered this outreach on time within the grant's parameters.

Many states' departments of health or education offer programs similar to First 5. Check state websites to view lists of grant recipients or call the school district to see if anyone in your area has special programs or funds in place to serve children. These groups may be willing to coordinate with you to deliver your outreach if it meets their own goals and grant requirements. They may even share some of their grant money to implement your project. I worked with my First 5 contact to arrange outreach to sixty children before my grant's deadline. Her group provided children with backpacks in which to take home their free books.

Sometimes one contact leads to another. Through a nearby elementary school, we discovered a nonprofit community partner of the Child Abuse Prevention Council of Sacramento. The group conducted free after-school care and a summer day camp across the street from the school. After corresponding with them and attending their meetings, I was able to outreach at their family health fair, with one of their counselors serving as my translator. This relationship continued to develop, as the day campers visited the library on a field trip, and I looked into securing books for their teen reading group.

Some libraries already have community partnerships. The Sacramento Public Library's Fair Oaks branch, for instance, participates in a yearly children's art fair that also involves the school district and a nearby church and is coordinated by the Fair Oaks Recreation and Park District. One could potentially build on any of these relationships. The same library also hosts a yearly in-house "teddy bear tea party" featuring bear-shaped cookies donated from the bakery around the corner.

This partnership might be extended into an outreach, such as a holiday storytime in a children's crisis center or hospital.

In addition to donating products or sharing space and time, community partners can provide funding. Many local and national retailers, including Macy's and Target, offer grants appropriate for library outreach. Another potential partner remains financial institutions, despite the economic crisis. The Wells Fargo Bank funded a one-book program at Sacramento State University for the 2008/2009 school year. The grant pays for each freshman's copy of Firoozeh Dumas's *Funny in Farsi*, which the campus community is reading together. Although large-scale funding like this might be more appropriate for a systemwide effort, it illuminates the possibility of a branch librarian approaching a teacher's credit union to assist with an early literacy outreach. Small businesses, especially those serving children, should also be considered. A children's dentist might fund an outreach during National Children's Dental Health Month, for instance. Consider which businesses are involved in the chamber of commerce, as these already demonstrate an interest in the community, and then consider how you can design an outreach that would appeal to them while serving your community.

State libraries, of course, offer outreach and early literacy grants. Librarians can also apply for literacy grants from the following national organizations:

Barbara Bush Foundation, www.barbarabushfoundation.com

Honor Society of Phi Kappa Phi, www.phikappaphi.org/Web/Scholarships/literacygrant.html

National Institute for Literacy, www.nifl.gov/nifl/grants_contracts.html

Keep in mind that not all outreach costs money. One of the most effective programs I've seen was a biweekly storytime delivered to a subsidized day care center down the street from a branch library where in-house storytimes had no attendance.

Finally, look within your own organization for partners. Colleagues can connect you with people if they know of your outreach needs. One challenge I faced was finding a bilingual partner, but through another librarian I found an ideal person within our system. Bilingualism is often a critical component of outreach, and the lack of a second language need not be a barrier. Frequently, you can find a coworker who speaks the language you need. If not, then approach volunteers or even patrons with whom you are familiar; their willingness to help may surprise you.

Community partnerships are the cornerstone of outreach. With some creativity, clear communication, and assertiveness, you can work with those around you to deliver the outreach your community needs.

55
CREATIVE PARTNERSHIPS WITH LOCAL ORGANIZATIONS

Ellen Mehling

QUEENS IS an ethnically diverse, expansive assortment of neighborhoods in the city of New York. It has its own public library system, Queens Library (QL), one of three systems serving the city, with sixty-two locations serving more than 2.2 million people.

It is a challenge for a library to reach out to such an enormous number of people, spread out over a large area (about 110 square miles), with multiple variables of age, language (more than one hundred languages are spoken in Queens), ethnicity, income, education, religion, ability/disability, and need. Despite recent and perhaps near-future budget cuts, the quantity, quality, and creativity of outreach done by QL, in cooperation with other local organizations, is considerable.

To one degree or another, each of QL's community libraries also works with groups in its local neighborhood. For other kinds of outreach, the outreach librarians have to strike a balance between continuing previously established partnerships with certain schools or organizations and forming new partnerships with other organizations.

In addition to outreach done by the local community libraries, QL has two full-time outreach librarians for all of Queens, and the outreach they do is both local to *their* library (Central, which is in Jamaica) and boroughwide; covers a wide variety of subjects, in English and other languages; and spans a continuum from straight education to education/entertainment. There are some outreach presentations that are given repeatedly in various locations in basically the same form and others that are customized for the partnering organization. Outreach services also include services to people with disabilities, and one of the goals of outreach (as well as of in-library programming) is to have educational programs about disabilities, for the general public or for children. Creativity is highly valuable in this kind of outreach work, both to keep the presentations interesting and relevant for the audiences and also to continue to come up with ideas for new outreach.

QUEENS LIBRARY HEALTHLINK

In partnership with the American Cancer Society, the Queens Cancer Center of Queens Hospital, and the Memorial Sloan-Kettering Cancer Center, HealthLink is a five-year, federally funded initiative to explore how the public library can reach medically underserved community residents. QL employs two HealthLink specialists who work with community libraries, local businesses, community groups and agencies, churches, and other organizations to form Cancer Action Councils. The Cancer Action Councils meet regularly to discuss how to identify that community's needs and to increase access to health information and cancer screenings for people who may be at risk in various neighborhoods.

OUTREACH TO SENIOR CENTERS AND NURSING HOMES

Outreach librarians serve the nursing homes and senior centers of Queens, with programs and events that include the following:

Partnering with a local university that provided a computer van for a genealogy workshop

Original reminiscing or educational programs—some topics are requested by the center; others are proposed by the QL outreach librarians. Topics include

- local history (Coney Island; people from Trinidad and Guyana living in New York City)

- memoir writing for older adults

- an intergenerational writing program with local seniors and schoolchildren

- presentations about celebrities or leaders (Frank Sinatra, George Gershwin, the Silent Comedians, Martin Luther King Jr.)

- introduction to American Sign Language

- poetry workshop/reading

- December holidays

A book discussion with author on speakerphone

Creation of a book club kit, to be given to organizations wishing to begin their own discussion group

English or bilingual/trilingual presentations (languages include Spanish, Chinese, and Russian) on library services

These presentations are multimedia whenever possible and may include verbal discussion, pictures, handouts, music, lyrics, multiple-choice questions, video/DVD clips, PowerPoint slides, or memorabilia to be passed around among the participants.

JOB-HUNTING OUTREACH

Another category of outreach is to patrons who are job-hunting or who will soon be seeking work; presentations and workshops address the needs of groups with certain challenges, for example:

Resume writing/job-hunting/interviewing workshops at high schools and colleges (including a bilingual English–American Sign Language presentation at a local school for the deaf; the school later sent a representative to speak to library staff about serving deaf patrons)

Job-hunting workshops (some English/Spanish bilingual) at correctional facilities and parole offices, drug and alcohol rehab centers, homeless shelters, and social services agencies; participation at job fairs that these organizations coordinate, with additional information provided about GED preparation, literacy, and computer classes

Presentations (some bilingual), with local organizations also serving job-hunters (and representatives from these organizations have also participated at QL events)

OTHER OUTREACH PARTNERSHIPS

Other kinds of outreach serve other groups and/or offer other kinds of services; for senior citizens, for example:

Participating in "older adult" fairs and celebrations and having representatives from the organizations that organized those fairs participate in similar events hosted by QL

Presentations at the local "Y" to groups of children attending summer day camp on "Communicating without Sound," which included an introduction to American Sign Language

OTHER TIPS FOR OUTREACH WORK

It is best to offer a *new* presentation at an organization with which a partnership has already been established. It's like banking goodwill; if the library already has a good working relationship with the organization and its staff, there is a greater chance of a positive response to a new proposal and a successful program. The collaboration also must be respectful; it is important not to push a certain program on a site or an activities director who is at all reluctant—the activities directors know the people they serve and are good judges of what will work.

It is also important to be flexible in terms of subject matter, length of program, availability and functioning of equipment, and any interruptions or unexpected occurrences during the presentation. A presenter who is unruffled by equipment failure or by the loss of some audience members due to an upcoming bingo game or lunch (!) is a presenter who is likely to be welcomed back. There may also be, especially at a senior center or nursing home, audience members who have visual, hearing, mobility, cognitive, or other impairments or for whom English is not the first language, and this may require some impromptu adjustments to a presentation: speaking louder and slower than usual, repeating or rephrasing information, and so on. Working *with* the staff and participants and adapting to the needs of that facility or organization makes for a more pleasant and beneficial partnership for all concerned.

The audience at outreach presentations can help the staff to brainstorm for new ideas: a few minutes of "getting to know you" questions immediately before or after a presentation can help generate innovative outreach for the future. General questions ("What are your hobbies/interests?" "How do you spend your free time?") are better than any that refer to what programs the *library may* provide, which may make the respondents limit their answers to services that they think are appropriate or possible for the library to provide.

QL's outreach librarians also attend community meetings regularly—this leads, of course, to networking opportunities but can also result in new outreach ideas and the discovery that previously known organizations are providing previously unknown services, which could make them ideal for partnership. Blogs written by other librarians can also yield fresh or adaptable ideas. It can be surprisingly easy for outreach staff to generate a long list of ideas and then be in the happy position of always having another idea ready to suggest to a new or existing partnering organization.

56

DINNER WITH THE PRESIDENTS
Teaming Up with the Yours Truly Restaurant Chain

Lynn Hawkins

YOURS TRULY Restaurants is a small seven-store family restaurant chain in northeast Ohio. The chain was established in 1981 with the intent of serving good food at fair prices, and each Yours Truly Restaurant maintains individuality through its programming and community involvement. Among the many awards given the restaurants have been *Cleveland Magazine*'s Top Comfort Foods in Northeast Ohio; Citysearch.com's Best Date Spot, Best Breakfast, and Best Hamburger; *Northern Ohio Live*'s Best Place to Take Kids; and the Lake County Chamber of Commerce Business of the Year Award. We were delighted when Jeffrey Shibley, the popular manager of the Yours Truly Restaurant in Mentor, Ohio, approached the Mentor Public Library about partnering with his store for Dinner with the Presidents. The concept was to entertain guests with stories and visits by some distinguished American presidents and expose them to library materials and staff. Guests weren't required to preregister; they were able to order whatever they liked, spend as much as they liked, or just have coffee.

THE STAR-STUDDED CAST

Mentor was home to James A. Garfield, the twentieth American president. President Garfield ran his campaign out of the house on "the Mentor Farm," and most everybody here likes the James Garfield story. Jeff Shibley chose James A. Garfield,

Mrs. Garfield, Teddy Roosevelt, and Abe Lincoln as his President's Day A-Team. Dinner with the Presidents took place on February 18, 2008, from 6:30 to 8:30 p.m. The professional presidential impersonators were longtime customers at the restaurant and were very comfortable meeting and greeting the Yours Truly guests, posing for photographs, and answering reporters' questions about the high points of their presidencies (true politicians, all!).

The Mentor Public Library sent a team of two to be our presence at the event: Dennis Heritage, head of Children's Services, and David Newyear, then a reference librarian. Dennis and David pulled relevant books, DVDs, and CD books from our collection to use for display and checkout at the event.

Our IT manager made arrangements to connect a tablet PC through our firewall so that we would have a connection to our then-Dynix patron database as well as to our online catalog. Our goals were to be able to register restaurant guests for new library cards, as well as to make the display items available to them for on-site checkout.

GETTING THE TECHNOLOGY RIGHT

David registered kids and adults for our library cards, and they were able to check out materials right on the spot. But getting the connection to the Dynix patron database through our firewall proved to be a pain. The first step in this process was to log into the firewall; the second step was to log into Dynix. We were using a tablet PC that was usually used for remote catalog deletions by a reference team, and David did not have a log-in established on the PC. We would strongly advise that interested libraries have an established log-in on the laptop that is used for this purpose. In our case it took a phone call to the IT manager and the trial of multiple IP/password/log-in combinations before we were able to establish the connection. Once we logged into the firewall, we were working on our domain controller. We suggest that interested libraries choose a staffer who is technically savvy enough to avoid getting into the wrong file, which could affect the website, calendar, or wiki, and making sure that the staffer logs off rather than shuts down; in our case, shutting down would have shut down our website. Our IT manager was adamant about this point!

INVITING KIDS TO THE CRAFT

Our team was busy nonstop, right from the start. The restaurant was packed; people were in line all the way out the door. Dennis brought a craft for the kids, and periodically the Yours Truly staff announced the Mentor Public Library's presence and invited kids to come to the craft. It was a simple craft, because the working space was quite tight; the craft area was set up in the restaurant's front office. The craft was giant-sized coins (actually three inches): realistic metallic replicas of pennies, nickels, dimes, quarters, and half-dollars. Each coin of course had a picture of a president on the front: Lincoln, Washington, Jefferson, Roosevelt, and Kennedy. Some had a picture of a president's home on the back, such as Monticello. Kids made rubbings of the faces of the presidents on precaptioned sheets. A second craft was Presidential Pendants, but it became impractical in the available space, so we suggest carefully considering the space that you may have to work in. The craft area was filled to capacity throughout the evening. A six-foot stand-up cutout of Abraham Lincoln added to the display.

Manager Jeffrey Shibley regarded the event as a huge business success, with restaurant receipts up 40 percent for the evening. He described it as a terrific connection between the business and the community and felt strongly that he wanted the library involved. For our part we were enthusiastic about everything: the venue, the subject matter, and the food. We love that we were able to do point-of-service checkout of our materials in a completely new venue and make new friends in the process. A quick video of the event is available at www.ytr.com/html/about_us.html. A repeat performance of Dinner with the Presidents in 2009 met with similar success.

57
FARAWAY PLACES
Uma Doraiswamy

WHO KNEW that fifty years after it was written, the song "Far Away Places" would echo in the region of western Kentucky? On a Thursday evening, if one were to stop by for a cup of coffee or browse through the stacks of Barnes and Noble bookstore around 7:00 p.m., one would hear lectures on various topics, from food to culture and places. Faraway Places (with strange-sounding names) is a community outreach project organized by Western Kentucky University (WKU) Libraries partnering with Barnes and Noble to educate and create awareness among students and the local community on different subjects and places. It started off in the year 1995 to educate the Bowling Green, Kentucky, community on the U.S. presidential elections. Then for four years it offered hands-on workshops to the community on the use of the Internet and other web skills, which brought in an average of more than twenty participants. The credits for the first series of Faraway Places go to the creative idea of Peggy Wright; to Brian Coutts, who thought the community might be interested in going around the world; and to Nancy Baird, who had visited and conducted research in Africa and made her first presentation on the Republic of South Africa, which attracted the attention of a lot of people to the bookstore. At present the Faraway Places program draws an audience of forty-five to seventy-five and sometimes even more than that.

Speakers from Western Kentucky University and also from other locations are invited on a regular basis. The program speakers are specialists and have conducted research in their respective subject or geographic location in recent years. The presentations combine lectures and PowerPoint presentations. The speaking session starts around 7:00 p.m. and goes on until 8:00 p.m. and often beyond that. There is a coffee shop close to the newspaper/current affairs section in the bookstore, which is the presentation area, so the audience can hear the lectures in a very relaxed setting. At the end of the presentation, prizes are given away to the speaker and the audience, based on a lucky draw. Maps of the region under discussion are distributed to the audience, along with a bibliography of books on that region available at WKU Libraries, as well as a list of ten new books available at Barnes and Noble. Although the topics of these sessions are on different regions of the world, the lectures do include other subjects as well; for instance, on November 20, 2008, Dr. Roger Launius from the National Air and Space Museum, Smithsonian Institution, talked on "Robots in Space."

During my first year as a catalog librarian at the Department of Library Technical Services of WKU Libraries, Brian Coutts suggested that I speak on South India for the Faraway Places series. I had just returned from South India with many art and architectural pictures and traditional clothes. So in October 2007 I had the opportunity of presenting South India to the local community. I could see the audience's interest in wanting to know about other regions and cultures as I spoke to them. It was interesting to share historical, political, and cultural information on southern India, which was new to many people in the audience. It was a new experience for me as well; someday in the future I hope to create awareness among librarians in India so that they will organize such educational outreach programs for their own communities. The students in the audience also learned that they could visit South India for research on ancient art, architecture, religion, and so on. The audience came up with interesting questions and looked at the colorful silk saris, jewelry, and books from South India with admiration. This will be a wonderful memory for me in the years to come, and it also demonstrated that librarians can get involved in the community and educate people through various outreach programs.

During the Faraway Places lectures, there is a table near the presentation area where books and artifacts from a particular country are displayed. If the speakers are authors, at the end of the session there is time for book signing. And in case anyone interested in these sessions missed any of the presentations, they can go to the WKU Libraries website (www.wku.edu/Library/) and check on the podcast. An important reason for the success of this outreach program is the relentless efforts of the WKU Libraries crew consisting of Brian Coutts, Peggy Wright, Haiwang Huan, and David Runner, assisted by Josten Wilson and Brandon Peters. In the past this event was sponsored by Coca-Cola. That company generously funded this program, helping to pay advertising costs such as the printing of posters and postcards and mailing them. The presenters were given fifty-dollar gift certificates. But recently funding has been provided entirely by WKU Libraries.

Faraway Places is targeted toward people who are interested in travel, students of Western Kentucky University, and people from the country under discussion living in the community. Bowling Green is known to have people from such diverse areas as Cambodia, Thailand, Albania, Bosnia, Romania, Russia, Somalia, and so on.

WKU Libraries was one of the first libraries to partner with Barnes and Noble, which advertises this program through its newsletter. WKU Libraries also does a lot of individual and group marketing for the success of this outreach project. Everything is done in-house for the publicity. Picture postcards are printed and distributed to WKU faculty, staff, and students, as well as other people in the community. There is also a web page exclusively for Faraway Places that highlights the featured speakers and the schedule of past and future events. Some faculty encourage their students to attend these sessions by giving extra credits. Prior to the presentation, university-wide e-mails are sent. The library staff come up with creative ways of putting out displays of books, pictures, and artifacts from the subject of the lecture close to the circulation area, which draws a lot of student and faculty attention.

This outreach program is beneficial to all participants. First, the local community gains new knowledge and awareness about the world and current events. Second, it brings in more users to WKU Libraries and enhances its public relations. A major focus of the university is international reach and encouraging its students to study abroad so that they can compete globally. Faraway Places is a potential avenue for them to learn more about the world and step into possible research areas. The lectures also help the Barnes and Noble bookstore to increase its sales; people who come to hear the presentation browse through their collection and end up buying books and other things. When authors are the lecturers, this event helps in the promotion and sale of their books.

Although challenges remain, such as finding new and creative ways to reach a wider target audience and keep people continuously interested in this program, the library crew behind the program are on their toes to make it better and better and increase awareness among the local community on diverse subject areas.

58

FOSTERING COMMUNITY ENGAGEMENT THROUGH A TOWN AND GOWN LECTURE SERIES

Susan M. Frey

INDIANA STATE University (ISU) is a doctoral/research institution that is committed to community engagement. Part of ISU's mission is the development of collaborative partnerships with educational, business, social service, cultural, and government concerns that contribute to the academic mission of the university and directly benefit the community. In line with this campus mission, the ISU Library adopted the "Borders bookstore" philosophy several years ago. Many scholarly and community events are held in the library and sponsored by a variety of university and community stakeholders. Although there are designated quiet study areas in the building, the first floor of the library is an open, fluid space that is regularly reconfigured with movable walls and screens to accommodate community and social activities such as lectures from internationally recognized scholars and authors, gaming tournaments, film series, symposia, poetry readings, impromptu group study, and casual gatherings.

One of the more popular events is the town and gown lectures series hosted by the library. These lectures are designed to build community between the campus and local surrounding areas by offering collaborative panels of speakers. Ideas for these lectures are diverse and come from many sources. Librarians, faculty, students, and members of the local community are encouraged to send their ideas to the library administration. Allowing anyone to make a suggestion has helped to create a wide variety of lectures. The library has hosted town and gown lectures on topics such as backyard astronomy, illiteracy, homelessness, the presidential election process, gardening, leisure and travel, home improvement, English as a new language, and recycling.

When a topic is cleared by the library administration, a team is set up for each event. If the person suggesting the topic is a library worker, then that person usually becomes the event organizer, who is responsible for identifying and inviting speakers. If the idea for the event comes from outside the library, then a librarian is assigned to be the event organizer. Also on the event team is a representative from our library's Systems Department, to handle Internet connection and equipment setup; our library events coordinator, who is responsible for oversight of all library programming; our library public relations coordinator, who will advertise the event campuswide and in the local media; and any faculty expressing an interest to serve. The team will initially meet from six months to a year before the actual event in order to set a date and discuss possible speakers. They will then meet a few more times before the event to firm up details. On the day or night of the lecture, library staff make sure that equipment and furniture are set up, while public relations staff handle temporary signage. The discussion panels usually comprise three to five experts from the university and surrounding area. Each panelist takes it in turn to present, and the event ends with panelwide discussion and an audience question-and-comment period. Some panelists supplement their lectures with video, PowerPoint slides, or artifacts, such as tools or reports. The event organizer usually serves as emcee and panel chair, making sure that the event runs smoothly and on time.

In 2006 ISU hosted one of its most successful town and gown lectures, called "Meth Valley: Why Here? Why Now?" bringing speakers together to discuss the methamphetamine problem in the local community and the country at large. A panel of experts, chaired by one of our reference librarians, reviewed the history of methamphetamine manufacture and abuse, including related social, legal, and economic issues. Panelists included a professor of criminology from ISU, a sergeant from the Indiana State Police Department, and a drug abuse counselor from a local rehabilitation center. An audience of about 40 was expected. Instead, 108 people showed up from the campus and surrounding local community. We did not have enough chairs, so many people sat on the carpeted floor. No one seemed to mind. Feedback from this program was extremely positive, demonstrating to us that we had provided a valued and important service in hosting this event. Another highly successful event was "What's at Stake in the State in 2008," in which a panel of faculty and community leaders discussed the gubernatorial and local electoral races.

Besides educating the local community, these events supplement the curriculum, because many professors bring their classes to these town and gown lectures.

Any academic library can host a lecture series. Because our campus is committed to community engagement, the ISU Library benefits from support mechanisms not in place in other libraries. Most academic libraries do not have their own public relations coordinator or events coordinator. But setting up a successful town and gown lecture series need not be difficult or costly. We offer no honoraria to town and gown speakers, because they are all local. As long as a laptop with Internet access, a projection screen, a large table, a microphone, and chairs are available, no new equipment need be purchased. For libraries that have not hosted such events before, offering just two town and gown lectures a year would be a good start. The benefits of doing so are many. Our experience has shown that we increased public awareness of our university by drawing in potential stakeholders who had never visited us before. We offered expert speakers for campus-bound students who don't have the time or money to hear off-site speakers. Our speakers benefit as well. Many have enjoyed presenting to new audiences, and they note their town and gown presentations on their resumes. A lecture series of this nature can provide rich opportunities for academic libraries to make connections and build partnerships with the local community.

59

A FRIEND IN NEED

Partnering with an Employment Center

Elaine Williams

THE LIBRARY'S partnership with the Highland County Employment Center began with a local crisis. In 2008, as gas prices rose and businesses in the area failed, life became difficult for our patrons in the rural village of Lynchburg, Ohio. The library itself suffered the economy's ill effects: our branch hours were slashed from sixty hours per week to only forty-four. Finally, the worst news came: our region's largest employer, ABX/Airborne Express, announced that they would be closing and laying off 8,000 workers in waves over the following months. This was devastating news in Lynchburg. Most new people who moved in had been transferred to ABX, and many new homes had been built to accommodate the incoming families. It seemed that every household in Lynchburg had someone employed at the airpark. Now the library's new challenge was to do something to help the scores of displaced workers created by ABX.

A NEW PARTNERSHIP

After a videoconference on a new state website for job seekers, the library director asked me to set up a meeting with the manager of the Highland County Employment

Center. During this meeting, which was attended by the director, the computer service librarian, and another branch manager, I learned what a terrific resource the employment center is, and I began to think about what more we could do. In the next month, we offered four computer classes and a resume workshop at our branch. Rick Thompson, the center's manager, had stated that one of the advantages the library has over the center is its hours of operation. I calculated that our branch in Lynchburg was actually open only one half hour more a week than the employment center. If our small branch was to support the center, we would have to develop some off-site programs.

COMPARING NOTES

In thinking about a partnership with the employment center, I listed what each party could bring to the table. The list looked like this:

EMPLOYMENT CENTER	LIBRARY
up-to-date collection of resources on one topic	trained researcher
more experience in partnering with agencies	passion to help others
more space, more computers, central location	open two evenings/Saturday
knowledge of funding sources	slightly larger staff
experience in working with nontraditional situations	experience with more topics
expertise in social services and job-seeking resources	larger collection of books

I also made a list of our respective limitations. These were factors that might hinder a partnership and would have to be overcome:

EMPLOYMENT CENTER	LIBRARY
small staff of 3: all full-time	small staff of 6: 2 full-time, 4 part-time
short hours	short hours; limited space
huge workload	busy: difficult to schedule off-site time
"stigma" of sharing building with welfare office	only four computers with Internet access

Next, I thought about the needs of each organization. The employment center's most pressing need was to find ways to meet requests for workshops on topics such as resume preparation, planning job searches, and interviewing skills. Over 9,000 people came through the center in 2007, and many more were expected soon. Many of the hours our branch lost were evening hours during which special events, group tours, and group meetings were scheduled. We needed to reach audiences with our programs, and we were always looking for ways to reach those citizens who neither use the library nor think of it as a job-hunting resource.

BRAINSTORMING

After this analysis of our respective missions, strengths, and weaknesses, I stopped by the employment center to brainstorm some ideas for off-site library services. Working together, we came up with several ideas. Thompson mentioned that an outside party had recently called to request more resume workshops. This immediate need gave us the idea for all-day resume workshops. The morning session would include information about resumes in general, and the afternoon would involve hands-on resume writing. Each attendee would leave with a resume. Those who came through the employment center also demonstrated needs for interviewing skills, dressing for success, and writing cover letters. We thought that these would be good topics for half-day workshops at the center. We also discussed placing pathfinders about library resources in the employment center and cowriting a small grant to help the center get a hundred copies of a certain workbook they used for their ongoing Job Club. We ended the meeting with the promise that we would look at our calendars for good times and dates to present workshops together.

This second meeting proved to be timely. Less than a week later, ABX announced that they would be permanently closing in February 2009. Thompson immediately scheduled me for two workshops on each of two consecutive Mondays, based on the available days we had discussed. Our new partnership is now well under way!

To summarize, the suggested steps needed to form a partnership between a library and a local employment center are as follows:

1. Talk with your supervisor about your idea for a partnership. Take a copy of the library's mission statement and that of the employment center.

2. Meet with the manager of the center to find out whether a partnership appeals to him. Find out what the center's needs are; brainstorm ways of meeting mutual needs.

3. Identify a time line. When are library staff available? What does the employment center already have on its schedule? Are there any upcoming special events that the library can cosponsor?

4. Once projects or joint events are scheduled, work out the details of what will happen that day and what each agency will be providing. The librarian and the manager might have different notions of how to present information to the public, so communicate your ideas clearly. Rely on what you know about each other's strengths and particular resources during these discussions.

5. Strengthen the new partnership by sharing the workload. Involve other interested staff members and outside experts for extra hands and fresh ideas.

Hopefully, most library partnerships are not necessitated by local economic crises. Find out what your community offers now, and the library will be better prepared to step right in should your community's needs begin to change quickly.

60
GUEST READER STORYTIME
Fenton Area Outreach Project

Christine K. Heron

"REAL READING readiness is accomplished quite simply; through exposure to language and print in all their forms."[1] The Fenton Area Librarians Committee began meeting in 1999, and the meetings were designed to allow collaboration on projects that encourage children to read. The committee comprised Fenton Area Public Schools media specialists and librarians from the Genesee District Library, the public library in Fenton, Michigan. One media specialist from each of the three elementary schools, the middle school, and the high school attended. Members from the Genesee District Library included the children's librarian, the adult services librarian, and the director of support services. On occasion, the Fenton school superintendent and the executive director from the Genesee District Library would attend. The meetings were held twice a year in the children's center of the public library. The three major projects were

1. Library card registration drive
2. Coordinating Accelerated Reader lists
3. Favorite Teachers Summer Story Hours

Favorite Teachers Summer Story Hours began with six to eight teachers who volunteered to read 30–40 minutes once a week over the eight-week Summer Reading Club period. Eventually the program evolved into Guest Reader Storytime featuring teachers, administrators, and staff from the Fenton Area Public Schools.

Beginning in 2003 the Guest Reader Storytime became an annual summer event that corresponded with the Summer Reading Club, which encouraged children to continue reading over the summer. Early in the spring, the children's librarian from the Genesee District Library contacted the high school media specialist to begin recruiting volunteers who would read to the children at the public library. She recruited volunteers by sending an e-mail to all employees of the Fenton Area Public Schools. Once she received the names of potential volunteers, she created an Excel spreadsheet to list the names, e-mails, addresses, and phone numbers of the volunteers. The children's librarian scheduled the dates and times the program would be held at the library. A school board member then met with each volunteer to coordinate the schedule of readers. The children's librarian contacted each volunteer ahead of time to confirm participation in the program. Occasionally, she would gather stories for the volunteers to read if the volunteers had not already selected stories. All publicity was handled by the Genesee District Library. Brochures and fliers were given to the public to announce the Guest Reader Storytime. Posters were displayed in the library. Press releases were given to the two local newspapers. Additional publicity was provided through the teachers, who included in their end-of-the-year student newsletters the dates they would be reading at the library. The children's librarian set up the room for each program and provided additional supplies as needed, like scissors or glue. When the summer ended and school resumed, the school board member met with each volunteer to express appreciation on behalf of the school district and the library. This school board member was in a unique position of serving for both organizations as a school board member and a library board member. In some years a small token of appreciation was given to each volunteer such as a bookmark, a paperback copy of a book, or a handmade thank-you card.

Attendance often varied from a small group of five to as many as twenty-five school- and preschool-age children. Regular audience participants were from the following groups:

- other teachers and their children
- friends and relatives of the volunteer readers
- neighborhood day care
- drop-in day care visitors

This Guest Reader program has continued to be a success over the past five years. The frequency of the storytimes has varied each summer based on other summer programs and the number of volunteers available. We've had as many as three sessions a week for twelve weeks and as few as two sessions a week for four weeks. There are a couple of teachers who return to read every year. The children have favorite teachers they want to hear. Providing a craft for the children is optional; however, some of the best-attended storytimes were by teachers who provided a fun activity along with the story. One teacher read the story *Me First* by Helen Lester. This story is about Pinkerton, who is a greedy little pig. He wants to be the first one to get a sandwich. Pinkerton is very surprised when he finds out what a sandwich really is. Following the story, each child received two pieces of bread and a variety of condiments to make an ultimate sandwich. Some children used peanut butter and marshmallows; others used grape jelly and lettuce. Another teacher read stories about ants and served watermelon to the children on red-and-white-checked tablecloths. Providing a craft or activity after the story helps children with the discovery and creative process in addition to fostering a love of reading.

We continue to offer this program as a way to outreach to the public school community. We reach the teachers, administrators, staff, students, and their families. Each summer we register hundreds of new patrons. In 2008 we registered 696 children for the Summer Reading Club. These statistics continue to go up each year. The Fenton Area Public Schools continue to enroll new students of all ages. There are over 3,700 students in the Fenton school system.[2] Working with the school district, the Guest Reader Storytime is an activity that helps "to form a relationship with agency personnel, building connections that can lead to further cooperative efforts and become a vehicle for the library to reach out to new family audiences."[3]

NOTES

1. Betty Farber, ed., *The Parents' and Teachers' Guide to Helping Young Children Learn: Creative Ideas from 35 Respected Experts* (Cutchogue, NY: Preschool Publications, 1997).
2. Fenton Area Public Schools, "2006–07 Fenton Area Public Schools Annual Report," www.fenton.k12.mi.us (accessed October 30, 2008).
3. Sandra Feinberg, Joan F. Kuchner, and Sari Feldman, *Learning Environments for Young Children: Rethinking Library Spaces and Services* (Chicago: American Library Association, 1998).

61

LOCAL ARTISTS-IN-RESIDENCE AT YOUR SCHOOL LIBRARY

Jan Siebold

"OUR WORK Is Child's Play." That is the motto of Fisher Price Toys, an internationally known toy company that is based in East Aurora, New York, the hometown of my school. Many of the company's designers and marketers reside in East Aurora, and some are parents of our students.

East Aurora is also known for the Roycroft, an arts and crafts guild that was founded by the philosopher Elbert Hubbard in the late nineteenth century. The guild was a thriving community of bookbinders, leather craftsmen, potters, weavers, and furniture makers whose products were known worldwide. Several of the original Roycroft buildings still stand and have been designated as national landmarks. A thriving group of master artisans actively keeps the Roycroft spirit alive through art festivals and demonstrations.

The proximity of these two valuable resources represented an opportunity for our students that was too important to ignore. As school library media specialist, I decided to investigate the possibility of an artist-in-residence program that would tap into local artistic talent. I enlisted several teachers and parents to serve on an Arts in Education Committee.

Having attended a New York Library Association/School Library Media Section conference at which the New York Foundation of the Arts (NYFA) was featured, I decided to explore that resource first. I discovered that NYFA would provide a consultant to help us plan our program if we could match their contribution toward the consultant's fee. My principal generously offered funding from her special programs account.

Our NYFA consultant flew in from New York City and spent three days in East Aurora. During her visit, she and the committee met with representatives from Fisher Price and the Roycroft to discuss possible partnerships. We also did long-range planning and determined ways to maintain support for an artist-in-residence program. NYFA places a major emphasis on finding ways to gain local funding and support so that programs will be sustained.

During the first year of our program, a Roycroft bookbinding artist who also specialized in marbled papers worked with our students to create exquisite accordion poetry books. We focused on connections with our school's language arts curriculum by incorporating the writing program into the residency. Funding for this program came from the PTO. Public relations played a huge role in capturing interest and funds for the following year.

The bookbinding project was so successful that we were able to invite a papermaking artist for our next residency. Imagine a large tent set up on the lawn behind our school. (There is a lot of water used in papermaking!) Inside the tent, every student and teacher had a chance to create five or six sheets of beautiful paper, which again was used in a variety of writing and art activities. Science and ecology connections were also woven into the project.

By the time our second residency was completed, the PTO had built funds into their budget to continue into the next year. For the third year of the program we decided to focus on the theme of toys and to take advantage of our Fisher Price partnership.

In terms of the curriculum, the toy theme fit nicely into social studies lessons about community, goods and services, careers, and inventions. Before the actual artist's residency, we invited a Fisher Price toy designer to speak to classes about the design process. Using poster boards, raw materials, and parts of unassembled toys, he showed the students all of the steps involved in the creation of a toy from the birth of the idea to the finished product.

We also hosted a visit by a local author who had written a book about toy trains. A teddy bear and doll expert came to show her collection to the students. Students conducted a survey to find out about their parents' and grandparents' favorite childhood toys. They compiled the survey results and used the information in several curriculum-related activities.

That spring I also applied for and received the Cultural Media Award sponsored by the School Library Media Section of the New York Library Association. With the award money I purchased a trunk and filled it with replicas of antique toys. Our Traveling Trunk is still used by teachers to give students a hands-on experience with toys that were used by children during the nineteenth and twentieth centuries. The trunk also contains lesson plans, books, and journal articles about the history of toys. It is cataloged and housed in the library and circulates within the school district and beyond.

Our artist-in-residence that year was a woman who created shadow dancers, which are silhouette toys that have movable arms and legs. Every student created and decorated a tag board shadow dancer to take home.

During the following school year we decided to add a performance aspect to our program. The Arts in Education Committee visited a neighboring school in which an active parent puppet troupe performed for students.

We came back home and set to work. For our first play we chose *The Tailor of Gloucester* by Beatrix Potter. The parents, some of whom are artists and designers, created amazing puppets and props. Our first season was a huge success. During the following year we added *Sylvester and the Magic Pebble* by William Steig to our repertoire. That play featured an interactive scene in which students in the audience used dog stick puppets (created in their art class) to "search" for the missing Sylvester.

The benefits of tapping into such local resources are immeasurable. After each residency was completed, the Arts in Education Committee heard countless stories about the carryover into students' lives. Many parents reported that their child's interest in the community was sparked by the programs. Teachers enjoyed creating lesson plans that integrated the residencies into the curriculum. Our students became much more knowledgeable about their community and about the creative process.

In every community there is a creative pool of talent from which to draw. The keys to a successful artist-in-residence program are planning, making meaningful curriculum connections, and involving administrators, parents, teachers, and community partners.

62

PARTNERING FOR LIFELONG LEARNING
A Unique Collaboration

Catherine Fraser Riehle

AS THE role of academic libraries transforms and diversifies in the digital information age, the role of academic librarians is changing as well. Audiences, resources, services, and spaces are changing, and the role of the academic librarian is morphing from traditionally passive to proactive, as outreach and engagement both on and off campus are on the rise. Many academic libraries are charging librarians with "outreach" as part of their primary job responsibilities and even their job titles. Academic libraries, like their public counterparts, are venturing into their communities more than ever, communicating their relevance and extending resources and services in ways many have not used before. This chapter will describe one such venture, in the form of a partnership between the Purdue University Libraries and the Lafayette Adult Resources Academy (LARA), a local social services organization.

KEY PLAYERS

Purdue University. Purdue University is a large, comprehensive research university in West Lafayette, Indiana. This land-grant institution has a long-standing reputation for contributions and engagement in the community. Faculty and staff in departments and offices across campus hail community outreach as a key goal and establish partnerships and develop programs with and for local schools, businesses, and other organizations in the community and region.

Purdue University Libraries: New Initiatives, New Roles. The Purdue Libraries have recently begun to increase efforts to engage the local community. One particular initiative was establishing my position, instructional outreach librarian, a new role created to extend and promote services and resources to underrepresented groups both on and off campus. In this new role I have developed and implemented programs and services for a wide range of audiences, from incoming international students to K–12 groups and local social services organizations. During my first year in this role I focused on campus, learning about the community and developing new services for incoming freshmen, honors and international students, and adult and nontraditional students. In my second year I began seeking and forming partnerships off campus and performing both formal and informal needs assessment. I began developing information sessions for school groups and collaborating with public librarians to offer research and information literacy programs for teens. One way I searched for potential partners was to watch the local news and skim the local newspaper, which is how I became acquainted with LARA in the summer of 2008.

The Lafayette Adult Resources Academy. I stumbled across LARA in a local news story that highlighted the organization's goals of encouraging and supporting lifelong learning, and it occurred to me that this was an organization with goals not unlike those of the Purdue Libraries. Founded in 1976, LARA exists "to teach academic and life skills to enable learners to make productive, ongoing changes in their personal lives, in society, and in public policy," according to their website.[1] LARA provides programs that help learners improve academic and life skills for successful entry or retention in the workforce, including work skills development, workplace literacy, ESL, corrections education, and special needs education.

PROGRAMMING WITH AND FOR LARA

Establishing a Partnership. Soon after reading about LARA, I sent an e-mail to the organization's assistant director to introduce myself and explain my role and the Purdue Libraries' new community engagement initiatives. I highlighted our shared goals and asked if she would be willing to meet and discuss ways we could potentially work together. When I met with LARA's director several weeks later, I realized I had found a special organization—one whose staff worked tirelessly to support adult education and workplace rehabilitation in the community—often with staff shortages and uncertain funding support. I was told that many LARA learners lacked computer skills, which often impeded them from entering or reentering the workforce, and we decided that I would explore the possibility of offering technology-related workshops for LARA learners. Thus I began the process of formal and informal needs assessment: I met with LARA teachers to share my initial ideas and to gather their feedback and suggestions; I began volunteering in an ESL class one evening a week to get to know learners and their needs; and I accepted an invitation to join LARA's advisory board, which provided a fantastic opportunity to learn about the challenges, work, and goals of the organization as well as other organizations in the community. Finally, I developed a survey to distribute to learners in order to determine their technology-related needs and interests.

Needs Assessment. Because of a wide range of literacy levels, I strove to be as concise and clear as possible while developing the survey. The tool consisted of three primary sections: one for basic demographic information and preferences (age, class time, and frequency); one on technologies available at home (computer/Internet); and one to gauge learners' interest in a variety of technology-related topics. Topics were divided into two sections: basic computer skills (MS Office, printing a document, installing a program) and another on Internet/research skills (evaluating information on the Web, research in college classes, and searching the Internet). While developing this survey, feedback from LARA teachers and administrators proved invaluable, as they reminded me of important considerations such as readability. I developed a survey that could be read at a fourth-grade level, so it would be readable for the majority of LARA learners. Within three weeks, over one hundred learners had completed the needs assessment. Findings revealed that the majority of respondents had access to both computers and the Internet at home. Although interest in nearly all the topics was consistently high, learners were most interested in topics pertaining to the Internet, especially searching for information, finding quality information, using social technologies, communicating via e-mail, and evaluating information online.

Program Planning. Based on the survey results, I began the process of planning a pilot series of classes to offer at LARA. The first series, geared toward beginning-level learners, included three sessions: one on Internet basics, one on finding and evaluating information online, and another on communicating online. After participating in the series, learners were able to access and navigate the Internet, use a search engine to find quality information, and send and retrieve e-mail. After evaluating the first pilot series, I hope to work with LARA to address some of the other needs and interests indicated in the survey results, by offering another series for intermediate learners or by offering stand-alone workshops on topics such as MS Office and research in secondary education. I look forward to continuing and strengthening this partnership while making a difference in the community by teaching skills for personal development and lifelong learning. The partnership between the Purdue Libraries and LARA also continues to open doors for additional partnerships and collaborations via my involvement in LARA's advisory board.

NOTE

1. Lafayette Adult Resources Academy, "Philosophy in a Nutshell," www.lsc
.k12.in.us/laraweb/mission/ (accessed October 14, 2008).

63

PARTNERING FOR DOLLARS
Using Grant Opportunities to Build Community and Provide Programming

Karen Brodsky

"I'M OFF to the Arts Council." "I will be at the public radio station." These are the excited statements from a busy librarian working to develop arts and lectures programs at an academic library. Academic libraries have a rich history of providing programs to enrich the lives of their students and faculty. For an academic library without an active Friends group, allocating librarian time to partner with the community is one way to ensure lively arts and lectures programs. By partnering for national grants, we have been able to expand the breadth of our offerings while maintaining energetic partnerships with the surrounding community. Such partnerships ensure meaningful and timely programs for the students, faculty, and people living within the Sonoma State University (SSU) area, which is located in Rohnert Park, California. This chapter will discuss the partnerships on two grants—the National Endowment for the Arts' Big Read project and the American Library Association's Let's Talk about It project.

WHERE DOES IT FIT? THE LIBRARY, THE COMMUNITY, AND THE GRANTS

One of the most important things a library must decide before beginning to work with the community, especially in applying for grants, is determining if the grant project and the community partnership align with the mission of the library.

SSU Library has several strategic initiatives, of which one is to provide a venue for the enrichment of student life and campus culture. One of the means for achieving this goal is providing dynamic art exhibits and lecture programs. We knew that participating with the community would expand our networks and, ultimately, add a unique element to our programs by drawing on a wider range of expertise.

Obviously, it is important to understand the needs of the community and be aware of projects in which collaboration makes good sense. In our community, there is a growing and committed arts and literary "scene," which made for perfect collaboration on numerous occasions and helped fulfill our mission. And while Sonoma County is a large area geographically, its small but growing population strongly participates in cultural activities.

The Big Read project was one example where the expectations of the funding opportunity matched the needs of the community *and* supported the mission of the library. The Big Read, a program sponsored by the National Endowment for the Arts in cooperation with Arts Midwest, brings together partners across a community to encourage citizens to read for pleasure and enlightenment. Our county had been working on something called "Sonoma County Reads" for several years with great success. The Big Read seemed a natural extension. Our community applied for Big Read grants for two consecutive years. The first Big Read grant encouraged all residents of Sonoma County to read Ray Bradbury's *Fahrenheit 451* and participate in a wide variety of activities. For the second Big Read grant, activities focused on Harper Lee's *To Kill a Mockingbird.*

The ALA's Let's Talk about It program is another national funding opportunity our library received. The Let's Talk about It program provides funding to present lecture and discussion groups on different topics surrounding Jewish literature. This particular project requires that libraries partner with a local scholar to lead discussions with community members on preselected books. It was another natural fit for both the library and the community's interests.

HOW TO PARTICIPATE

Community partnerships seem to work best when each group plays to its own strengths. For example, the Big Read project was administered overall through the local public radio and television station, which had the capacity to handle the administrative execution of the project. Our library hosted and coordinated an art exhibition titled "Those Who Don't Build Must Burn: An Installation in Response to Ray Bradbury's *Fahrenheit 451*" by local artist Brooke Holve, whose interpretation of the book challenged college students and local high school students whose classes read the book. The public library coordinated book readings in each community, and the local independent film house sponsored showings of the film version of the book. The unique perspectives each organization brought to the discussions helped ensure that the programs created reflected the diverse interests of the community. On a side note, it was fascinating to work with school, public, and academic libraries.

The Let's Talk about It project didn't have the community involved in developing a wide variety of programs but rather in helping to ensure the series attracted a wide audience. The community partners in this case who helped in the promotion of the series included local synagogues, senior centers, student groups, and the networks established from our participation in programs such as the Big Read.

EVALUATION

For both grants, the visions and insights shared by a wide range of participants helped ensure that the goals of each program were met. For each project, specific evaluation outcomes were provided as required by the funder. Assessment on the local level included quantitative data such as numbers of participants, media queries, and hits to websites and qualitative data such as survey responses from students and teachers and at events, which were used to evaluate the success of the overall program. Each participating group also had individual evaluation tools. We evaluated such things as the number of people attending events in our building, comments from program participants, and the number of new community borrowers.

CONCLUSION

For our library, where community means supporting our users through engaging services and collections, bringing people into our facility, friend building, and being a good member of the larger community, local participation helps us meet our library's mission in ways we could not have done alone—perhaps the ultimate meaning of community.

64
PARTNERING WITH A LOCAL PARK OR HISTORICAL AGENCY

Florence M. Turcotte

DO YOU see a natural fit between materials in your library and the theme of a local historical landmark or park? If so, then you may want to consider collaborating with the folks who run the park, museum, or landmark to supplement the experience for their visitors and help promote your collection at the same time. Literary landmarks, you might imagine, have a natural connection to books and printed materials. An example of one such successful partnership is described below. On the other hand, your library might have a collection related to a historical figure with local roots or an event that took place in your area, for example, a Civil War battle. People visiting a park or landmark related to that person or event may want to learn more as a result of their visit, and your library might be a good place for them to turn. Once you have your idea, follow these steps for setting up a collaboration.

Identify Related Materials. You may want to produce a bibliography, brochure, or even an exhibit to publicize your collection to visitors of the park or historic landmark. Rare, unique materials or collections of unusual objects are good candidates. Are there materials in your collection that complement the holdings of a local museum?

Meet with Interested Stakeholders. Talk to the director or public relations person at the park or landmark about setting up your collaboration. Find out if school groups are regular visitors. If they are, you may want to tailor your promotional material for an elementary- or middle-school-age group. If retirees are their mainstay visitor group, then ideas for collaborative activities might include lectures, demonstrations, and exhibit-type activities.

Identify Common Goals and Strategies. Try to identify common goals, communicate them to each other, and figure out how to achieve them together. Your approach will be significantly different depending on whether your goal is to encourage serious researchers on a particular subject or to have local children have an enjoyable encounter with a historical person or place. Would access to your collections or attendance at a special workshop help park rangers improve their interpretive programs? Can you produce an FAQ document that would help docents with their training?

Get Some Funding. Local tourist development councils, Friends groups, and state and local granting agencies are all sources of funding for such programs. Many collaborative activities cost next to nothing to produce; they just need creative energy and time.

It's a Win-Win Situation! With a successful collaboration, park visitors will have a better experience, and you will facilitate and increase access to your collections.

A LITERARY COLLABORATION

A good example of a successful community partnership between an archival repository and a historic landmark is the one established between the Marjorie Kinnan Rawlings Manuscript Collection at the University of Florida and the Marjorie Kinnan Rawlings Historic State Park in Cross Creek, Florida, about twenty miles southeast of the campus.

Pulitzer Prize–winning author Marjorie Kinnan Rawlings came to north-central Florida in 1928 on vacation with her first husband Charles, who was also an aspiring writer. Marjorie instantly fell in love with the place, and at her urging she and Charles sold all they had, bought a dilapidated farmhouse and a neglected grove in the tiny community of Cross Creek, and moved there in November 1928. Marjorie stayed on after their divorce and eventually married hotel man Norton Baskin. She made Florida her primary home until her death and recorded her impressions of the subtropical landscape and the colorful cast of characters living in it.

When she died in 1953 at age fifty-seven, Rawlings left her manuscripts and correspondence to the University of Florida Library, as the core of the Creative Writing Collection. Since then, archivists at the university have processed, described, and added to this collection to build a comprehensive archive of the Rawlings's literary heritage.

Visitors to the Marjorie Kinnan Rawlings Historic State Park can walk back in time to 1930s farm life on a Florida homestead. Cross Creek has changed very little since Rawlings lived there. Her house is a notable example of the Cracker (descendants of pioneer settlers) style of architecture, derived from a variety of influences to suit the climate and available technology of the rural South. The actual home and farm where she lived for twenty-five years has been restored and is preserved as it was when she lived there. Visitors can tour Rawlings's farmyard, grove, and nature trails with a ranger in period costume. There is no air-conditioning, no visitor center, and no gift shop on the premises.

One of the priorities of the Rawlings Historic State Park staff is to maintain the authenticity of the park and provide interpretive programs that will transport visitors into Rawlings's world. Much of the success of these programs is attributable to the *research and comprehensive training of the interpretive staff*. This training is accomplished by allowing staff access to the archive material firsthand and through published versions. Tour guides are encouraged to visit the collection and do their own research and writing about Rawlings. All of this requires a close *cooperative relationship* between the archives staff and the park personnel.

Other collaborative activities include developing promotional materials together, arranging tours for students and researchers by park personnel at Cross Creek, and referring visitors with questions to the manuscripts curator. Interpretive tour leaders do their research in the manuscript collection on a regular basis, and the curator participates on many levels in activities and events at Rawlings Historic State Park and at the Marjorie Kinnan Rawlings Elementary School. The curator of the collection at the University of Florida serves on the board of trustees of both the Citizens Support Organization of the park and the Marjorie Kinnan Rawlings Literary Society, which is charged with promoting the Rawlings's literary legacy and also publishes the *Marjorie Kinnan Rawlings Journal of Florida Literature*. These partnerships serve to broaden the community of stakeholders in both locations and to enrich research, educational, and interpretive programs.

A significant outcome of this collaboration was the conferral of National Historic Landmark status on the park. The National Historic Landmark designation is the highest such recognition accorded by our nation to historic properties determined to be of exceptional value in representing or illustrating an important theme, event, or person in the history of the nation. National Historic Landmarks can be actual sites where significant historic events occurred, places where prominent Americans worked, or sites that represent the ideas that shaped our nation. Fewer than 2,500 historic places carry the title of National Historic Landmark. During the application process, support documentation was gathered from the collection, from the library administration, and from the Marjorie Kinnan Rawlings Society, as well as from major Rawlings scholars. Without the combined efforts of all these parties, the application would not have been successful.

This partnership has helped to cultivate a community interested in Marjorie Kinnan Rawlings as a writer, as a Floridian, as a twentieth-century woman, and as a major literary figure on the national scene. As is the case with every successful collaboration, both parties accomplished their goals more effectively and benefited from the community partnership.

65

PARTNERING WITH YOUR LOCAL HISTORICAL SOCIETY

Elaine Williams

DURING MY career as a librarian, my library's most fruitful partnership has been with the local historical society. As a twenty-something "new kid in town," it took a while for my relationship with the historical society to blossom. I wasn't confident enough to venture out into the community at first. Befriending the unofficial town historians helped me learn enough local history to be able to answer simple reference questions. I became a member of the fledgling Lynchburg (OH) Historical Society after having been involved, at their behest, in a few projects at the beginning of their incarnation. I soon became aware that the library's mission and that of the historical society are mutually inclusive.

A SHARED MISSION

The Lynchburg Branch Library's pledge to "provide materials and access to resources in order to meet the educational and informational needs of its users" is a good match for three of the stated purposes of the Lynchburg Historical Society:

- to gather and preserve historical information . . . of Lynchburg and the surrounding area
- to make the information and materials available to the public
- to educate and instill a sense of appreciation of the . . . history and heritage of the area

This was the first step in our partnership—the decision to work together due to a shared interest in meeting common goals.

BRINGING SOMETHING TO THE TABLE

The first programs jointly sponsored by the library and the historical society took place in the library building. The first two years of the society's meetings were held in the library's meeting room. The library also received donations such as artifacts and reference books for pickup by historical society members. We held receptions for local artists and veterans, undertook oral history interviews, and hosted guests who spoke on historical topics. The historical society used the library building as a sign-up location for volunteers and events and our office equipment to fax, copy, and type up information. These particular library resources solved many problems for the historical society. The society has no building, nor any hours of operation;

therefore, without the library, its mission of making materials available to the public would be difficult to meet. Although our historical society members have riches of Lynchburg history stored in their memories and attics, few are comfortable with computers, and so the work of e-mailing announcements and making fliers is another task for which I volunteered.

BRANCHING OUT

The most effective joint offerings of the library and historical society have been off-site. The library's small meeting room could not hold everyone who took part in some of the Ohio Bicentennial events, such as the following.

A two-day Building Doctors program, in which experts from Columbus, Ohio, came to Lynchburg and gave general tips about restoring old homes. The Building Doctors visited homes over fifty years old to diagnose and prescribe treatment for structural and interior problems. The library wrote the application essay and organized the event with Columbus, and the historical society recruited people with older homes and provided the costs of lodging the experts.

A Historic House Tour of thirteen homes in and around Lynchburg. Society members provided photos and information, and the library designed and printed the color brochures and provided a place for attendees to sign up.

Recovering an old cemetery with Make a Difference Day grant monies. The library wrote the grant, researched tombstone care, and signed up volunteers; the society provided matching funds, helped create the budget, and purchased supplies.

The society identified citizens of the village to be interviewed and then paid my expenses for a three-day Oral History Institute. They also purchased interviewing equipment. In return, I conducted the interviews, transcribed and printed the transcripts, and delivered copies to the library, the historical society, and the interviewees' family members.

More examples of successful off-site events: opening of a 1917 time capsule, unveiling of a mural painted on a historic building, and visiting third-grade classes to present "Lynchburg Then and Now" local history units.

All of these plans came to fruition because the library and the historical society shared a passion for preserving local history and getting information to the public.

CONSIDERATIONS

There are several thoughts to keep in mind when forging a relationship with the local historical society.

1. Support from the library administration is essential. Involvement with outside agencies will take time and staff away from in-house library duties.

2. Cosponsored programs should satisfy the goals of both organizations. For example, the library decided not to share the cost of expensive advertising in a regional tourist publication, so the historical society went ahead on its own. We also have no input into awarding the historical society scholarship besides reading and rating the student essays.

3. Be careful with funding issues. I was asked to purchase two prints of a painting of the Lynchburg Covered Bridge for the society. The library director authorized me to buy one for the library as well. Unfortunately, I paid for all three prints with library money and caused problems for our library's clerk-treasurer. Make sure you have approval for anything that requires funding from the library.

4. Remain as neutral as possible. Just as history delves far into the past, so do grudges between longtime residents. When calling veterans for interviews, I unwittingly unearthed some volatile feelings. Apparently there was a rivalry between vets who had seen foreign combat and those who had stayed stateside. Those with hurt feelings wanted to vent; I listened and politely ended the conversation. Similarly, it's best to ignore gossip and stay out of disputes between society members.

MUTUAL BENEFITS

Ideally, both the library and the historical society should reap multiple benefits from their partnership. The library has gained knowledge and important friends. We are better equipped to answer questions such as "Can you tell me the history of my house?" and "What can you tell me about Lynchburg?" because of the historical society. The library has joined the society in becoming a strong link between village natives, longtime residents, and newcomers. Finally, the library has become an essential link between the historical society and the public. Without a building, open hours, or an official phone number, the society would not be able to achieve many of its goals without partnerships. However, the goal of the partnership itself is not to create one agency's dependence on another but to become interdependent. Libraries and historical societies should never be mutually exclusive. We all need each other in this work of satisfying the public's desire for information.

Librarians just getting started with this work may be surprised by outcomes stemming from a single introductory e-mail. With persistence, enthusiasm, careful planning, and a commitment from both partners to shared goals, much can be done to the benefit of both the public library and the community.

66

A UNIVERSITY LIBRARY REACHES OUT TO AN ENTIRE COMMUNITY

Iona R. Malanchuk

WOULD YOU like to offer a program that has the potential to attract the participation of local politicians, young children, American and international college students, professors and administrators, public, school, and college library staff, a local disc jockey, and an author or two? Consider organizing a Readathon in April in celebration of National Library Week. Or perhaps you could promote your library during another major event at a time when the weather will permit a similar outdoor program. Invite diverse groups of children and adults from your large community. You won't regret it. As word of this event spreads further each year, enthusiasm and support for your library will follow.

Six years ago a University of Florida Libraries committee organized a Readathon in celebration of literacy and libraries. Embraced by both the campus and the Gainesville, Florida, community at large, this successful program continues on an annual basis each April in conjunction with National Library Week. A diverse group of over fifty volunteers read aloud during this outdoor event. Students, local elected officials, campus administrators, international visitors, authors, and media personalities from both TV and radio sign up each year on our Readathon website. Some have returned each year to share a favorite book with others. They all help in the celebration of the valuable programs, services, and collections found in the many libraries located throughout their community.

HOW IS THE READATHON ORGANIZED?

A large canopy is put in place on the front lawn of the main library for the four days of the program. Volunteer readers stand at the front podium while reading aloud to those assembled on chairs in the audience. If it rains, the Readathon is moved inside the library. There is a different theme for each day of the Readathon. On Monday the theme might be Politics or International Day; on Tuesday it is frequently Children's Literature Day; on Wednesday the theme might be Southern Living Day or Humor Day; and Thursday is open microphone day, which sometimes includes readings of short stories or poetry. Food is provided at the lunch hour thanks to generous donations from local pizza restaurants, coffee shops, ice-cream stores, and supermarkets.

On Children's Literature Day we conclude the morning story hours with donated juice and cookies. Donated bottles of water are kept on hand for all readers, and many attendees bring their own morning coffee or lunch to enjoy outside while listening to many excellent interpretive readers. Be sure to choose a month when you normally have reliable weather for an outside event and one that is convenient for your staff.

WHERE DO THE VOLUNTEER READERS COME FROM?

University administrators, professors, undergraduate and graduate students, local politicians, public librarians, school media specialists, and local authors readily volunteer each year to spend anywhere from ten to twenty minutes reading from a favorite author or work of literature. A favorite couple on the faculty returns each year and elicits laugher each time they share reading aloud from Miss Manners.

If you are inviting your town mayor, the university president's wife, or a popular local disc jockey or author, they should receive a personal invitation from a designated committee member at least two months in advance. These are all busy people who need to get your Readathon into their full schedules early.

CHILDREN'S LITERATURE DAY

University faculty, students, and community political figures readily volunteer to read aloud in the morning from the works of Trina Schart Hyman, Louis Sachar, Tedd Arnold, Don and Audrey Wood, Ian Falconer, Dr. Seuss, and many other favorite young children's authors. Children sit on over a hundred donated carpet squares and are split into two groups, each group with a volunteer reader. This requires two speakers every ten minutes on Children's Literature Day instead of the customary single reader. The children arrive by foot, by bus, and, in some cases, by van. They enjoy being read to in the mid- to late morning hours. A local supermarket donates free drinks and cookies for the children's snack, and oftentimes, when they leave the canopy, they assemble on a lawn nearby to enjoy the picnic lunch brought by the preschool staff before they return to their school. The readers in the afternoon on this same day choose young adult novels. We frequently have groups from the English Language Institute at that time. The international students experience a new and challenging language activity while sitting among American students outside on the lawn in front of the main library.

THE ORGANIZING COMMITTEE

The eleven volunteer committee members represent library faculty and staff from both the public services and technical service areas of the library. Some committee members have served willingly since the first Readathon was organized in 2003. Each year every committee member is prepared to read aloud in case there are any no-shows or the volunteer reader does not take up his full ten-minute slot as scheduled.

The purpose of the Readathon is to promote reading and libraries, and it has been one favorite activity that people begin looking forward to months in advance.

AFTERWORD

THOSE OF you reaching this point in *Librarians as Community Partners: An Outreach Handbook* might have several outreach programs under your belt, while others might be exploring an outreach partnership with new potential for your school, public, or academic library. Some of you have been impressed by the breadth of work contained in these chapters, and others have searched to find ideas that will work to support a specific outreach. In any case, the creativity, commitment, and thoroughness of the many librarians in this volume are causing your mind to race with a plethora of ideas as to what you can do to increase your library's services and meet its mission. The ideas have been conceived, the outlines have been put forth, and the goals have been reached. Where to begin, what resources are needed, and which partners to approach are much clearer now. The information has been concise enough to allow for the duplication of these exemplary programs or to tailor them to fit your own specific needs. Authors have been timely as they have spoken to environmental issues, economizing costs, collaborating with schools, digitizing collections, developing one book–one read programs, and addressing diverse populations. Outreach partners ranging from local beaches to prisons have been identified in successful programs, and the steps for creating these programs have been laid out. The programs are enjoyable activities that are quite purposeful. More important, we as librarians are reaffirmed in our efforts to serve our communities, and our need to keep expanding our own knowledge base is satisfied.

This dynamic array of accomplishments makes one realize that librarians are not alone in our quest to make information accessible and reading more enjoyable.

Edith Campbell
Media Director, Arlington High School, Indianapolis

CONTRIBUTORS

Tiffany Auxier is youth and young adult services manager and assistant director of the Hinsdale Public Library, Hinsdale, Illinois. She obtained her MLS from Dominican University. Auxier has been awarded several outreach grants, and she developed an early literacy initiative that has served as a model for local organizations. She received a 50 under 50 Community Leadership award from the Community House in 2007 and participated in Synergy: The Illinois Library Leadership Initiative in 2005.

Kathy Barco is the author of *READiscover New Mexico: A Tri-Lingual Adventure in Literacy* (2007), winner of the 2008 New Mexico Book Award, Children's Activity Book category. She is also the coauthor (with Valerie Nye) of *Breakfast Santa Fe Style* (2006) and *Breakfast New Mexico Style* (2009). Barco is children's librarian at Albuquerque/Bernalillo County Public Library; she is also vice chair of the New Mexico Library Foundation Board of Trustees.

Bob Blanchard has been adult services librarian at the Des Plaines (IL) Public Library since 2000. He obtained his MLIS from Northern Illinois University. Blanchard is the 2008 recipient of the Illinois Library Association's Alexander J. Skrzypek award for his contributions to the advancement of library services for the blind or physically disabled in Illinois. His work has appeared in the Illinois Library Association's *Reporter* and in *Thinking Outside the Book: Essays for Innovative Librarians* (2008).

Karen Brodsky is an associate librarian who has worked at Sonoma State University in Rohnert Park, California, since 1997. Since 2000 she has directed the Library Arts and Lectures program, which includes lecture and discussion series, art exhibitions, and events. From 1998 to 2008 she was also library instruction coordinator at SSU, working toward the integration of information competence learning outcomes into the curriculum. She received her MLS from Simmons College in 1997.

Maureen Brunsdale has been an academic librarian since 1993 serving in distance education, reference and instruction, access services, and special collections. Since 1996 she has worked at the Milner Library, Illinois State University. Her work has appeared in *Reference and User Services Quarterly*, *Popular Culture in Libraries*, and in *Digital versus Nondigital Reference* (2004). Her library recently was awarded the John Cotton Dana Award for Public Relations.

John R. Burch Jr. is presently serving as director of library services at Campbellsville University. He reviews books for *American Reference Books Annual, CHOICE: Current Reviews for Academic Libraries,* and *Library Journal.* He is the author of *Owsley County, Kentucky, and the Perpetuation of Poverty* (2007) and the compiler of *The Bibliography of Appalachia* (2009). With Tim Hooper, he coauthored *Campbellsville University* (2008).

Edith Campbell has been media director at Arlington Community High School, Indianapolis, Indiana, since 2004. She obtained her MLS from Indiana University. Her writings have appeared in *Indiana Libraries* and *Viewpoints.* In 2006 she participated in the Leading Edge Librarian Academy through the Library Fund of the Indianapolis Foundation. She recently returned to her library after a year of teaching English in Taiwan and currently maintains the blog *Crazy Quilts* (http://camp bele.wordpress.com).

Delores Carlito is reference librarian for instruction and outreach at the Mervyn H. Sterne Library, University of Alabama at Birmingham. She has an MLIS from the University of Alabama, an MA in English from the University of Alabama at Birmingham, and an MAEd from the University of Alabama at Birmingham. Carlito frequently instructs area classes and professional development workshops. In addition to her library responsibilities, she teaches a course on critical thinking skills.

Sharon Carlson is director of the Western Michigan University Archives and Regional History Collections in Kalamazoo, Michigan. Her MLIS is from Wayne State University, and she holds a PhD in American history from Western Michigan University. She teaches courses on archival administration and research methods in archives and special collections. Her research interests include the use of archives and the history of women's organizations and public library development.

Chelsea Dinsmore holds an MA in history from the University of Florida. After obtaining her MLIS, she worked at the Harry Ransom Humanities Research Center, University of Texas. Her Gator roots pulled her back to Gainesville, Florida, and she became the international documents librarian at the University of Florida Libraries in 2004. She enjoys organizing bake sales and promoting her library in any way possible.

Mark Donnelly is an outreach librarian with the Special Services unit of Queens Library in New York City. The groups he works with include older adults, the disabled, the unemployed, and the incarcerated. He conducts memoir-writing workshops at senior centers and libraries, as well as oral history projects, drawing on his writing and teaching background. He serves as programmer for the New York Library Association's Roundtable for Special Populations.

Uma Doraiswamy is a librarian at Western Kentucky University, Bowling Green, Kentucky. She has a BA degree from Bangalore University, India, and worked as an instructor in English before coming to the United States. After getting her MLS from Emporia State University, Kansas, she worked for the Flint Hills Technical College Library, Kansas, and then for the State Library of Kansas. She writes book reviews for *Library Journal*.

Katya B. Dunatov is outreach language librarian (Russian) at the Arapahoe Library District, Colorado. She obtained her MLIS from the University of Illinois at Urbana-Champaign and has a PhD in Russian language. Before she became a librarian, Katya taught Russian language and culture courses in Russia, Norway, and the United States. The U.S. State Department has long recognized the Glendale branch of Arapahoe Library District where she works as exemplary in serving its Russian-speaking patrons.

Susan M. Frey is reference/instruction librarian at Indiana State University in Terre Haute. She contributed "Constructing Narrative to Situate Learning in Library Instruction" to *Practical Pedagogy for Library Instructors* (2008). She served as coordinator of one of the university's information literacy programs for elders, Bits 'n' Bytes, and works with others on the university library's town and gown lecture series.

Vera Gubnitskaia is youth services manager of the Orange County Library System, Orlando, Florida. She obtained her MLS from Florida State University. Her library received the ULC/Highsmith Award of Excellence for work with teen volunteers in 2006, LAMA Best of Show Awards in 2006 and 2007 for middle and high school reading lists, and the Community Partnership Award for Outstanding Support of and Dedication to the Orange County Citizens' Commission for Children in 2006.

Lynn Hawkins is executive director of the Mentor Public Library on the shores of Lake Erie, Ohio. She is coauthor of *High Tech, High Touch: Library Customer Service through Technology* (2003). Her articles on library collaborations and board-director relationships have been published in *Indiana Libraries*, and she has presented at state and national library conferences. During her tenure as director of the Mooresville Public Library in Indiana, her library received the Outstanding Indiana Library Award in 2004.

Christine K. Heron is senior librarian of children's services for the nineteen-branch library system of the Genesee District Library in Michigan. She has served on several outreach committees, including Reach Out and Read of Genesee County and the Michigan Reads! 0–5 Years Old: One Book, One Community initiative. Her professional activities include service on the Youth Library Services Advisory Committee to the state librarian and the Fenton Area Librarians Committee.

Margaret Keys has served as an instruction librarian at California State University, Sacramento, since 2007. She earned her MLIS from San Jose State University and her MA in English literature from California State University, Northridge. A former college English instructor and youth services librarian, her interest in education at all levels continues to inspire and inform her work.

Meryle Leonard is outreach manager for the Public Library of Charlotte and Mecklenburg County, North Carolina, and coordinates the design, development, and evaluation of a centralized delivery of outreach services for the twenty-four-branch system. Leonard was a 2007 Life Long Access Institute Fellow. Her library has received the 2006 National Award for Museum and Library Services, the John Cotton Dana Library Public Relations Award, and the 2008 Mora Award.

Iona R. Malanchuk is associate university librarian and head of the Education Library at the University of Florida, Gainesville. She has held academic library positions at Indiana University, Western Michigan University, and the University of Florida. She has recently been selected to receive the I Love My Librarian national award sponsored by the Carnegie Corporation, the *New York Times*, and the American Library Association.

Marian Matyn is archivist of the Clarke Historical Library and an assistant professor at Central Michigan University. She obtained her MLIS from the University of Michigan at Ann Arbor. She has been an archivist for nearly twenty years in Pennsylvania and Michigan and has worked with a variety of manuscripts dating from the late eighteenth century on. She is currently working on two books examining Michigan circuses and carnivals.

Nancy Kalikow Maxwell is library director at Miami Dade College's North Campus. She is the author of *Sacred Stacks: The Higher Purpose of Libraries and Librarianship* (2006), which explores the spiritual aspects of librarianship. She is a frequent contributor to *American Libraries*, and her writing has also appeared in the *Journal of Access Services*, *National Catholic Reporter*, and *Reform Judaism*, among others. She is working on a book entitled *The Reluctant Leader*.

Ellen Mehling is outreach librarian at Queens Library in New York City, where she conducts outreach for schools, community organizations, and senior centers on topics including job-hunting, reminiscing, health information, and customized presentations. Mehling's expertise includes serving patrons with disabilities, particularly those with visual or hearing impairment. She is a 2008 fellow of Libraries for the Future's Lifelong Access Libraries Institute, and she attended the 2008 conference, Creating Aging-Friendly Communities.

Maryann Mori is director of the Waukee (IN) Public Library. Formerly teen specialist librarian at the Evansville (IN) Vanderburgh Public Library, she expanded outreach efforts there to include information literacy instruction at schools. She has presented at the Internet Librarian Conference (2007), the American Library Association (2008), and elsewhere. Her work has appeared in *Public Libraries, Indiana Librarians,* and in *Social Networking Communities and e-Dating Services* (2008).

Mary H. Nino is interim associate dean at the San Jose State University Library, San Jose, California. She obtained her MLS from San Jose State University's School of Library and Information Science in 1988 and has worked in academic, public, and school libraries. Her interests include strategic planning, community outreach, and information literacy with young adults. Her work has appeared in the *Journal of Web Librarianship* and *Performance Measurement and Metrics.*

Catherine Fraser Riehle is instructional outreach librarian and an assistant professor at Purdue University. She has partnered with and developed programs for adult learners, homeschooling families, and K–12 groups, among others. She received the 2008 Indiana Library Federation's Collaboration Award with partners at the Tippecanoe County Public Library and Ivy Tech Community College, and she was named a 2008 ALA Emerging Leader. She is active in committees in the American Library Association and the Association of College and Research Libraries.

Loriene Roy is a professor in the School of Information of the University of Texas at Austin, where she teaches graduate courses in reference and public librarianship. She is Anishinabe, enrolled on the White Earth Reservation, a member of the Minnesota Chippewa tribe. She was the 2007–2008 president of the American Library Association. She is the director and founder of "If I Can Read, I Can Do Anything," a reading club for Native children.

Jamie Seeholzer is first-year experience librarian at Kent State University's Main Library in Kent, Ohio, where she provides outreach efforts to incoming freshmen in order to support the university's goal of providing a learner-centered environment that contributes to student retention and success. She is a member of Phi Beta Kappa and is working on a second master's degree in instructional technology. Her work appears in *Our New Public, A Changing Clientele* (2008).

Barbara A. Shatara has been outreach librarian at the Fletcher Free Library, Burlington, Vermont, since 1998. She received an MLS from the State University of New York at Albany. Prior to coming to Burlington, she was cataloger for the Williams College Slide Library in Williamstown, Massachusetts. She thanks the very talented AmeriCorps VISTA members Amber Gaster and Colleen Wright without whom the library's ESL services and this article would have been impossible.

Glennor Shirley is library coordinator for the Maryland State Department of Education's Correctional Education Libraries. She has an MAS from Johns Hopkins University and an MLS from the University of Maryland. She is a contributor to *Behind the Walls, A Day in the Life: Career Options in Library and Information Sciences* (2007), and she was the recipient of the 2008 James Partridge Award for

Outstanding African American Information Professional. Her blog is at http://prison librarian.blogspot.com.

Melissa Shoop is coordinator of instruction and outreach at Humanities and Social Sciences Library West, University of Florida at Gainesville. She earned an MA in English from Northern Illinois University and an MS in information studies from Florida State University. She joined the faculty at the University of Florida in 2006. Shoop coordinates the libraries' mentoring program with the University Writing program, working closely with the Dean of Students Office in library outreach.

Jan Siebold has been school library media specialist at Parkdale Elementary School in East Aurora, New York, since 1977. She received her MLS from the University of Buffalo. Siebold has served as secretary of the New York Library Association, and she received the New York Library Association/School Library Media Section's Cultural Media Award in 1992. She is the author of *Rope Burn* (1998), *Doing Time Online* (2002), and *My Nights at the Improv* (2005); these middle-grade novels have been named to numerous award lists.

Licia Slimon is reference/teen services librarian at the Whitehall Public Library, Pittsburgh. She earned her MLS from the University of Pittsburgh in 2006. In the past year her literacy program, Homework Club for English Language Learners, has doubled in size. Slimon's Teen Advisory Group has just completed their first video, which can be viewed on YouTube. She is a contributor to the online publication *Library Student Journal* and writes the blog *Librarian with a Purse* (http://librarian withapurse.blogspot.com).

Felicia A. Smith earned an MLIS and is outreach and Latino studies librarian at the University of Notre Dame. She previously worked as a criminal defense private investigator specializing in homicide and narcotics. She carried a .357 Magnum, which fellow librarians think may be useful in this profession. Her interest in criminal justice combined with her current job as outreach librarian naturally led to the creation of a Correctional Facility Literacy program.

Florence M. Turcotte is research services archivist and curator of literary manuscripts in Special Collections at the University of Florida. She was a contributor to *Academic Library Outreach: Beyond the Campus Walls* (2008), and she received the 2008 Employee Excellence Award for Outreach from the George A. Smathers Libraries, University of Florida, Gainesville. She received her MLIS degree from the University of South Florida and her BS and MA from Georgetown University.

Elaine Williams is a branch manager and youth librarian in the Highland County (OH) District Library System. Her eighteen-year library career includes work in both academic and public libraries, and she is an Ohio certified public librarian. Williams has been recognized locally for her work on behalf of the Lynchburg Historical Society and by the Ohio Memory Project, the Ohio Association of Community Action Agencies, and the Ohio Reads program.

INDEX

A

Abbott, Polly, 98
ABX/Airborne Express, 167
Academic Search Premier, 109
Academic STARS program, 146–147
The Adventures of Captain Underpants
    (Pilkey), 134
advertising
    for library docent program, 8
    for low-vision fair, 98–99
    Storytime @ the Pools, 16
    for studying at the library, 50
African Americans
    outreach to college students, 146–147
    Voice and Images project, 129–132
Agriculture, Department of, 121
Alachua County Library District (Florida),
    103–105
Albom, Mitch, 102
American Cancer Society, 17, 158
American Girl magazine, 136
American Library Association
    Let's Talk about It program, 18, 178
    Libraries Build Community theme, 137
    Presidential Citation on Innovation in
        International Librarianship, 133–134
    program grants, 18–19
American River College, 109–110
AmeriCorps VISTA program, 140, 142
An Na, 143
anniversary celebrations, library, 13–15
Appalachian State University, 88
Arapahoe Library District (Colorado),
    144–145, 148–150
Arcadia Publishing, 19
archival outreach
    integrating manuscripts into curriculum,
        110–114
    partnering with oral historians, 129–132
    Teaching American History Grants,
        119–121
Arlington Heights Memorial Library
    (Illinois), 97
Arnold, Tedd, 186
art galleries, library, 79–81

artists-in-residence program, 172–174
Arts Midwest, 102, 178
assistive technology, 98
Association of Africans Living in Vermont,
    140
athletes, student, 53–55
Auxier, Tiffany, 48–51, 153–155
Avi, 102

B

baby boomer outreach, future of, 37–40
Baird, Nancy, 163
Baldacci, David, 102
Baldwin Public Library (Pennsylvania),
    135
Barbara Bush Foundation, 157
Barnes and Noble Booksellers, 102, 163–
    165
Barnett, Cynthia, 105
Barnyard Song (Greene), 93
Barris, Chuck, 102
Baskin, Norton, 180
Bayside Library (Queens, NY), 29
Beach Reads program, 16–17
Bed Hogs (DiPucchio), 93–94
Beginning, Middle, and End game, 36
Benjamin and His Brother (film), 143
Berg, Elizabeth, 34
Bi-Folkal Kit, 34
Big Chickens (Helakoski), 93–94
Big Read project, 178
Bits 'n' Bytes program, 27–28
Black Beauty (Sewell), 96
Blanchard, Bob, 33–35, 97–99
Blast Off to Reading game, 72
Blume, Judy, 96
book festivals
    childhood favorites, 95–97
    Michigan Reads! project, 93–95
    One Community, One Story program,
        99–101
    SOKY Book Fest, 101–103
book flood, 137–139
book giveaway programs, 9–11, 16

book production
for community outreach, 19–21
Ethiopia Reads organization, 133
for memoir writing, 29–32
bookbinding project, 173
Books and Baskets event, 102–103
Bowling Green Public Library (Kentucky), 102
Bradbury, Ray, 178
Bragg, Rick, 102
Bread and Jam for Frances (Hoban), 95
Brittingham, June, 72
broadcasting industry, 85–87
Brodsky, Karen, 79–81, 177–179
Brothers, Nancy, 97
Brown, Marc, 102
Brunsdale, Maureen, 53–55, 75–77
Bryson, Bill, 34
budgets
Ethiopia Reads organization, 133
library anniversary celebrations, 14
for library art galleries, 81
for snacks and supplies, 50
Building Doctors program, 183
Burch, John R., Jr., 19–21, 87–89
Burhanna, Ken, 146–147
Burlington High School (Vermont), 142
Burton, LeVar, 102
Byrd, Robert, 119

C

California Library Association, 39
California State Library, 39
California State University, 109–110
"California: Transforming Life after 50" initiative, 39
Campbellsville University, 19–21, 87–89
Carle, Eric, 96
Carlito, Delores, 114–116
Carlson, Sharon, 119–121, 129–132
Carnegie Foundation, 27
Carpenter, John, 102
Central Kentucky News-Journal, 87
Central Michigan University, 110–114
chambers of commerce, 156–157
childhood favorites, 95–97
Children's Initiative, 45–48
Children's Literature Day, 186
circus collection, 75–77

Circus, 1870–1950 (Daniel), 76–77
Circus Fans Association, 77
Circus Historical Society, 77
Clarke Historical Library (Michigan), 110–114
classic books, 96–97
classroom outreach
archival outreach, 110–114
to middle schools, 109–110
science projects, 121–123
secondary classroom instruction, 116–118
teacher workshops, 114–116
teaching American history, 119–121
See also public school systems
Cleary, Beverly, 96
Cleveland Magazine, 161
Clewiston News (Florida), 78
CNN Hero, 133
Coben, Harlan, 102
Coca-Cola Corporation, 164
collaboration
on circus collection, 77
involving historical newspapers, 77–79
low-vision fair, 97–99
Teaching American History Grants, 119–121
See also community collaboration and outreach
Comerford, Kim, 97
Common Reading program, 103–105
community collaboration and outreach
artists-in-residence program, 172–174
Dinner with the Presidents event, 161–163
with employment centers, 167–170
to entire community, 185–186
Family Fun Fest, 153–155
Faraway Places project, 163–165
grant opportunities, 177–179
Guest Reader Storytime, 170–172
for lifelong learning, 174–177
with local historical society, 182–184
with local organizations, 158–161
with local park or historical agency, 179–181
One Community, One Story program, 99–101
for storytimes, 155–157
town and gown lecture series, 165–167

computer skills
  academic library outreach, 109–110
  for digitizing historical photographs, 88
  local history and, 78
  for refugees, 139–141
  senior outreach programs, 27–28, 35
Conroy, Pat, 102
Conti, Stephen, 98
Cooper, Floyd, 102
copyrights, 87
Coral Reef Senior High School (Florida),
  121–123
correctional facilities
  Flip the Script activity, 67
  Freedom Readers program, 65–68
  journal writing, 67
  shared grant projects, 72
  summer reading games, 68–72
  Word Find and Define activity, 67
Council of State Archivists, 89
Coutts, Brian, 163–164
Covey, Stephen, 66
Creech, Sharon, 102
Culinary Arts program, 5
Cultural Media Award, 173

D

Daniel, Noel, 76–77
DARE (Drug Abuse Resistance Education),
  155
DATmanager, 88–89
Day of the Children / Day of the Books
  program, 127–129
Department of Agriculture, 121
Department of Education, 119, 138
Des Moines Public Library (Iowa), 52
Des Plaines Public Library (Illinois), 33–35,
  97–99
Día de los Niños / Día de los Libros
  program, 127–129
digital images
  digitization projects, 19–21
  historical newspapers, 77–79
  historical photographs, 87–89
  Shutterbug Club, 36
Dinner with the Presidents event, 161–
  163
Dinsmore, Chelsea, 17–19, 21–23
DiPucchio, Kelly, 93

diversity outreach
  Academic STARS program, 146–147
  African American college students,
    146–147
  building community, 141–143
  Día de los Niños / Día de los Libros
    program, 127–129
  Ethiopia Reads organization, 132–134
  Homework Club for English Language
    Learners, 134–136
  If I Can Read, I Can Do Anything
    program, 137–139
  laptop literacy, 139–141
  to Russian-speaking community, 144–
    145
  serving multicultural patrons, 148–150
  Sí Se Puede! / Yes We Can! program,
    35–38
  Voice and Images project, 129–132
docent program, 5–8
Donkey Mobile Library (Ethiopia), 133–134
Donnelly, Mark, 29–32
Doraiswamy, Uma, 101–103, 163–165
Duke University, 88
Dunatov, Katya B., 144–145, 148–150
Dynix patron database, 162

E

Eddie and the Fire Engine (Haywood), 136
Edible Book Contest, 3–5
Education, Department of, 119, 138
Ellington, Cynthia, 29–30
employment centers, 159–160, 167–170
English language learners, 134–136,
  139–140
Enoch Pratt Free Library (Maryland),
  69–71
Ephemeral Cities Project, 77–79
Ernst, Kathleen, 102
Ethiopia Reads organization, 132–134
The Ethiopian Bee (newsletter), 133
Evansville Vanderburgh Public Library
  (Indiana), 51–53, 58–59
Every Child Ready to Read initiative, 52–53

F

Fahrenheit 451 (Bradbury), 178
Falconer, Ian, 186

Family Fun Fest, 153–155

Fantom, Laura, 97

Faraway Places project, 163–165

Farley, Walter, 96

Fenton Area Public Schools (Michigan), 170–172

Filipovic, Zlata, 143

First They Killed My Father (Ung), 143

Fisher Price Toys, 172–173

Fletcher Free Library (Vermont), 139–142

Flip the Script activity, 67

Four Directions Technology Innovation Grant, 138

Four Mile Family Resource Center (Colorado), 150

Freedom Readers Literacy Outreach program, 65–68

The Freedom Writers Diary, 65–67

Freeman, Kathleen, 30

Frey, Susan M., 27–28, 165–167

Friends of Ethiopia Reads Partner Program, 133

Friends of the Library, 9–11

Frisbie, Dodie, 97

Frontline World (television program), 18

fund-raising for library art galleries, 81

G

Gamma Phi Circus, 75–77

Garcia-Febo, Loida, 29

Garfield, James A., 161–162

Gaster, Amber, 140

A Gathering of Readers event, 138

Gebregeorgis, Yohannes, 132–134

Genesee District Library (Michigan), 93–95, 170–172

Girl from Kosovo (Mead), 134

Glenview Public Library (Illinois), 97

Graduate Research Association, 138

Grafton, Sue, 102

grant projects
for building community, 177–179
employment center, 169
Four Directions Technology Innovation Grant, 138
Immigrants Integration grant, 150
The Long Journey discussion series, 142
for low-vision fair, 99
mini-grants, 17–19
shared grants, 72

storytime outreach, 155–157

Teaching American History Grants, 119–121

teaching refugees computer skills, 140

Greater Pittsburgh Literacy Council, 135

Greene, Rhonda Gowler, 93–94

Gubnitskaia, Vera, 9–11, 45–48

Guess Whose Photograph That Is program, 29

Guico, Karina, 97

Guild for the Blind, 98

Gustin, Gary, 97

H

Halberstam, David, 102

Harrison Middle School (Pennsylvania), 134–136

Hawkins, Lynn, 15–17, 161–163

Haywood, Carolyn, 136

Head Start program, 9, 93, 156

HealthLink initiative, 158–161

Helakoski, Leslie, 93

Hendricks, Roy, 30–31

Hendry County Library Cooperative, 78

Heritage, Dennis, 162

Heron, Christine K., 93–95, 170–172

Hickam, Homer, 102

Highland County Employment Center (Ohio), 167–170

Hillel at University of Florida, 18

Hinsdale Public Library (Illinois), 48–51, 153–155

historical agencies, 179–184

historical newspapers, 77–79

Hoban, Russell, 95

Hoffer, Deborah, 29

Holve, Brooke, 178

homeschooled teens, 43–45

Homework Club for English Language Learners, 134–136

Hooper, Tim, 19–21, 87–89

Howard County libraries (Maryland), 69–70

Huan, Haiwang, 164

Hubbard, Elbert, 172

Hyman, Trina Schart, 186

I

If I Can Read, I Can Do Anything program, 137–139

Illinois Library Association, 98
Illinois State University Milner Library, 53–55, 75–77
image digitization project, 19–21
Immigrants Integration grant, 150
Indiana State University, 27–28, 165–167
information literacy instruction, 27–28
Institute of Museum and Library Services, 102
Ivy Tech Community Campus Library (Indiana), 43–45

J

job descriptions for library docents, 6–7
job-hunting outreach, 159–160, 167–170
Johnston, Dedee DeLongpre, 104
journal writing, 67

K

Kalamazoo Regional Educational Service Agency, 119
Kalamazoo Valley Museum, 130–132
Keats, Ezra Jack, 96
Keene, Carolyn, 96
Kent State University (Ohio), 59–61, 146–147
Keys, Margaret, 109–110, 155–157
King, Cassandra, 102
Kiss the Dust (Laird), 143
Kurtz, Jane, 133

L

Lafayette Adult Resources Academy (Indiana), 174–177
Laguna Elementary School (New Mexico), 137
Lahiri, Jhumpa, 34
Laird, Elizabeth, 143
Lance Armstrong Foundation, 138
laptop literacy, 139–141
Launius, Roger, 164
Lee, Harper, 178
Leonard, Meryle, 35–38, 127–129
Lester, Helen, 171
Let's Talk about It program, 18, 178
Libraries Build Community theme, 137
Libraries for the Future, 39, 142
library anniversary celebrations, 13–15

library art galleries, 79–81
library docent program, 5–8
Library Gateway Project, 121–123
Library Honor Roll, 46–47
Library Matters (local cable television program), 85–87
Library of Congress, 77, 118
License to Learn Library Card Contest, 46
lifelong learning, 174–177
Lincoln, Abraham, 162
Lindsey, Marty, 137
literacy skills
    for early childhood, 52–53
    for homeschooled teens, 44
    Homework Club for English Language Learners, 134–136
    in juvenile correctional facilities, 69–72
    Michigan Reads! project, 93–95
    for refugees, 139–141
    SOKY Book Fest, 102
local media
    circus collection and, 76
    digitizing historical photographs, 87–89
    promoting library services via, 85–87
    town and gown lecture series, 166
local parks, 179–181
Long, Sarah Ann, 137–138
The Long Journey discussion series, 141–143
Lynchburg Branch Library (Ohio), 182–184
Lynchburg Historical Society (Ohio), 182

M

Macy's department stores, 102–103
Malanchuk, Iona R., 3–5, 185–186
Mallillin, Connie, 30–31
manuscripts
    defined, 111
    integrating into curriculum, 110–114
    introduction in classroom, 111–112
    tips for using, 113–114
    topical, 112–113
Maori in Libraries and Information Management, 138
Marjorie Kinnan Rawlings Literary Society, 181
Marjorie Rawlings Elementary School (Florida), 181
marketing/promoting
    awareness of library services, 11–13

marketing/promoting (cont.)
  digital collections, 79
  Guest Reader Storytime, 171
  for library anniversary celebration, 14
  library art galleries, 80
  via local media, 85–87
  The Long Journey discussion series, 143
  for low-vision fair, 98
  Michigan Reads! project, 94–95
  One Community, One Story program,
    100–101
  outreach for homeschooled teens, 43–44
Maryland Correctional Education Libraries,
  68–72
Maryland Library Association, 71
Mason, Marsha, 102
Matyn, Marian, 110–114
Maxwell, Nancy Kalikow, 85–87, 121–123
McCloskey, Robert, 96
McIntyre, Jane, 97
McKinney, Stan, 87
MCRMedia Associates, 88–89
MDC TV, 85–87
Me First (Lester), 171
Mead, Alice, 134
media. See local media
media centers, partnerships with, 121–123,
  170–172
Mehling, Ellen, 37–40, 158–161
memoir writing, 29–32
Memorial Sloan-Kettering Cancer Center,
  158
Memories in Poetry and Prose, 30
Memories of the Mind, 29
Mentor Public Library (Ohio), 15–17,
  161–163
Mervyn H. Sterne Library (Alabama),
  114–118
MetLife, 143
Mexican Americans, 129–132
Miami Dade College (Florida), 85–87,
  121–123
Michigan Reads! project, 93–95
microfilm collections, 78–79
middle school outreach, 109–110, 134–136
Milner Go To program, 54
mini-grant programs, 17–19
Mirage (Barnett), 105
modern classics, 96–97
Montgomery Library (Kentucky), 87
Mora, Pat, 127

Mori, Maryann, 51–53, 57–59
Morton Grove Public Library (Illinois), 97
multicultural outreach, 148–150

N
The Namesake (Lahiri), 34
National Agricultural Library, 122
National Air and Space Museum, 164
National Center for Education Statistics, 68
National Digital Newspaper Program, 77
National Endowment for the Arts, 102, 178
National Endowment for the Humanities,
  77
National Historic Landmark, 181
National Institute for Literacy, 157
National Library Week, 3–5, 137–138
national reading club, 137–139
Native Americans
  If I Can Read, I Can Do Anything
    program, 137–139
  Voice and Images project, 129–132
New York Foundation of the Arts, 172–173
New York Library Association, 172–173
newspapers
  digitizing historical photographs, 87–89
  historical, 77–79
  Michigan Reads! project, 94
Newyear, David, 162
Nextbook program grant, 18
Niles Public Library District (Illinois),
  97–99
Nino, Mary H., 5–8, 13–15
North Suburban Library Association
  (Illinois), 137
Northeast Florida Library Information
  Network, 78
Northern Ohio Live, 161

O
Oke, Janette, 102
One Book, One Community program, 93
One Campus–One Community–One Book
  event, 102–103
One Community, One Story program,
  99–101
oral historians, 129–132
Orange County Library System (Florida),
  9–11, 45–48
Otaku Anonymous, 58

P

Park Ridge Public Library (Illinois), 97
parks, local, 179–181
Pearce, Fred, 103
Perceptions of Libraries and Information Resources (De Rosa), 11
Peters, Brandon, 164
photographs. *See* digital images
Pilkey, Dav, 134
pilot projects, 21–23
planning
    Día de los Niños / Día de los Libros program, 127–129
    library anniversary celebration, 13–14
    for library art galleries, 80
    library docent program, 6
    for lifelong learning program, 176
    for low-vision fair, 97–98
    Michigan Reads! project, 93
    One Community, One Story program, 100–101
    outreach for homeschooled teens, 43–44
    partnering with historical agency, 179–181
    partnering with local park, 179–181
    television show, 86–87
    town and gown lecture series, 166
    Voice and Images project, 130
Potter, Beatrix, 174
PTA/PTO, 156, 173
public access television stations, 85–87
Public Library of Charlotte and Mecklenburg County (North Carolina), 35–38
    Día de los Niños / Día de los Libros, 127–129
public readings, memoir writing project, 30
public school systems
    academic library outreach to, 109–110
    If I Can Read, I Can Do Anything program, 137–139
    Michigan Reads! project, 93–95
    partnerships with, 45–48
    science project partnership, 121–123
    teacher workshops, 114–116
    Teaching American History Grants, 119–121
The Pull of the Moon (Berg), 34
Purdue University Libraries (Indiana), 43–45, 174–177

Q

Queens Hospital, 158
Queens Library (New York), 29–32, 158–161

R

Raccoon Tune (Shaw), 93–94
Race to Read game, 72
Randall, Cara, 155
Rawlings, Charles, 180
Rawlings, Marjorie Kinnan, 180–181
Rawlings Historic State Park, 180–181
Readathon, 185–186
Readers Rule game, 72
Reading Is Fundamental (RIF), 69
Reaves, Tracy, 29
Rebuilding the Temple (film), 143
recruiting library docents, 7–8
Remembering School Days program, 34
Remembering When program, 35
researching
    archival outreach and, 110–114
    classroom outreach for, 109–110
    for homeschooled teens, 44
    outreach to college students, 146–147
    for student athletes, 55
    teacher workshops on, 114–116
retaining library docents, 8
Riehle, Catherine Fraser, 43–45, 174–177
Robards, Karen, 102
Rochdale Village Library (Queens, NY), 30
Rockpoint Community School (Arizona), 137
Roosevelt, Theodore, 162
Rosetta Stone program, 140–141
Ross, Ann B., 102
Rowling, J. K., 96
Roy, Loriene, 132–134, 137–139
Roycroft guild, 172–173
Runner, David, 164
Russian-speaking refugees, 144–145, 148
Rutherford, Clifton, 30

S

Sachar, Louis, 186
Sacramento Public Library (California), 155–157
Sacramento State University, 157
San Francisco Public Library, 132

San Juan Unified School District
(California), 156
Schaap, Dick, 102
school library media centers. *See* media
centers
School Readiness First 5 program, 156
science projects, 121–123
Seeholzer, Jamie, 59–61, 146–147
senior outreach
baby boomers and, 37–40
Beginning, Middle, and End game, 36
Bits 'n' Bytes program, 27
computer instruction, 27–28, 35
HealthLink initiative, 159
information literacy instruction, 27–28
memoir writing, 29–32
Remembering School Days program, 34
Remembering When program, 35
Senior Celebration, 33
Senior Housing and Resource Fair, 33
Shutterbug Club, 36
Sí Se Puede! / Yes We Can! program,
35–38
Telling Our Stories program, 36–37
service learning, 54–55
Seuss, Dr., 96, 186
Sewell, Anna, 96
shadow-dancers, 174
Shatara, Barbara A., 139–141, 141–143
Shaw, Nancy, 93–94
Shibley, Jeffrey, 161, 163
Shirley, Glennor, 68–72
Shola Children's Library (Ethiopia), 133
Shoop, Melissa, 77–79, 103–105
Shutterbug Club, 36
Sí Se Puede! / Yes We Can! program, 35–38
Siebold, Jan, 95–97, 172–174
Silly Mammo (Gebregeorgis), 133
Silverstein, Shel, 96
SKIP (Successful Kids Involve Parents)
program, 94
Skokie Public Library (Illinois), 97
Slimon, Licia, 55–57, 134–136
Smith, Felicia A., 11–13, 65–68
Smithsonian Institution, 164
Smokey Hill High School (Colorado), 150
Snee, Sharon, 135–136
Society of American Archivists, 89
SOKY Book Fest, 101–103
Somali Bantu Association, 140

Somerset County Library System
(Maryland), 72
Sonoma State University Library
(California), 79–81, 177–179
South Hills Interfaith Ministry
(Pennsylvania), 135
special collections
circus collection, 75–77
digital collections, 77–79
historical newspapers, 77–79
library art galleries, 79–81
Spring Institute, 149–150
St. Michael's College (Vermont), 142
staffing
for library art galleries, 80
for library docent program, 8
studying at the library and, 49
Steele, Tony, 76
Steig, William, 174
A Step from Heaven (An Na), 143
Stine, R. L., 102
storytimes
Guest Reader Storytime, 170–172
partnering to deliver, 155–157
Storytime @ the Pools, 16
Stroop effect chart, 66
student athletes, 53–55
studying at library, 48–51
summer reading games, 68–72
Sylvester and the Magic Pebble (Steig), 174

T

The Tailor of Gloucester (Potter), 174
Target Corporation, 93–94, 155
Taschen Press, 76–77
Te Ropu Whakahau, 138
Teaching American History Grants, 119–
121
teen outreach. *See* youth outreach
Teen Read Week, 137
Teen Tech Week, 137
teen thespians, 55–59
television, promoting library services via,
85–87
Telles-Irvin, Patricia, 104
Telling Our Stories program, 36–37
Texas Information Literacy Tutorial, 43–44
Texas Library Association, 137
theater productions, teens and, 55–59

Thomas Gale/Library Journal Library of the
    Year, 5, 13
Thompson, Cathy, 97
Thompson, Rick, 168
Tippecanoe County Public Library, 43–45
To Kill a Mockingbird (Lee), 178
Tocker Foundation, 138
town and gown lecture series, 165–167
training program for library docents, 6–7
Turcotte, Florence M., 99–101, 179–181
Turow, Scott, 102

U
Ung, Loung, 143
University of Alabama at Birmingham,
    114–116, 116–118
University of Buffalo (New York), 132
University of Florida Center for Jewish
    Studies, 18
University of Florida Libraries
    Children's Initiative, 45–48
    Children's Literature Day, 186
    Common Reading program, 103–105
    digital collection, 77–79
    Edible Book Contest, 3–5
    Library Honor Roll, 46–47
    License to Learn Library Card Contest,
        46
    Marjorie Kinnan Rawlings Manuscript
        Collection, 180
    mini-grants and, 17–19
    outreach to entire community, 185–186
    pilot projects and, 21–23
    Weeks of Welcome program, 17–19,
        22–23
University of North Carolina, 88
University of Notre Dame, 11–13, 65–68
University of Texas at Austin, 132, 137
University of Vermont, 142–143
Upward Bound program, 59–61

V
Vermont Adult Learning, 139
Vermont Public Library Foundation, 140
Vermont Refugee Resettlement Program,
    139–140
Vernon Area Public Library District
    (Illinois), 97

vision impairment, 97–99
Voice and Images project, 129–132
Voss, Joyce, 97

W
A Walk in the Woods (Bryson), 34
web conferencing, 78–79
Weeks of Welcome program, 17–19, 22–23
Welch, Eleanor, 75
Wells Fargo Bank, 157
Western Kentucky University, 101–103,
    163–165
Western Michigan University, 119–121,
    130–132
Western Union, 150
When the Rivers Run Dry (Pearce), 103–105
White, E. B., 96
Whitehall Public Library (Pennsylvania),
    55–57, 134–136
Wilder, Laura Ingalls, 96
Williams, Elaine, 167–170, 182–184
Wilson, Josten, 164
Winona State University (Minnesota), 140
Wood, Don and Audrey, 186
Word Find and Define activity, 67
Wright, Colleen, 142–143
Wright, Peggy, 163–164

Y
YES (Youth Enrichment Services), 153–155
Yes We Can! program, 35–38
Yours Truly restaurants, 161–163
youth outreach
    book giveaway program, 9–11
    Children's Initiative, 45–48
    to correctional facilities, 65–72
    creating teen patron programs, 51–53
    Every Child Ready to Read initiative,
        52–53
    Flip the Script activity, 67
    for homeschooled teens, 43–45
    journal writing, 67
    partnerships with public school systems,
        45–48
    at pools and beaches, 15–17
    service learning, 54–55
    to student athletes, 53–55
    studying at the library, 48–51

youth outreach (cont.)
    summer reading games, 68–72
    teen response to, 57–59
    teen theater groups, 55–59
    Upward Bound program, 59–61
    Word Find and Define activity, 67
    Youth Enrichment Services, 153–155

Z

Zlata's Diary (Filipovic), 143

You may also be interested in

Writing and Publishing: If you are interested in writing or reviewing for the library community or in publishing a book, or if you need to write and publish for tenure, then *Writing and Publishing* is for you. This book includes practical how-to guidance covering fiction, poetry, children's books/magazines, self-publishing, literary agents, personal blogging, and other topics.

Building a Buzz: Want to get the word out about your library in the most cost-effective way possible? You can achieve this with the effective word-of-mouth marketing (WOMM) strategies laid out in this book.

Bite-Sized Marketing: Written and designed to reflect the way people read today, this book is structured to quickly impart simple and cost-effective ideas on marketing your library.

Creating Your Library Brand: This resource covers everything from working with outside experts to evaluating and maintaining your library's brand. Illustrated by case studies from real-life libraries, this book includes tips, suggestions for success, answers to frequently asked questions, and more.

Order today at www.alastore.ala.org or 866-746-7252!